Blended Learning
Research Perspectives

Edited by Anthony G. Picciano and Charles D. Dziuban

THE SLOAN CONSORTIUM
A Consortium of Institutions and Organizations
Committed to Quality Online Education

Blended Learning
Research Perspectives

This book was made possible by a grant from the
Alfred P. Sloan Foundation.

SCOLE
Sloan Center for OnLine Education
at Olin and Babson Colleges

Sloan-C has its administrative home at the Sloan Center for OnLine Education (SCOLE) at Olin and Babson Colleges. SCOLE has been established as a center that spans the two campuses of Olin College and Babson College. SCOLE's purpose is to support the activities of the Sloan Consortium, a consortium of higher-education providers sharing the common bonds of understanding, supporting and delivering education via asynchronous learning networks (ALNs). With the mission of providing learning to anyone anywhere, SCOLE seeks to provide new levels of learning capability to people seeking higher and continuing education. For more information about Sloan-C, visit www.sloan-c.org.

For more information about Olin and Babson Colleges, visit www.olin.edu and www.babson.edu.

Preface

This book emerged from a series of blended learning workshops, sponsored by the Alfred P. Sloan Foundation in 2004 and 2005 at the University of Illinois-Chicago (UIC). Thirty professional educators with online learning experience were invited to share their expertise in blended learning and to develop a national perspective. The planning committee of individuals associated with the Sloan-C Consortium developed an agenda in 2004 that focused on the definitions, types, and nature of blended learning. In 2005, the committee established working groups to discuss institutional perspectives, best practices, and research.

The research group consisted of 10 members, who were published authors and researchers in the field of online learning, and who had begun studies of or were contemplating research on blended learning. A preliminary review of the literature indicated that there were very few studies that concentrated on blended learning in higher education, confirming that no research base existed.

Each member agreed to contribute a book chapter of original research in blending learning during the next year. This book shares their findings and conclusions, provides a forum for issues associated with the emergence of blended learning in higher education, and addresses the need to develop foundations of research on blended learning. The studies in this volume relate to the first four pillars of the Sloan-C Pillars Quality Framework that includes learning effectiveness, student satisfaction, faculty satisfaction, student access, and cost effectiveness.

Terminology

Chapter 1 presents a definition of blended learning discussed at the 2004 and 2005 Blending Learning Workshops at the University of Illinois, Chicago. This definition, however, serves as a guiding principle, not a strict definition. In some colleges and universities, other terminologies, such as "hybrid" or "mixed-mode" learning, are used; each, however, describes essentially the same concept. In Chapter 6, for example, *Discovering, Designing, and Delivering Hybrid Courses*, the authors Robert Kaleta, Karen Skibba, and Tanya Joosten, use the word "hybrid" because the University of Wisconsin-Milwaukee and other institutions involved in this study, use that term.

Audience

This book is geared primarily to higher education professionals that include policy makers, administrators, faculty, and support personnel, and may be of particular interest to educators responsible for planning and integrating online learning into academic programs. A wider audience, however, will find elements of pertinent, important, and timely information

i

about blended learning that will appeal to experienced researchers and those new to online learning.

Acknowledgments

This effort would not have been possible without significant support and assistance by a number of organizations and individuals.

The Alfred P. Sloan Foundation is an inspiration among philanthropies promoting the development of quality online programs in American higher education. The *Anytime, Anyplace Grant Program* has provided tens of millions of dollars to colleges and universities to support online technology to access learning opportunities. A. Frank Mayadas, the program officer for this initiative, is a visionary, who saw, early on, the potential for learning with technology, and who continues to nurture its development. The generous funding provided by the Sloan Foundation to the workshops at the University of Illinois-Chicago made this book possible.

The Sloan Consortium (Sloan-C) is an organization of more than 1,500 colleges and universities dedicated to promoting quality online learning. Started in 2001, Sloan-C has developed an ambitious agenda, based on quality and research that builds an academic community of organizations and individuals, who believe online learning to be an important vehicle to extend learning beyond the traditional classroom. Through its Board of Directors and operations staff, Sloan-C provided invaluable technical and planning assistance to produce this book. The authors especially thank John Bourne, Janet Moore, and Katie Fife.

The Planning Committee for the 2004 and 2005 Blended Learning Workshops also provided very valuable advice and suggestions for the development of this book. In particular:

Mary Niemiec — University of Illinois, Chicago, Chair
Tana Bishop — University of Maryland University College
Chuck Dziuban — University of Central Florida
Joel Hartman — University of Central Florida
George Otte — City University of New York
Anthony G. Picciano — Hunter College and Graduate Center, City University of New York
Steve Sorg — University of Central Florida
Karen Swan — Kent State University
Karen Vignare — Michigan State University

The authors also extend a sincere thank you to a number of individuals, who assisted in data collection, editing, and the final production of this book. Especially noted from the Research Initiative for Teaching Effectiveness at the University of Central Florida are: Patsy Moskal, Marcella Bush, Sara Wood. Rut Serra-Roldan, Rosalie Luby, and Yuiza Arce.

Blended Learning
Research Perspectives

Contents

Introductory Chapters

Introduction

Setting the Stage

Scenario One

D.G. is an associate professor at a small community college where she teaches chemistry. Four years ago she applied for and received a grant to develop an online course. Her technology skills are well-developed and she had used WebCT to develop online materials including several simulations of chemical lab experiments. As part of her grant, she refined her online course materials and developed an entire course in inorganic chemistry. The most difficult part of her online course development was simulating complex experiments that normally were conducted in "wet" laboratories. To solve this problem, D.G. decided to use a commercially-available software program to supplement her own "home-grown" simulations. D.G. offered the fully online inorganic chemistry course for two semesters, and while she was happy with the result, she also was conflicted: perhaps students would be better served by doing lab experiments in face-to-face situations. When the grant expired, she decided that she preferred to teach part of the course online and part (the lab component) face-to-face.

Scenario Two

The program coordinator (C.S.) of an online Masters of Business Administration (MBA) at a college that specializes in adult and distance learning, brought her full-time faculty together to consider offering a variation of the program that will require students to meet face-to-face. Although the fully online MBA program was well enrolled and considered successful, student evaluations of the program indicated that they would like opportunities to meet with their fellow students. The faculty were well-experienced in online learning but tended to agree with C.S.'s suggestion. A small committee was formed to work out the logistics and details. One year later a second "blended" version of the online MBA program was offered that requires students to meet once a month on Saturdays in face-to-face mode at the College is offered. During the Saturday meetings, two-hours in the mornings are reserved for traditional face-to-face classroom instruction, and the rest of the day including lunch are reserved for group work, to do project presentations, and to socialize/bond with one another. The new "blended" program has been very successful especially among students within a one hundred and fifty mile radius from the college. While the enrollment in the fully online MBA program has decreased, the number of students in the blended program has more than made up for this decrease.

Scenario Three

The president (G.M.) of a major university has been meeting with his executive staff regarding the infusion of technology into all of its academic programs. The university has done a great deal of work in online learning including establishing a world-class fully online distance learning center. On the other hand, while many of the programs at the main campus use technology, they have evolved through the initiatives of individual departments and faculty and not as the result of a coordinated university effort. After several months of meetings, the decision is made that online technology components are to be integrated or "blended" into all academic programs within the next two years. A new office is established at the university that will coordinate pedagogical and technological support for this new initiative. To lead this initiative the present director of the distance learning center is transferred to the Provost's Office and promoted to the position of associate provost. Working with academic deans, department chairs, and program coordinators, the associate provost is in the process of developing a five-year plan to implement the blended learning initiative.

Scenario Four

A public urban university in the sunbelt has been experiencing unprecedented growth as a result of a population boom that has been continuing for more than ten years. Enrollments in its programs are increasing at the rate of 5–8% per year, while state funding has been stagnant. Although there has been some funding for building construction, there is a dire shortage of classrooms and other teaching spaces. The university has an excellent technology infrastructure and has been offering online courses since 1997, and more recently, there has been a significant increase in blended courses where part of the class time is replaced by an online component. The president's cabinet has been discussing the classroom shortage, and one suggestion has been made to expand and formalize the blended learning activities to recapture classroom space. Presently faculty determine what they will do online, but there is no system in place to recapture the classroom space freed up as a result of the online component of any given course. The Provost and Chief Information Officer propose that required courses normally taken in the freshmen year include at least a one-third online component. Many of these courses are taught in large lecture classes with 100 to 400 students. Class room space would be reassigned to take advantage of the one-third portion of the class taught online. This would provide a significant increase of classroom space with little additional expense.

Scenarios such as these are playing themselves out throughout higher education as colleges and universities attempt to take advantage of online technology for instruction. They represent a variation of online learning in which courses and programs are not fully online but contain multiple (some face-to-face and some online) modalities. The term "blended" refers to this form of instruction that combines online instruction with traditional face-to-face instruction. Also known as "hybrid", "mixed-mode", and "flexible learning", blended learning appears to be gaining in popularity.

During the past decade, a substantive body of research on fully online learning emanating mostly from faculty participating in distance learning programs has evolved. More recently, books and articles (e.g., Bonk and Graham, 2006) have begun to appear which provide descriptions of blended learning models that herald them as growing rapidly among institutions throughout the world. However, most of the published work on blended learning is based on case studies and best practices rather than empirical studies. A search of several major databases such as ERIC, Applied Science, and Wilson Education reveals less than twenty empirical studies that specifically examine blended learning. In the *Journal for Asynchronous Learning Networks (JALN)*, a refereed journal dedicated exclusively to online learning, 35 of 165 articles published since 1997, refer to blended or hybrid learning but only six of these can be considered empirical studies.

For more than a decade the Alfred P. Sloan Foundation has funded a very successful "Anytime, Anyplace" program directed primarily at colleges and universities interested in developing fully online learning courses and programs. In 2004 and 2005, in response to the growth of interest in blended learning, the Foundation, provided funding for two workshops to examine issues associated with blended learning. The invitational workshops held at the University of Illinois-Chicago (UIC) brought together thirty participants from the United States and Canada with expertise in online learning to consider issues associated with blended learning. A planning committee was established in consultation with the Sloan Consortium (Sloan-C) to develop the agenda for these workshops. The recommendation of this committee was that the workshops be organized around three themes and work groups as follows:

1. institutional perspectives;
2. best practices;
3. research.

Each of the thirty members of the 2005 workshop were assigned to one of these work groups. The ten members of the research work group were selected because they had recently been engaged in or expressed an interest in research in blended learning. Early on they realized that the extent of published research on blended learning was very limited and decided to collaborate on a project to produce a book on blended learning research. Other researchers were invited to work with the original ten members so that twenty-five researchers representing sixteen different colleges and organizations contributed their talents to the project resulting in this book. As indicated in the Preface, the essential purpose of this project/book is to begin to fill the need for developing a research base on blended learning.

Defining "Blended Learning"

Blended learning means different things to different people. The word "blended" implies a mixture or combination. When a picture is pasted above a paragraph of text, a presentation is created that may be more informative to the viewer or reader but the picture and text remain intact and can be individually discerned. On the other hand, when two cans of different colored paints are mixed, the new paint will look different from either of the original colors. In fact, if the new paint is mixed well, neither of the original colors will continue to exist. Similar situations exist in blended learning. The mix can be a simple separation of part of a course into an online component. In a course that meets for three weekly contact hours, two hours might meet in a traditional classroom and the equivalent of one weekly hour conducted online. The two modalities for this course are carefully separated and while they may overlap, they can still be differentiated. In other forms of blended courses and programs, the modalities are not so easy to distinguish. For example, consider an online program that offers three online courses in a semester that all students are required to take. The courses meet for three consecutive five week sessions. However, students do a collaborative semester (fifteen week) project that overlaps the courses. The students are expected to maintain regular communication with one another through email and group discussion boards. They also are required to meet once a month on Saturdays at the college in face-to-face settings where during the morning sessions, course material from the online courses are further presented and discussed, and afternoon sessions are devoted to in-person group project work. These activities begin to blur the modalities in a new mixture or blend where the individual parts are not as discernable as they once were. Add to this, the increasing popularity of integrating videoconferencing, podcasting, wikis, blogs, and other media into class work and the definition of blended learning becomes very fluid.

The participants in the Sloan workshops recognized the difficulty in formulating a simple definition of blended learning. In fact, the discussion of a definition continued during both workshops and alternated between a broad versus a narrow definition. Gary Miller (2005), Associate Vice President for Outreach, and former Executive Director of The World Campus, the Pennsylvania State University, described a lengthy process at his university which resulted in a definition containing five variations of "blended learning" environments. In the broadest sense, blended learning (see Figure can be defined or conceptualized as a wide variety of technology/media grated with conventional, face-to-face classroom activities. However,

8

some workshop participants wanted to focus on a narrower definition that centered on an online component that replaced seat time in the conventional classroom (see Figure 2). The issue of a broad or narrow definition was discussed extensively and the two core elements (online and face-to-face instruction) were deemed critical to blended learning. At the 2005 Sloan-C Workshop, the following definition of blended learning was adopted by the participants:

1. Courses that integrate online with traditional face-to-face class activities in a planned, pedagogically valuable manner; and
2. Where a portion (institutionally defined) of face-to-face time is replaced by online activity. (Laster, Otte, Picciano, and Sorg, 2005).

This definition serves as a guideline for the researchers represented in this book. This definition eliminates, for example, a face-to-face course utilizing certain forms of stand-alone media such as videotape, CD-ROM, or DVD. It would not eliminate a course utilizing these media that had both an online and a face-to-face component.

Figure 1. **Broad Conceptualization of Blended Learning**

Blended Learning Conceptualization

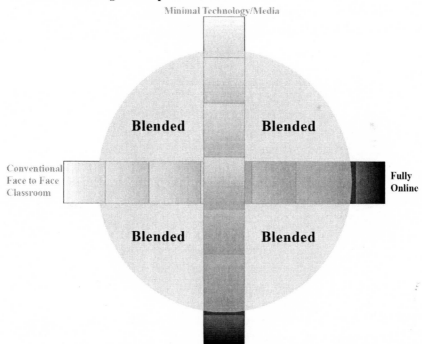

*Source: Picciano, A.G. (February 9, 2005). Posting to the Official Website of the 2005 Sloan-C Summer Workshop held in Victoria, British Columbia.

(Note: Conceptualization discussed at meetings of the Planning Committee for the 2005 Sloan-C Workshop on Blended Learning held in Chicago.)

Figure 2. **Online-Specific Conceptualization of Blended Learning**

Blended Learning Conceptualization

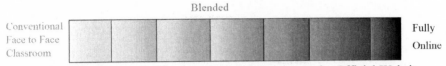

*Source: Picciano, A.G. (January 22, 2005). Posting to the Official Website of the 2005 Sloan-C Summer Workshop held in Victoria, British Columbia. (Note: Conceptualization discussed at meetings of the Planning Committee for the 2005 Sloan-C Workshop on Blended Learning held in Chicago.)

What We Know and Don't Know

While the research base on blended learning is sparse, indications are that many faculty in American colleges and universities are willing to incorporate blended learning into their pedagogical repertoire. However, the extent, the basis, and the nature of this willingness have not been well-established for several reasons.

First, it is generally believed that blended learning has reached well into the mainstream of American higher education. Unfortunately, little data are available that document this reach. For example, the Sloan Consortium conducts annual national surveys on online learning at American colleges (Allen & Seaman 2004, 2005). The findings of these surveys represent important baseline data on student enrollments in fully online courses including the percentage and nature of colleges and universities offering these courses. While these surveys are well-respected and frequently cited in studies and articles on online learning, very little data are presented on blended learning. Jeff Seaman, one of the authors of these studies, is concerned and a bit frustrated that these data are not being systematically collected at most colleges and universities. In effect, faculty might be teaching blended courses but many administrators do not necessarily know who these faculty are or what they actually are doing in these courses. The lack of mechanisms for identifying blended courses in college databases creates a situation in which a large-scale study becomes difficult to conduct and vulnerable to misinformation.

A second issue related to the lack of data on blended learning relates back to definitions. While thirty educators invited to the Sloan Workshops reached a consensus on a relatively stream-lined definition of blended, the thousands of college administrators representing American higher education have not. There are many forms of blended and a generally accepted taxonomy does not exist. One school's blended is another school's hybrid, or another school's mixed-mode. Furthermore, the issue is not just one of labels but the lack of agreement on a broad versus a narrow definition as well.

Third, there is little reason to believe that faculty are identifying themselves as teaching blended learning courses. For many younger faculty who grew up fully immersed in online technology, using Internet tools for instruction is second nature. They use these tools as many older faculty would use overhead projectors. The mystique and aura of teaching online that was present in the mid to late 1990s is disappearing. As online learning becomes more commonplace, faculty do not necessarily see themselves as doing something unique and special when teaching online, particularly in blended learning environments where a small portion of the class may be conducted online. As Eliot Masie, president of the Masie Center for Learning and Technology, has observed: the "e" in e-learning is disappearing and it is all just learning (Masie, 2003).

In sum, without administrative systems in place for identifying blended learning courses and without a widely-accepted definition, collecting data on blended learning becomes difficult. These factors combined with the relative newness of this instructional phenomenon make it easy to understand why there is a dearth of empirical research on the subject. It is the hope of the twenty-five contributing researchers to this project to address and provide insight into these issues with this book.

Organization of this Book

This book is organized into three parts as follows:

Part I — Introductory Chapters (1 through 4)
Part II — Research Chapters (5 through 12)
Part III — Concluding Comments (Chapter 13)

As mentioned earlier, this book evolved from discussions among members of the research group that met at the 2005 Sloan Workshop on Blended Learning held at UIC. The research foci of the chapters in Part II represent their interests in blended learning, and are based on the individual research they either were undertaking or decided to undertake at the time of these workshops.

In determining the content of Part I, there was substantial interest in attempting to ground this work within a pedagogically appropriate conceptual framework (Chapter 2) and a review of the literature (Chapter 3) that would encompass a broad spectrum of blended learning and not only the elements that individual researchers would be studying in each of the chapters of Part II. In addition, a question that all of the participants in this project were interested in exploring was why faculty are adopting blended

11

learning in their courses. I. Elaine Allen and Jeff Seaman agreed to conduct a survey of participants in Sloan-C workshops to determine some of the "whys" they and their institutions were interested in blended learning (Chapter 4).

It was not the intention of the editors of this book to require its sequential reading. To the contrary, it was assumed that many readers would want to read the chapters in an order of their choosing or move around and select material that was of most interest to them. Below are short summaries that highlight key aspects of each chapter so that readers may navigate through this book in a way that best meets their interests.

Towards A Conceptual Framework for Learning in Blended Environments (Chapter 2)

Peter Shea, in developing a conceptual framework, asks fundamental questions about the nature and purpose of blended learning:

What is the problem to which blended learning is the solution?

Why would we want to move instruction out of the classroom and put some, but not all of it into an online format?

What are the benefits? What are the losses?

What happens to cognition, motivation, and affect when learning occurs partly in the classroom and partly online?

Shea uses multiple lenses drawing on the work of a number of theorists to demonstrate the complexity of these queries and their answers. The work of Bransford, Brown, and Cocking (*How People Learn*), Vygotsky (zone of proximal development), Knowles (andragogy), and Garrison, Anderson, and Archer (Community of Inquiry) are identified as appropriate frameworks within which to consider phenomena such as cognition, interaction, and experiences as related to blended learning. Learner centeredness emerges as an important element within all of these frameworks. Shea also emphasizes the role of community, collaboration, and cooperation as essential mechanisms for producing desired learning outcomes. Echoing the work of a number of other researchers, he concludes by proposing a grounded model for blended learning environments.

Review of the Literature on Blended Learning (Chapter 3)

Karen Vignare has perhaps drawn one of the toughest assignments for this project. A review of the literature for any topic is a time-consuming task. For a topic such as blended learning where a definition is problematic and overlaps with other topics, it becomes a Herculean task. By necessity, Vignare has had to examine also the literature on online learning in general, much of which provides a foundation for studying blended learning.

In this chapter, a review of the literature on blended learning is presented using the Sloan Consortium's Five Pillars quality framework for online asynchronous learning networks. Vignare attempts to sift out the evidence as to whether blended learning is truly a unique learning environment or just a simple combination of traditional face-to-face and online instructional approaches. She also concludes that the early research indicates that blended learning can be as successful as either online or face-to-face instruction, but that there is a great need for more study.

Blending In: The Extent and Promise of Blended Education in the United States (Chapter 4)

I. Elaine Allen and Jeff Seaman made a valuable contribution to this project by sharing their work from two national surveys (N=1025 and N=1170) of chief academic officers of colleges and universities that they had conducted in 2004 and 2005. This chapter was extracted from their report, *Blending In: The Extent and Promise of Blended Education in the United States*, Needham, MA: Sloan-C, 2006. The findings examine the extent and nature of fully online and blended courses and programs. Their data indicate that the majority of all higher education institutions were offering some form of both fully online and blended learning courses by 2003. Their chapter also provides comparisons based on size and type of institution (public, private, for-profit), level of programs (associate, baccalaureate, graduate, doctoral), program disciplines, and the nature of the faculty teaching fully online and blended courses. They concluded their surveys by asking the chief academic officers for their opinions of the future, or the "promise," of online and blended learning for their colleges and universities.

Realizing the Transformational Potential of Blended Learning (Chapter 5)

Charles R. Graham and Reid Robison attempt to identify the nature of blended learning at Brigham Young University. They identify, characterize, and compare three major categories of blends:

1. Enabling blends — focus primarily on providing access and convenience to students;
2. Enhancing blends — focus on increasing instructor or student productivity (e.g., increasing the amount of information students are able to cover or increasing the richness of the material covered); and
3. Transforming blends — focus on facilitating an improvement in pedagogy by moving from a more information transmission focused pedagogy to a more active learning pedagogy.

Using a mixed-methods research approach and multiple data sources, Graham and Reid show that there is a broad range of perceptions and practices regarding blended learning among university faculty. Graham and Reid also consider the provocative question of whether blended learning is fundamentally changing instructional practice at BYU.

13

Discovering, Designing, and Delivering Hybrid Courses (Chapter 6)

Robert Kaleta, Karen Skibba, and Tanya Joosten examined faculty experiences in discovering, designing, and delivering hybrid courses. They observed that while there are a number of articles that cite the reasons why faculty like hybrid courses and continue to teach them, there is little information about what prompted faculty to initially try the hybrid course model, why they adopted this format, and how they designed and taught these courses. One of the major goals of this study was to understand why faculty adopt and implement the hybrid instructional model. Using a qualitative interpretive research methodology, they interviewed ten faculty at three institutions of higher learning who had training and experience in teaching hybrid courses. The major factors affecting the decision to adopt hybrid courses were identified including how faculty development can be used as a change agent. This study also investigated how faculty roles expand when teaching hybrid courses to include pedagogical, social, managerial, and technological roles. These faculty experiences are a source of very valuable lessons learned that can be used to inform institutional hybrid course initiatives, enhance faculty development programs, and guide faculty who are preparing a hybrid course.

Student Perceptions of Assessment Efficacy in Online and Blended Learning Classes (Chapter 7)

Gary Brown, Tamara Smith, and Tom Henderson examined the timely issue of assessment in online and blended learning environments. Student age and types of assessment were specifically considered as part of this study. Brown, Smith, and Henderson used survey research of instructors (N=200) and students (N=900) engaged in fully online (N=44) and blended learning (N=31) courses at Washington State University. The data gathered included responses from both quantitative and qualitative (open-ended) questions. Significant differences in preferences for assessment activities were found depending upon the age of the learners. Novice learners (18–20 years) were more likely than older students to report that multiple-choice questions best reflected their learning. Novice learners also reported more confidence in essays and other assessment strategies including simulations, homework, and term papers performed primarily as an individual activity associated with "school." Conversely, more experienced or older students reported that "community" assessment activities better reflected their learning than did "school" assessment activities, and their comments illuminate the implications of the richness of a learning experience that extends beyond traditional "school" boundaries. Many of their findings have important implications for practice and how assessment should be viewed in online and blended learning environments.

Enhancing Student Interaction and Sustaining Faculty Instructional Innovations through Blended Learning (Chapter 8)

Michael Starenko, Karen Vignare, and Joeann Humbert report on the results of the Blended Learning Pilot Project at the Rochester Institute of Technology (R.I.T.). This two-year pilot included 69 faculty, 80 unique courses and 115 sections. A mixed-methods research design using multiple data sources was employed. Data sources including capturing qualitative input from faculty regarding initial course design for their blended courses, faculty narratives reflecting upon their experiences teaching a blended course, and interviews with the faculty participants. Issues such as sustainable faculty instructional innovation and student interaction were specifically considered as important variables for the pilot program's success. One of RIT's eight colleges is the National Technical Institute for the Deaf (NTID), the world's first and largest technological college for students who are deaf or hard-of-hearing. As a result, Starenko, Vignare, and Humbert also provide important insights into the satisfaction of students in blended learning environments who are deaf or hard of hearing.

Reactive Behavior, Ambivalence, and the Generations: Emerging Patterns in Student Evaluation of Blended Learning (Chapter 9)

Charles Dziuban, Patsy Moskal, and Linda Futch undertook a sophisticated study of student satisfaction in blended learning courses at the University of Central Florida. Three separate theories and three research methods were integrated and used for this study. The theories were based on sociological, psychological and metaphorical frameworks and the methods relied on component analysis, Monte Carlo studies and decisions trees. The major data collection instrument was a survey (N=969) completed by students at UCF who had enrolled in at least three blended learning courses. Dziuban, Moskal, and Futch specifically examined students' satisfaction with their blended learning experiences mediated by the political, economic and social influences of the time period in which they passed from early childhood to adulthood. The smallest number of students expressed outright dissatisfaction with blended learning by giving it a non ambiguous "thumbs down". The majority of students had mixed feelings, finding both positive and negative experiences in the blended learning environment.

Student Perceptions of Blended Learning in a Traditional Undergraduate Environment (Chapter 10)

Robert Woods, Diane M. Badzinski, and Jason Baker explored students' patterns of use, perceptions of usefulness, and outcomes related to instructor use of a web-based course management program in a blended learning environment. Woods, Badzinski, and Baker adopted a mixed research methodology using a convenience sample (N=151) of students enrolled in a media literacy course taught by one of the researchers. Content analysis was also performed on available Blackboard CMS course areas to determine frequency and patterns of use. The findings revealed the most popular features and which features were perceived to be most important for learning. Student perceptions of web-based instruction as enhancing the quality and quantity of class discussion were also studied. Woods, Badzinski, and Baker concluded with a discussion of the implications of on-campus students' willingness to embrace blended instruction.

Educational Equivalency (Chapter 11)

Renee Welch examined one of the more important policy issues associated with online and blended learning namely, the educational equivalency of a "contact hour" in courses where students do not meet in a particular place and time. Welch specifically questioned the relevance of the time-on-task-based Carnegie Unit as an appropriate measure of course participation and completion. Citing the work of Watkins and Schlosser, Welch suggests that a Competency Based Education Equivalent (CBEE) is a more practical instrument and can be used for both traditional, blended, and online courses relying on academic achievement rather than time to measure the class equivalency. A case study methodology was followed using the redesign of a single, large-lecture course in criminal justice at the University of Illinois-Chicago. Data sources were triangulated and included an end-of the course survey, peer assessment techniques, and analysis of course management system's course statistics and web-based student responses and activities. Welch recommended that while the Carnegie Unit has been a convenient standard of equivalency since 1902 and purports to gauge faculty effort and student accomplishment, it does not measure learning based on goals or results.

Blended Learning—Complexity in Corporate and Higher Education (Chapter 12)

Robert Albrecht and Judy Pirani, working with the EDUCAUSE Center for Applied Research, compared the development of blended learning in two very different organizations. They observe that managing blended learning and incorporating it into the strategic goals of the organization presents challenges for an entity of any size. The complexities of large organizations, such as those in this study—IBM and Arizona State University—offered even greater challenges. Case studies of these two organizations provided insights into the management of blended learning in such structures and suggested even broader comparisons between corporate training/education and higher education. Albrecht and Pirani concluded by offering summaries of these comparisons, focusing on convenience, satisfaction, cost, learning effectiveness and marketing.

Everything I Need to Know about Blended Learning I Learned from Books (Chapter 13)

Chuck Dziuban, Joel Hartman, and Patsy Moskal conclude this book with powerful commentary on blended learning by framing the issues raised in the earlier chapters within broader organizational concepts and ideas. Readers will find insights into these issues integrated with the work of Senge, Bates, Rogers, Christensen, Forrester, Friedman, and others. Dzuiban, Hartman, and Moskal correctly remind the reader that what may appear as simpler technical issues on the surface relate to complex institutional processes, attitudes, and culture. This chapter concludes with a call to readers "to sustain the inquiry base" on blended learning and provides a plethora of questions that lay out a research agenda on blended learning for years to come.

A Final Comment on Educational Research

The studies in this book represent the dedicated work of a group of researchers who identify a problem and work with modest resources to design, develop, and carry out a project. They epitomize the curiosity and zest of individuals willing to invest significant time in pursuing answers to questions and issues of importance not only to themselves but to many others interested in the nexus of education and technology. To reach their findings and conclusions, the researchers who participated in this project were free to develop any research methodology that would best meet the needs of their study. Readers interested in educational research per se will appreciate the variety of methods used in these studies. Both qualitative and quantitative methods using surveys, content analysis, interviews, case studies, multi-organizational approaches, etc. were employed. A number of studies also used the increasingly popular mixed-methods approach combining both qualitative and quantitative techniques and relying on multiple data sources. In sum, the work of the project's researchers provides a wealth of information not only on the substantive educational issues explored but also on the manner and methods in which such explorations can be carried out.

References

Allen, I. E. & Seaman, J. (2005). *Growing by degrees: Online education in the United States, 2005.* Needham, MA: Sloan-C.

Allen, I. E. & Seaman, J. (2004). *Entering the mainstream: The quality and extent of online education in the United States 2003, and 2004.* Needham, MA: Sloan-C.

Bonk, C. J., & Graham, C. R. (Eds.). (2005). *Handbook of blended learning: Global perspectives, local designs.* San Francisco, CA: Pfeiffer.

Masie, E. (2003). The AMA Handbook of E-Learning Chapter 26: E-Learning, the Near Future http://www.amanet.org/books/catalog/0814407218 _ch26.htm. Accessed February 22, 2006.

Miller, G. Blended learning and Sloan-C. Posting to the Official Website of the 2005 Sloan-C Summer Workshop held in Victoria, British Columbia, June 30, 2005.

Laster, S., Otte, G., Picciano, A.G., & Sorg, S. Redefining blended learning. Presentation at the 2005 Sloan-C Workshop on Blended Learning, Chicago, IL, April 18, 2005.

Towards A Conceptual Framework for Learning in Blended Environments

Peter Shea Ph.D.
University at Albany

What problem does blended learning solve? Why would we want to move instruction out of the classroom and put some, but not all of it into an online format? What are the benefits? What are the losses? What happens to cognition, motivation, and affect when learning occurs partly in the classroom and partly online? These are some of the questions for which a conceptual framework for blended learning should provide direction.

One common answer to the "problem" question is access. If an institution is able to exchange some of the contact hours or "seat-time" that normally occurs in the classroom for contact and interaction that occurs in an online setting, that institution has made two changes that increase access. First it has reduced a student's need to be at a particular place at a particular time. This can free the student to pursue alternative goals, some of which might include work, child rearing or other activities that are necessary to, or highly valued by the student—but which are also more time and place bound. The second access issue addressed by the transition of instruction to an online environment is the freeing up of classroom space. Given enough blended courses, it has been documented that an institution may significantly increase capacity to serve additional students, assuming the availability of human and physical resources (i.e. willing faculty, technical and pedagogical support, technical capacity to offer blended learning, leadership to support and sustain it in a rational manner). Such increased instructional capacity without a simultaneous increase in physical capacity may be seen as a mechanism by which higher education is made more accessible with less additional investment in physical infrastructure. There *is* a need to shift investment and energy to the virtual infrastructure and to the development and sustenance of a culture of innovation—but the investment and maintenance of some additional physical infrastructure may be avoided, thus aiding the institution to maintain or thrive in an increasingly resource constrained and competitive environment.

Framing access as the problem blending solves assumes that the quality of the instruction before and after the transition remains equivalent (or improves)—otherwise the transition will result in a net loss. The issue of quality is essential to solving the problem of access with blended learning. If quality suffers, increased access is no benefit. No institution can afford to reduce the quality of its academic programs to increase access and expect to achieve the goal—students do not want access to low quality programs:

faculty do not wish to teach in such programs, and alumni do not wish to support such programs.

The issue of quality raises a number of questions germane to a book on the topic of blended learning research. The first is "how are institutions managing to maintain or increase the quality of instruction in blended learning environments"? Another might be "From a theoretical perspective what are the preconditions and activities that would likely lead to high quality"? What do we mean by "quality" blended instruction? This is where a conceptual or theoretical model can become beneficial. Here is why—a conceptual model (ideally) allows us to make testable hypotheses about the preconditions and activities likely to result in high levels of learning and high levels of student, faculty satisfaction, and ultimately increased access and more efficient deployment of existing physical resources.

What do we mean by a conceptual or theoretical framework? An example may prove useful to the discussion. Think of other theories with which you are familiar. Certainly one with which many of us are familiar (and which is still able to produce public controversy) is Darwin's theory of evolution. What does such a theory do for us? In very clear and concise terms it allows us to understand the origin and development of plant and animal life on this and all other hypothetical worlds. That is a very powerful tool. With a few premises the theory of evolution explains how it is that all living things "got that way". While the theory has its detractors both within and outside the academy it remains the most cogent and elegant solution to the questions it addresses. Imagine a similar approach to the questions we seek to address here: how do people learn in higher education in (partially) technology-mediated environments? Working toward a conceptual model allows us to better understand, describe, explain and ultimately improve upon the design of blended learning—benefiting all participants in the enterprise and providing justification for utilizing blended learning to meet the goals of increasing access.

To understand learning in a blended environment we need to have an understanding of several underlying and interrelated questions. These include: how learning occurs generally, how it occurs among adult learners, and how it occurs in technology-mediated environments. Answering these questions is no small task. There is a great deal we do not know about each of those underlying questions. But we do have some knowledge—we know for example that learning is, in many ways, a social activity. We know that it must also be viewed as a cognitive activity. We also know that learning is shaped by affect. We know that students learn better in environments that attend to or support certain principles or pre-conditions. So, in order to understand blended learning in higher education it is beneficial to consider what we know in each of these arenas: what we know about learning generally, what we know about *adult* learning and what we know about *technology-mediated* teaching and learning. One lens through which to view learning generally in a blended environment is the "How People Learn" (HPL) framework

Figure 1. **Bransford, et al. (2000) "How People Learn"**

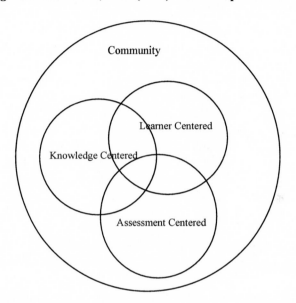

To understand how people learn, Bransford and his colleagues, Brown and Cocking (2000), reviewed elements of successful learning environments and concluded that they share certain characteristics (see Figure 1). Good learning environments are learner-centered, knowledge-centered, assessment-centered, and community centered. The HPL framework has spurred the work of other models looking at psychological, social, and developmental influences on e-learning specifically, (e.g. McCombs & Vakili, 2005; Shea, Fredericksen, Pickett, and Pelz, 2003).

A second lens through which to analyze blended learning, and one which carries the added benefit of addressing the needs of adult, college age learners is the Principles of Good Practice in Undergraduate Education (Chickering & Gamson, 1987). This strand summarizes decades of investigations in the undergraduate experience and distills this research into seven principles for fostering good, higher-education learning environments. These include frequent contact between students and faculty, reciprocity and cooperation among students, active learning, prompt feedback, time on task, the communication of high expectations, and respect for diverse talents and ways of learning. Another resource for considering blended learning for adult students is Knowles' (1980, 1984, 1998) work on the concept of andragor Briefly Knowles (and others working in this arena, e.g. Brookfield

21

Fellenz & Conti, 1989; Merriam & Caffarella, 1999) suggest that utility of learning goals, immediacy of learning application, independence, autonomy, self direction, and ownership of learning are all components of learning environments likely to lead to satisfactory experiences for adult learners. Added to this are needs for collaboration and the sharing of life experiences in effective communities of practice (e.g. Wenger, 1991, 2002). Each of these needs aligns well with suggestions arising from other frameworks, such as the goals of learner-centeredness and knowledge-centeredness in the HPL framework as well as elements of the principles of good practice in undergraduate education.

A third lens through which to view blended learning, one that also focuses directly on issues relevant to online pedagogy and processes, is the Community of Inquiry Model for online teaching and learning (Garrison, Anderson, and Archer, 2000). This model emphasizes the need to attend to various forms of "presence" to achieve quality teaching and learning in the absence of face-to-face interaction. Among these are teaching presence, social presence and cognitive presence, which will be described in more detail below.

Each of the previously mentioned "lenses" share an emphasis on the role of community, collaboration, and cooperation as a mechanism for producing desired learning outcomes. Here it may be useful to review the conditions that each of these conceptual frameworks place on a theory of quality blended learning.

For a blended learning environment to meet the first condition of the HPL model—"learner-centeredness"—the activities and pre-conditions in that environment need to focus on the goals, objectives, needs and interests of the learner. Instructors and designers involved in creating a learner-centered blended environment need to concentrate on understanding what students know—that their approach to learning may vary, and that it is possible and desirable to help learners understand how they learn through strategic guidance. For instructors and designers to achieve quality in a blended learning environment energy and activity needs to be applied to understanding who students are, learning about their abilities, passions, and goals and creating blended learning activities that align with these. A book which purports to seek to understand the phenomena of blended learning through research should, therefore, examine these issues. We need a framework through which to determine how and whether such environments may enable or constrain our abilities to put learners in active roles, at the center of the teaching and learning transaction. This concern is also implied in the principles of good practice in undergraduate education—for example ·nles calling for active roles for learners, and frequent contact between ·d with instructors. Can learning activities in blended environments ·n give learners more responsibility, ownership, and understanding of their learning relative to face-to-face instruction? Can blended environments be designed to enhance learner motivation and engagement levels with meaningful and worthwhile content? How? Are instructors using blended environments to understand and leverage learners' different strengths and approaches, to assist learners to be strategic about their learning, and in what ways?

For blended environments to meet the condition of "knowledge-centeredness" they must be designed to leverage the affordances of online and face-to-face settings in ways that support understanding and subsequently transfer to new settings (Bransford et al., 2000). To accomplish this we need to know first what knowledge learners bring to learning environments. A theory of blended learning should account for mechanisms by which online and face-to-face instruction can be combined to effectively and efficiently determine and build upon incoming abilities. Knowledge-centered learning environments also seek to enhance understanding rather than memorization; it is frequently recommended, therefore, that learners be encouraged to "do" the work of the discipline rather than memorize facts about it. A theory of blended learning should account for how such environments encourage the development of active learning that focuses on depth rather than primarily on breadth. "Ideas are best introduced when students see a need or a reason for their use—this helps them see relevant uses of knowledge to make sense of what they are learning" (Bransford et al., 2000, p. 139). Understanding how environments can be designed to introduce ideas when they are most needed is a useful element for a theory of blended learning from this perspective. Understanding how to assist learners to enter and participate in the work of a discipline rather than to learn "about" it is another goal towards which a theory of blended learning should strive. What are the characteristics of online learning, which, when combined with face-to-face instruction, can promote learning with understanding—meaningful learning?

In order for blended environments to meet the goal of "assessment centeredness" they need to help learners make their thinking visible, so that feedback and revision are more likely. Such environments also align instruction and assessment. A theory of blended learning should account for the ways in which online and face-to-face environments can be effectively orchestrated to accomplish this goal. Are certain types of assessment more appropriate or more easily accomplished online—why? how? For example, the use of automatically graded multiple-choice type assessments is "easier" to implement in computer mediated environments. Perhaps even quicker checks of comprehension can be conducted in the classroom. Is there a good rationale for choosing one environment over another to facilitate frequent and constructive assessment of understanding? Can we design blended environments to utilize such formative feedback to develop opportunities for more productive and substantive interaction rather than just the conventional (summative) quiz? Finally, how can self-assessment of understanding be effectively facilitated in blended environments? A theory of blended learning should accommodate these considerations given their significance in regards to HPL and other established theoretical frameworks for quality learning environments.

To meet the fourth criterion for effective learning environments design in the HPL framework (as well as others—see Garrison, 2000 e.g.), blended learning needs to be "community centered." Questions that we need to address include how we can promote the development of a sense of connectedness, collaboration, and a sense of safety through the integration of online and offline learning activities. Learning environments that are characterized by these qualities are considered to be more effective in promoting learning (e.g. Bransford et al., 2000; Johnson, Johnson, and Smith, 1991). How do we design blended instruction to promote collaboration and community? Can blended activities be designed to increase cooperation to achieve learning rather than competition for grades? Can we help learners to collaboratively construct knowledge in a community of practice through integration of different modalities? How?

To begin to create a conceptual framework we need to reflect on results of investigations undertaken to date on the impact of technology mediated teaching and learning. For example, why do we see, from a conceptual standpoint, the replication of the finding regarding the importance of learner interaction? As has been pointed out through extensive research in traditional learning environments, one need look no further than the work of Vygotsky for an explanation. Vygotsky argued that learning occurs in two stages (and also posits a powerful explanation for the development of the elements of all psychological functioning). The two stages or "planes" are the inter-psychological and the intra-psychological. Vygotsky (1978) states it relatively simply:

> We propose that a central feature of learning is that it creates a zone of proximal development that is, learning awakens a variety of internal development processes that are able to operate only when the child is interacting with people in his environment and in cooperation with peers. Once these processes are internalized they become part of the child's internal development achievement (p. 90).

If we replace "child" with "learner" we can see why interaction, both online and offline, is so critical to learning. It is the process by which new abilities are internalized—how they transform from the inter-psychological to the intra-psychological plane. Vygotsky (1979) states elsewhere,

We could formulate the general genetic law of cultural development as follows: any function in the child's cultural development appears twice, or on two planes. First it appears on the social plane, and then on the psychological plane. First it appears between people as an inter-psychological category and then within the child as an intra-psychological category. This is equally true of voluntary attention, logical memory, the formation of concepts and the development of volition (p.163).

If we are to take seriously the notion of a conceptual framework through which we can better understand, study, and design blended learning environments, we need to take seriously the notion that it is through thoughtful design of the interaction that most learning occurs. Whether we set out to create scenarios by which cognitive conflict may be resolved, as in a Piagetian perspective, or to construct a productive, shared zone of proximal development (in Vygotskian terms), the extent to which we enable productive discourse between learners with new technological tools is the extent to which we will promote better learning in these new environments. This may be accomplished through the re-design of collaborative learning activities known to sustain rich, productive dialogue in traditional environments, with attention paid to the affordances and constraints of the blended environment. A blended-learning environment offers us a new opportunity for such reflection—to carefully consider how both curriculum and instruction are carried out—designed, re-designed, and implemented in higher education.

There is some concern, however, that blended learning environments, even those designed for collaboration, will fail to support the kind of sustained and challenging discourse known to facilitate learning. One strand of research suggests that learners frequently do not participate very intensively in collaborative blended environments. Guzdial (1997) and Guzdial and Turns (2000) for example found that students wrote, on average, only 4.8 messages in a ten-week academic period. Hara, Bonk, and Angeli (2000) found that graduate students posted, on average, only fifteen notes in as many weeks. Others (e.g. Hsi (1997)) studied 8th graders and found that they wrote, on average, fewer than five notes in an eighteen-week period.

In addition to the limited numbers of initial postings described in this line of research on collaborative, blended environments, the number of response messages written was also limited and very brief. A number of investigators found that the average discussion thread in computer supported collaborative learning environments was only 2.8–3 notes (Guzdial, 1997; Guzdial & Turns, 2000; Hewitt & Tevlops, 1999). Hara et al. (2000) reported similar results with nine university courses—the average thread length was

2.7 messages. Lipponen, Rahkainene, Hakkarainen and Palonen (2002) reported that the average thread length among education students studying in blended environments was 3.8, indicating that interaction in these environments tended not to be intense or sustained. Stahl (1999, 2001) found that computer supported collaborative learning was mainly used for the exchange of opinions and for delivering surface knowledge and not for collaborative knowledge building. This finding is supported to a certain extent by Garrison (2000). Feldman, Konold, Coulter, Conroy, Hutchinson, and London (2000) found that most messages posted in discussion spaces appear to be social in nature, rather than about content.

This paucity of participation and depth in blended environments reported by these researchers is disappointing. From a conceptual perspective, greater levels of participation is more desirable. In addition to the general learning benefits of interaction outlined above, participation in online threaded discussions is a form of writing and writing is known to play an essential part in explication and articulation of one's thinking (e.g. Bereiter & Scardamalia, 1987; Olson, 1994). The externalization of cognition through writing makes thinking visible and gives students opportunities to reflect and share their ideas and emerging expertise (Collins, Brown, & Holum, 1991).

Integration and Interaction

One could hypothesize that these findings reflect a common problem. The missing instructional element in this line of research line seems to be "integration". It appears that students in these studies viewed the online learning activities as either supplemental or irrelevant to their learning in the face-to-face activities—i.e. they were not integral. Other researchers (see Vignare in this volume) have reported much better results when blending integrates and clearly values online activities on par with classroom activities. Promoting, facilitating, and integrating online and face-to-face interactions are essential to blended learning. Without integration of interactions in the different modalities blended environments will fail to achieve their potential. The analysis of integration of face-to-face and online interaction will, therefore, be a crucial component of theory building for effective blended learning. Such analysis needs to be accomplished on several levels in order to inform the development and evolution of a conceptual model. Online interaction on a macro level can be examined through analysis of thread patterns. Graphically depicting and mapping interaction as seen in Howell, Richardson and Mellar (1996) and Hara et al. (2000) will be useful in understanding and learning how better to guide and structure instruction in blended environments and to avoid limited or feeble interaction. Online interaction can also be analyzed at the micro level through discourse analysis (e.g. Anderson, Rourke, Garrison and Archer,

2001). Such analysis allows us to understand underlying processes and meanings inherent in online communication and to adjust the design of instruction based on findings.

A number of researchers have made a case for investigating how well-designed and integrated blended learning environments can further the goal of supporting higher order thinking and learning. Several methodological approaches have been used for this purpose—each of which may contribute to the development of a conceptual model for blended learning and provide direction to avoid weak or unproductive interaction levels in blended environments. As previously mentioned, the manifest content of messages can be measured through such indices as word count of message length (indicating message complexity) as well as methods that evaluate latent content related to cognition. Bloom's taxonomy (as well as later interpretations—e.g. Anderson & Krathwohl, 2001) may be applied to message content to determine levels of cognition (e.g. for evidence of thinking at the higher levels of analysis, synthesis, and evaluation). When this level of analysis is combined with investigation of course design features, we may begin to better comprehend how blended environments can facilitate higher order thinking.

Another approach to the analysis of higher order thinking is Biggs and Collins (1982) SOLO Taxonomy which assesses structural complexity reflected in writing and allows for discrimination between in-depth and surface processing of learning. The taxonomy is comprised of five categories: pre-structural, uni-structural, multi-structural, relational and extended abstract. The latter two categories are considered to reflect in-depth as opposed to surface processing. Identifying the course design and interaction patterns that result in deeper processing will advance our understanding of effective blended learning.

Garrison's Practical Inquiry Model of Cognitive Processing is yet another methodological framework through which cognition in blended environments may be assessed. In Garrison's model, online discussion can progress through four phases: a triggering event, an exploratory phase, (leading to cognitive conflict) an integration phase and a resolution phase. Garrison suggests that online discourse should cycle through these phases if higher order learning is to occur.

The analyses of interaction at the macro and micro levels and the analysis of higher order thinking reflect just a few of the methodological approaches through which the development of a theory or conceptual framework for blended learning might be developed and tested. Others working in this arena have looked at existing theories that might inform the development of a conceptual framework for high-quality blended teaching and learning environments. The theories of human cognition that underlie an emphasis on such technology-mediated collaborative learning are varied and include social psychology, distributed cognition, situated cognition, situated learning, activity theory, and constructivism. One of the promises of hybrid learning is the potential for technology support for facilitating collaboration. This kind of support includes overcoming physical barriers, more efficient computational support, and new models of interaction that enable richer, more productive communication, learning, and work (Stahl, 2001).

Future Directions

So far it has been argued that blended learning may be considered one solution to expanding access to higher education if the quality of the learning experience is maintained or improved, and that research into "interaction" is a promising direction for the development of a framework for quality blended environments. Further, a key to ensuring the instructional quality of blended learning is to attend to what we know about quality learning environments generally, to keep in mind what we know about adult learners, and to integrate our burgeoning knowledge of online learning processes. While this is no small feat in itself, a degree of additional complexity arises when we consider what can actually be "blended" in blended learning. While common notions of blended learning consider the integration of activities that occur online with those that occur in face to face settings, several other options exist. Blending of pedagogy (e.g. from cooperative to competitive), blending of synchronous and non-synchronous technologies, blending instructional formats (e.g. from cohort to more independent models), blending of modalities (from text-based to more multimodal technologies), even blending of institutions providing the courses (students may seek/bring courses from other institutions to a program). Finally, through the use of communication technologies it is also possible to bring learners or faculty (or guest speakers) from other institutions into the teaching and learning occurring locally. Thus participant in courses may also be "blended". A non-exhaustive list of blending options might then include the frequencies along which activities occur on several spectra:

Time	(Synchronous – Asynchronous)
Place	(Face-to-Face – Online)
Pedagogy	(Cooperative – Competitive)
Technologies	(Text – Multimodal)
Format	(Cohort – Self paced)
Courses	(Home-institution's courses – Others)
Participants	(Local – Distant)

Learner and faculty characteristics as well as learning objectives and available resources enable and constrain decisions about when, why, and what to blend. All exist within an institutional culture that may encourage or discourage such innovation. A sketch of the components and influences impacting decisions that may come into play in a blended learning environment is presented in Figure 2 below.

Figure 2. **Blended Learning Design Decisions: Components and Influences**

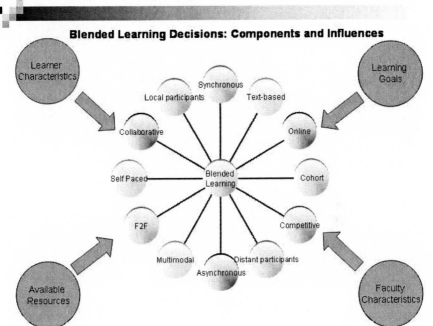

Each of the impacts of these blending options should be considered in a conceptual framework for blended or hybrid teaching and learning. The relative balance of synchronous and asynchronous online activities in blended environments, for example, may be mediated by the backgrounds of learners—some may want blended learning environment because of their need for flexibility—activities that require them to be time and place bound are not desirable.

The balance of cooperative and traditional pedagogies may also be mediated by types of learning and theoretically complementary instructional approaches. Jonassen (1993) argued that at the introductory level, in which learners have little directly transferable knowledge about a content area, classical instructional design, characterized by its pre-determined, constrained, sequential and criterion-referenced methodology would be most appropriate. As learners approach more advanced knowledge levels, constructivist approaches may be more appropriate. A theory of blended learning should specify other relationships that support decisions regarding how to blend elements identified here (and others that may be added) to maximal educational benefit.

     In the final analysis, however, it might be conceded that application and integration of communication technologies, modalities, people, temporalities, locations, and pedagogies etc. (blending in this larger sense) are not the units of analysis most useful for making decisions about how to ensure instructional quality while increasing access to higher education via blended learning. A growing chorus of researchers (e.g. Hannafin & Land, 2000; Hannafin, Hannafin, Land and Olliver, 1997; Hakkinen, 2002; Mishra, 2002; Whitehouse, 2004; Dabbagh, 2005) are advocating new approaches to online and distributed instructional design. From a pedagogical standpoint, to ensure quality of learning environments, ultimately, we need practices that are grounded. To achieve this we need to articulate our epistemological beliefs, identify the theories of learning that support these beliefs, specify pedagogical models that attempt to bridge theory and practice, define instructional strategies that provide general guidance for particular learners in particular contexts, and design specific learning activities that achieve the goals of these instructional strategies for the learners and their contexts. Examining and communicating what we know, believe, or choose at each of these levels will provide guidance that helps accommodate each of the elements that may be blended. Such a model might take this form (see Figure 3):

Figure 3. A Grounded Model for Blended Environments

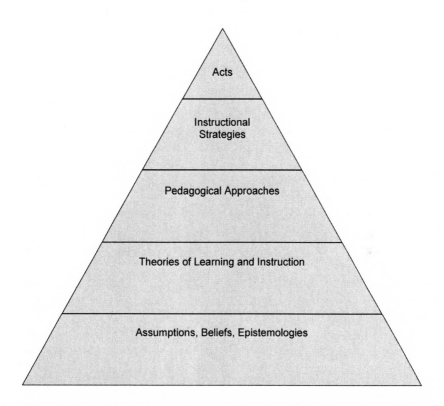

The process in such a model would begin with stating our assumptions and beliefs about the nature of knowledge. We would then identify the theories of learning that reflect these philosophical underpinnings. Following this we would articulate complementary pedagogical approaches, from which instructional strategies and, ultimately, specific learning activities flow. Such a grounded-design approach avoids the dogmatic application of specific instructional methods, forces us to articulate the basis for instructional choices, and provides a firmer foundation for curricular and pedagogic decisions in blended environments.

Media and Methods

This grounded approach can be extended beyond the curricular and pedagogic. We can also apply it to what we know about technology mediation in learning. Consequently, we should also identify and articulate our assumptions and beliefs about particular forms of technology that may be utilized in the blended teaching and learning transaction and specify their likely impact on motivation, cognition, affect, learning and other outcomes important in education when integrated into a complementary pedagogic approach, and within specific learning activities. These should serve to remind us that the media by which the instruction and learning occur may be less important than the design decisions made within such a grounded framework—especially when we consider the history of media comparison research:

> Past research on media has shown quite clearly that no medium enhances learning more than any other medium regardless of learning task, learner traits, symbolic elements, curriculum content or setting (Clark & Salomon, 2001, p. 37).

While many feel this overstates the case and that specific technologies do have unique cognitive consequences when applied in specific contexts with specific learners, the record so far has not been good. This may be an artifact of the approach to research. To paraphrase Clark and Salomon (2001), *gross* comparisons of instruction via blended-learning technologies versus conventional instruction are unlikely to prove more useful in the future than similar investigations of previous innovations were in the past. Assessment of blending is unlikely to show a positive effect on the quality of learning unless blending is employed with well designed regard for complementary pedagogies and the potential of specific media attributes in the blend to impact some aspect of cognition, motivation, affect or other essential learning element. Medium and method are integral parts of the design of instruction (Kozma, 1991), and nowhere may this prove to be more accurate than in blended learning environments. Focusing on a grounded instructional approach before considering which technologies to employ can help avoid a "technology-driven" design and the mistakes of the past associated with such models.

Conclusion

From a quality perspective, the ultimate potential of blended learning may be to make possible novel and productive instructional methods that may be difficult or impossible to implement in the absence of blending (Kozma, 1991). Such progress would satisfy the condition put forth recently (e.g. Twigg, 2001; Hannafin & Land, 2000) to go beyond the "no significant difference" status into which research in online- and technology-mediated teaching and learning appears to have settled. To arrive at that potential, however, we will need better road maps than we currently have. It is hoped that the articulation here of the preconditions and requirements of a theoretical framework for blended learning; the specification of promising research methodologies regarding successful application of blending; advice regarding how the results of such research can contribute to theory building;

the description of the fuller spectrum and intricacies of what may be blended, and the identification of a grounded "theory-to-practice-in-context model" for blending may help the dialogue and mapping to proceed.

References

Anderson, L. & Krathwohl, D. (2001). A taxonomy for learning, teaching and assessing: A revision of Bloom's Taxonomy of educational objectives. New York: Longman.

Anderson, T., Rourke, L., Garrison, D. R., & Archer W. (2001). Assessing teaching presence in a computer conferencing context. Journal of Asynchronous Learning Networks, 5(2), 1–17.

Biggs, J. & Collins, K. (1982). Evaluating the quality of learning: The SOLO taxonomy. New York: Academic Press.

Bereiter, C. & Scardamalia, M. (1987). The psychology of written composition. Hillsdale, NJ: Lawrence Erlbaum.

Bransford, D., Brown, A., & Cocking, R. (2000). How people learn: Brain, mind, experience and school. Committee on Developments in the Science of Learning, Commission on Behavioral and Social Sciences and Education, National Research Council. Washington, D.C.: National Academy Press.

Brookfield, S. (1986).Understanding and facilitating adult learning. San Francisco: Jossey-Bass.

Chickering, A. W., & Gamson, A. F. (1987). Seven principles for good practice in undergraduate education. Racine, WI: The Johnson Foundation, Inc. Wingspread.

Clark, R. & Salomon G. (2001). Why should we expect media to teach anyone anything? In R. Clark (Ed.), Learning from media: Arguments, analysis, and evidence (pp. 37–71). Greenwich CT: Information Age Publishing.

Collins, A, Brown, J. S. & Holum, A. (1991, Winter). Cognitive apprenticeship: Making thinking visible. American Educator, 15(6–11), 38–46.

Dabbagh, N. (2005) The instructional design knowledge base. Retrieved September 3, 2005, from http://classweb.gmu.edu/ndabbagh/Resources /IDKB/index.htm.

Feldman, A. Konold, B. Coulter, B. Conroy, B. Hutchison, C. & London, N. (2000). Network science, a decade later. The Internet and classroom learning. Mahwah, NJ: Lawrence Erlbaum.

Fellenz, R. & Conti, G. (1989). Learning and reality: Reflections on trends in adult learning. ERIC Clearing House on Adult Career and Education and Training Information Series (No. 336).

Garrison, D. R., Anderson, T., & Archer, W. (2000). Critical inquiry in a text-based environment: Computer conferencing in higher education [Electronic version]. Internet and Higher Education, 11(2):1–14. Retrieved from http://communitiesofinquiry.com/documents/CTinTextEnvFinal.pdf.

Guzdial, M. (1997). Information ecology of collaboration in educational settings: Influence of tool. In R. Hall, N. Miyake & N. Enyedy (Eds.), Proceedings of

CSCL '97: The second international conference on computer support for collaborative learning (83–90). Mahwah, NJ: Erlbaum.

Guzdial M. & J. Turns (2000). Effective discussion through a computer-mediated anchored forum. Journal of the Learning Sciences, 9, 437–469.

Häkkinen P. (2002). Challenges for design of computer–based learning environments. British Journal of Educational Technology, 33(4), 461–469.

Hannafin, M. J., Hannafin, K. M., Land, S. L. & Oliver, K.(1997). Grounded practice and the design of constructivist learning environments. Educational Technology, Research and Development, 45(3), 101–117.

Hannafin, M. J., & Land S. (2000, Fall). Technology and student-centered learning in higher education: Issues and practices. Journal of Computing in Higher Education, 12(1), 3–30.

Hara, N. Bonk C. J. & Angeli, C. J. (2000). Content analysis of online discussion in an applied educational psychology course. Instructional Science, 28 (20), 115–152.

Hewitt, J. & Tevlops, C., (1999). An analysis of growth patterns in computer conferencing threreads. In C. Hoadley (Ed), Proceedings of CSCL '99: The third international conference on computer support for collaborative learning, (232–241). Mahwah, NJ: Erlbaum.

Hsi, S. (1997). Facilitating knowledge integration in science through electronic discussion: The multimedia kiosk forum. Berkley, CA: University of California at Berkeley.

Johnson, D. W., Johnson, R. T. & Smith, K. A. (1991). Active learning: Cooperation in the college classroom. Edina, MN: Interaction Book Co.

Jonassen, D., Mayes, T, & McAleese, R. (1993). A manifesto for a constructivist approach to uses of technology in higher education. In T. M. Duffy, J. Lowyck, & D. H. Jonassen (Eds.), Designing environments for constructive learning (232–247). Heidelberg, Germany: Springer-Verlag Berlin.

Knowles, M. (1980). The modern practice of adult education: From pedagogy to andragogy (2nd ed). Englewood Cliffs, NJ: Prentice Hall, Cambridge.

Knowles, M. (1984). Andragogy in action: Applying modern principles of adult education. San Francisco, CA: Jossey-Bass.

Knowles, M. (1998). Holton, E. & Swanson, R. The adult learner. Houston, TX: Gulf.

Kozma, R. (1991) Learning with media. Review of Educational Research, 61(2), 179–212.

Lipponen, L., Rahikainen, M., Hakkarainen, K., & Palonen, T. (2002). Effective participation and discourse through a computer network: Investigating elementary students' computer-supported interaction. Journal of Educational Computing Research, 27(4), 355–84.

McCombs, B. & Vakili, D. (2005). A learner-centered framework for e-learning. Teachers College Record, 107(8), 1582–1600.

Merriam, S. & Caffarella, R. (1999). Learning in adulthood: A comprehensive guide. San Francisco, CA: Jossey-Bass.

Mishra, S. (2002). A design framework for online learning environments. British Journal of Educational Technology, 33(4), 493.

Olson, D. (1994). The world on paper: The conceptual and cognitive implications of writing and reading. Cambridge, MA: Cambridge University Press.

Shea, P., Fredericksen, E., Pickett, A., & Pelz, W. (2003). Faculty development, student satisfaction, and reported learning in The SUNY Learning Network. In T. Duffy, T. & J. Kirkley (Eds.), Learner Centered Theory and Practice in Distance Education. Mahwah, NJ: Lawrence Erlbaum.

Stahl, G. (1999). Reflections on WebGuide. Seven issues for the next generation of collaborative knowledge-building environments. In C. Hoadley (Ed), Proceedings of CSCL '99: The third international conference on computer support for collaborative learning, 600–610. Mahwah, NJ: Erlbaum.

Stahl, G. (2001). Rediscovering CSCL. In T. Koschmann, R. Hall, & N. Miyake (Eds.), CSCL2: Carrying forward the conversation, (pp. 169–183). Mahwah, NJ: Erlbaum.

Twigg, C. A. (2001). Innovations in online learning: Moving beyond no significant difference. Taylor, NY: Pew Learning and Technology.

Vygotsky, L.S. (1978). Mind in society. London: Harvard University Press.

Vygotsky, L. (1979). The genesis of higher mental functions. In J.V. Wertsch (Ed) The concept of activity in Soviet psychology. Armonk, NY: M. E. Sharpe.

Wenger, E. (1991). Situated learning: Legitimate peripheral participation. Cambridge, UK: Cambridge University Press.

Wenger, E. (2002). Cultivating communities of practice: A guide to managing knowledge. Boston: Harvard Business School Publishing.

Whitehouse, P. (2004). Women's studies online: An oxymoron? Teaching with technology today, 10(5).

Review of Literature
Blended Learning: Using ALN to
Change the Classroom—Will it Work?

Karen Vignare
Michigan State University

Abstract

Blended learning, also known as hybrid, mixed mode, flexible or distributed learning, is gaining acceptance and being adopted throughout higher education. In this chapter, a review of the literature on blended learning is presented using the Sloan Consortium's Five Pillars quality framework for online asynchronous learning networks. Evidence is mixed as to whether blended learning is truly a unique learning environment or just a simple combination of traditional face to face and online instructional approaches. The early research indicates that blended learning can be as successful as either online or face to face instruction; however, there is a great need for more study on its effectiveness.

Review of Literature Blended Learning:
Using ALN to Change the Classroom—Will it Work?

Blended learning is gaining acceptance and being adopted at college campuses throughout the US (Bonk & Graham, 2005; Allen & Seaman, 2004). The availability of online technologies like course management systems, the recognition that the Internet is a valuable communications tool, the convenience and flexibility of having fewer campus meetings, and research on how we learn all seem to support the growth of blended learning. Some scholars argue blended learning could be more powerful than other forms of learning and transformative for higher education (Garrison & Kanuka, 2004; Bransford, Brown & Cocking, 2000; McCombs & Vakili, 2005). Existing evidence of such a transformation is limited but not without promise. This chapter will provide an investigation of the research currently available on blended learning and what research is needed to gain a more comprehensive understanding of blended learning and its potential in education. Research from asynchronous learning networks (ALNs) and how that research applies to the blended learning format will be the primary source of information. The Sloan-Consortium (Sloan-C) quality framework, built around the Five Pillars of learning effectiveness, faculty satisfaction, student satisfaction, access, and cost effectiveness/institutional commitment, provides the organization for reviewing the literature (Moore, 2002). It is clear that it is important to consider other sources of information and effort is undertaken to connect ALN research to the use of educational technologies, to established research for the traditional, face to face classroom, and to learning theories; however, the driving phenomenon for blended learning is the advent of ALN and Internet communications technologies. While other technologies and different types of blended learning experiences are viable (see definitions below), the focus of this chapter is limited to the planned integration of ALN and the traditional classroom.

Defining Blended Learning

Definitions for blended learning vary considerably. For example, corporate blended learning could be a mixture of face to face instructor led and self-paced online learning (Graham, 2005). Some educational researchers believe blended learning should include the use of mixed media as a definition (Osguthorpe & Graham, 2003). In another generic example, a course which uses a web-site or a course management system plus a classroom experience would be blended learning. However, a significant group of educational scholars seem to prefer defining blended as simply the combination of online (mostly asynchronous) learning with face to face learning environments. The definition for blended courses that emerged from research workshops sponsored by the Sloan-Consortium is:

1. Blended courses integrate online with face to face instruction in a planned, pedagogically valuable manner; and
2. Do not just combine but trade-off face to face time with online activity (or vice versa) (Niemiec & Otte, in press).

This definition helps focus this literature review. Since 1998, the University of Central Florida (UCF) has been using a similar definition for its blended learning courses, termed mixed-mode courses (Dziuban, Hartman, Moskal, Sorg, & Truman, 2004). The UCF data reveal that blended learning is effective and can lead to higher student success rates (grades) in specific academic disciplines (Dziuban et al., 2004). In addition, faculty seem to be very satisfied with teaching either blended or online as long as they receive training and academic support (Schroeder & Oakley, 2005). Research by Garrison and Kanuka (2004) posited that blended learning is not only an acceptable methodology but a transformative one for higher education. This view that online learning technology could transform learning was also suggested by Bransford et al. (2000) in their book on how people learn. Hiltz and Turoff (2005) strongly support the view that the introduction of asynchronous learning networks to campus courses will be viewed as a critical breakthrough in improving learning. McCombs & Vakili (2005) reached a similar conclusion because blended learning can lead to a more learner-centered education environment.

However, not all of the research is positive. A recent experiment of a course taught in all three modalities concluded that fully online was the best of all the approaches—better than blended and better than face to face (Reasons, Valadares & Slavkin, 2005). Vaughn and Garrison (2005) did not find any evidence that blended learning improved student cognitive presence while exclusive ALN environments did show that evidence. Wu and Hiltz's (2004) study of students in blended courses found that online discussions were meaningful, but no evidence was shown to support the hypothesis that blended was significantly better than fully online. Proponents of learner-centered design and institutional transformation would argue that the focus must be on individuals and on changing the educational progress from a course by course set of outcomes to a competency based criteria for a curriculum or discipline (Weimer, 2002; Tagg, 2003; McCombs & Vakili, 2005). Instructional technologists might also argue that educational improvement comes from more highly interactive technologies such as gaming and simulations (Dede, 2005). However, institutional limitations such as funding, user-friendly technology, culture, organizational structure, and staff are not always available to support those kinds of dramatic changes. Blended learning is a relatively simple and effective change that institutions can indeed adopt.

The student mix and demand for technology is very different than it was ten years ago. Today's students of traditional age essentially grew up on the Internet but represent only a small portion of the total college population. Seventy-five percent of all students in higher education would be called non-traditional, they work full-time; are older than 18–22; delayed going to college, etc. (Oblinger & Oblinger, 2005; Snyder, 2005). The differences in these populations are striking. The Net Generation expects technology integration and having something online is not enough (Kravik & Caruso, 2005). Contrary to the headlines and misperceptions, the evidence from UCF's work is that student's 25 years and older seem to be more satisfied than younger students with online and blended learning (Hartman, Moskal & Dziuban, 2005). It is also important to remember that not all college students have ready access to the Internet (Oblinger & Oblinger). Requiring online learning for students who lack Internet access is problematic. Approximately 20% of all higher education students now take online courses, thereby allowing students with busy lives another way of completing courses and degrees (Allen & Seaman, 2005). Students often can be persuaded about the benefits of new ways of learning if they understand what they are supposed to gain as a result of using these techniques (Hartman et al.).

Sloan-C Quality Pillars Framework

The organization of this chapter is based on the Sloan-C Five Pillars quality framework (see Figure 1). Sloan-C describes these pillars as:

> The Sloan-C principles, known as the pillars or elements of quality, parallel the familiar principles of continuous quality

improvement (CQI), using metrics to improve products and processes. In higher education, the quality goal is scalability to achieve capacity and breadth through attention to learning effectiveness, access and affordability for learners and providers, and faculty and student satisfaction. These elements are interdependent (Moore, 2002).

Figure 1. **Sloan-C Five Pillars Framework.**

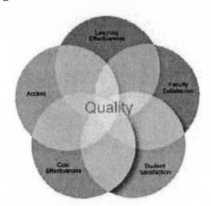

Beginning with learning effectiveness, the pillars offer researchers and higher education concepts to begin to benchmark. It is important to note that while each of the pillars has individual characteristics, they are also related to each other. Much of the research in one pillar overlaps or impacts other pillars. Learning effectiveness includes demonstrating that learners are given the tools to be good students. Research in the area often starts with global measures of effectiveness like retention and completion but certainly includes much more. Student satisfaction begins the preparation needed to prepare students for online learning. It also includes the services that are needed to support learners and community elements needed for students to feel satisfied about their online learning experiences. Faculty satisfaction is interwoven in learning effectiveness and other pillars and focuses on what is needed to make sure that faculty feel prepared and satisfied with their online teaching. Access has to do with providing opportunities for students to pursue an education. Cost effectiveness and institutional commitment have to do with the institutional cost and benefit analysis of integrating ALN or blended learning into its operations.

Learning Effectiveness

One of the larger questions facing the field is whether blended learning is effective as measured through traditional methods of grades, course completion, retention, and graduation rates. An even greater question is whether blended learning is "better" than other learning environments. The results from fully online learning courses show mixed results but overall meta-analyses show that online courses are at least as effective as traditional classroom instruction (Russell, 2001; Zhao, Lei, Lai, & Tan, 2005). In the Zhao et al. research the meta-analyses certainly support no significant difference findings, but they also supports the fact that distance learning can be better than face to face when instructor involvement, interaction, content studied, learner capabilities, and the right mix of human interaction and technology are combined. While the focus of this meta-analysis was on distance learning, Zhao et al. included blended learning research studies. Others would argue that comparing the two environments does not allow education to move beyond the comparison trap to look for new and different outcomes (Sener, 2004). According to the Sloan-C Five Pillars framework, the appropriate measure for learning effectiveness is to make sure the quality of online learning is as good as the quality of classroom learning. Research does support that fully online ALN is effective, especially when looking at measures of retention, completion, course outcomes, perceived learning, shifts in cognitive presence, and deeper learning. The research available on blended learning that measures these same attributes is harder to find and currently more ambiguous.

Retention of students is important for most universities and is measured by course completion rates, program completions, and graduation. Buried in the data are course drop-outs, stop-outs, and student withdrawals. Much of the data on fully online ALNs suggest that retention rates are not as high as for face to face instruction. Some research suggests that the comparisons are not as easy to make as the headlines have indicated data reported are inconsistent (Howell, Laws & Lindsay, 2004). The best extrapolations come from the Department of Education's Institutional Postsecondary Educational Data and Statistics, where graduation rates must be reported for all four- and two-year programs. Associate degree colleges graduate approximately 35% of their students versus a 50% graduation rate at traditional four-year colleges. No similar data is yet reported for fully online programs. What is known though from Allen and Seaman's (2004, 2005) work is that nearly 50% of the institutions offering ALN courses are associate degree colleges. Thus, when comparisons of graduation rates are made, it should be noted that more ALN courses and programs are offered by colleges which already have a low rate of graduation. Until more accurate data appear for ALN courses, it is simply premature to say graduation rates are lower for ALN.

Moving to the course level data, Ingle (2005) reports completion rates for fully online courses of 57% for two-year schools, 84% for four-year schools, 85% upper division programs only, and 86% for graduate schools. In Vignare (2002) and Starenko, Vignare, & Humbert (2006), cour completion rates of 95% were almost exactly the same for both fully o

41

and blended courses offered at the Rochester Institute of Technology. It is again difficult to locate comparable face to face data on course completion, so until accurate and equitable comparisons can be found either in single institutions like the RIT data reported above or across multiple campuses it is simply too early to indicate that course completion data show that ALN is lower than face to face. Using course outcomes as measured by grades or drops, withdrawals and failures (DWFs), Dziuban et al. (2004) data show that blended learning completion rates at UCF are higher than fully online, and in some cases higher than traditional face to face learning, but that there are significant differences among the disciplines. In Reasons et al. (2005) the data on course grades and tests showed students in the fully online courses doing better than either face to face or blended courses. There are also a number of case studies which report that outcomes were very similar for blended learning courses versus face to face or ALN courses (Carroll, 2003; Christensen, 2003; King & Hildreth, 2001; Johnson, 2002). Much like the distance learning effectiveness research, there are studies which show blended learning to be more effective (Boyle, Bradley, Chalk, Jones & Pickard, 2003; Cottrell & Robinson, 2003; Dowling, Godfrey & Gyles, 2003).

Other measures of blended learning effectiveness tend to show weak but positive results that blended learning is enhancing the learning environment. Garrison and Kanuka (2004) concluded that data from their survey research show that students believe that they are learning from discussions but their actual performance is only slightly positive and not statistically significant (Wu & Hiltz, 2004; Vaughan & Garrison, 2005). For example, analysis of online discourse supports that more knowledge construction occurs online but it is no different in the amount of triggering events or the resolution phase (Swan, 2005; Vaughan & Garrison). Students perceive both learning and satisfaction as higher in the fully online ALN environment provided the faculty have been prepared to teach online (Shea, Pickett & Pelz, 2003).

The McCombs and Valiki (2005) approach that applies the learner centered framework from the American Psychological Association (APA) includes 14 principles organized into four research validated domains of cognitive and meta-cognitive, motivational and affective, developmental and social, and individual differences. The APA defines learner-centered as follows:

> 'Learner-centered' is the perspective that couples a focus on individuals learners—their heredity, experiences, perspectives, backgrounds, talents, interests, capacities, and needs—with a focus on learning—the best available knowledge about learning and how it occurs and about ᵗching practices that are most effective in promoting the ᵗst levels of motivation, learning, and achievement for

all learners. This dual focus then informs and drives education decision making. Learner-centered is a reflection in practice of the Learner-Centered Psychological Principles—in the programs, practices, policies, and people that support learning for all (McCombs & Vakili, 2005, p. 1564).

The APA, McCombs and Vakili (2005), and Weimer (2002) identify principles, practices and teaching ideas to make instruction more student centered as well as effective. Online learning technologies enable most of these teaching ideas, but many learner-centered proponents do not mention using fully online ALN or blended learning as strategies for implementing better instruction. McCombs and Vakili use case studies and research from online learning to identify how strategies used online learning to enable a learner centered framework.

The 14 principles of learner centered psychological principles as published from the APA work group include: under cognitive and metacognitive factors—nature of learning process, goals of the learning process, construction of knowledge, strategic thinking, thinking about thinking and context of learning; under motivation and affective factors—motivation and emotional influences on learning, intrinsic motivation to learn, and effects of motivation on effort; under developmental and social factors—developmental influences on learning and social influences on learning; and under individual-difference factors—individual differences in learning, learning and diversity and standards and assessment (as reprinted in McCombs & Vakili, 2005). All of these principles of learning are typically guidelines for good ALN design as well. In ALN there has been a clear indication that applying instructional design principles while also allowing some just in time adjustment results in greater student satisfaction with the outcomes of the courses (Graff, 2003; Karagiorgi & Symeou, 2005; Lohr & Ku, 2003). There are clear differences between the proponents of instructional design and ALN learning effectiveness. Instructional design has been more aligned with the learning theory of behaviorism (Gagne & Driscoll, 1988). ALN recognizes the importance of constructivism and social constructivism (Hiltz & Goldman, 2005; Swan, 2005). Examples of how online learning can be structured to enhance all learning theories are also a current research topic of discussion (Hung, 2001). Learning theories have also been attached to specific academic disciplines that can be taught through behaviorism (Hung; Zhao et al., 2005; Dziuban et al., 2004). Allen and Seaman (2005) further document that business, liberal arts, computer and information sciences, and health professions and related sciences are mo*~* prevalent as fully online degree programs. It is clear that academic/ *~* across the country are reaching a consensus that certain online inst*~* strategies align easier to certain content. The research does not r *~* fully online and blended can be introduced in other field*~*

instructional reasons these academic disciplines have found online more effective at this early juncture in certain fields.

Faculty Satisfaction

According to the Sloan-C framework, faculty satisfaction factors include administrative and technical support, quality control, institutional rewards, research opportunities, access to new populations of students and participation in interactive learning communities (Moore, 2005). In much of the research, faculty satisfaction seems to be tied to two things: choice and preparedness. Faculty who are required rather than choose to teach online or blended learning are often more reluctant to redesign courses. Recent research also dispels the notion that core faculty do not teach online (Allen & Seaman, 2005). Faculty who are given the instructional support and the preparation time to learn how to teach online indicate they are more satisfied with their online teaching experience (Shea et al., 2003; Dziuban et al., 2004). In addition, there appears to be no difference in the level of faculty satisfaction regardless of whether faculty teach fully online courses or blended courses (Dziuban et al., 2004). Case study research from faculty also points to high levels of satisfaction when faculty feel that their teaching strategies have impacted students positively. Evidence proves that meeting students' needs for flexibility and multiple learning styles through using blended learning strategies also increase faculty satisfaction (Shea et al., 2003).

Of critical importance to faculty is continuing success at the many tasks they have been assigned—typically teaching, research, publication, grantsmanship, participation in learning communities, and participation in college governance. Done well, each of these functions takes time, and to get faculty to improve or try new teaching methodologies requires efficient academic support mechanisms. Providing the right level of support and providing it the best way for faculty is a clear concern to institutions and as important as student support and technology infrastructure needs (Arabacz, Pirani & Fawcett, 2003).

Administrative departments that support online learning on campus must find ways to appeal to faculty to get them to come to training (Otte, 2005; Hitt & Hartman, 2002). Training varies greatly in some institutions and can consist of learning to use basic technology tools as well as learning to develop effective pedagogical techniques (Arabacz & Baker, 2003; Ives & Steinbrenner, 2005). However, a lack of sufficient support is likely a main reason why many faculty do not participate in online and blended instruction.

So what kind of support seems to help faculty more? The evidence for this question seems to come from faculty themselves. Faculty engage in new learning methodologies for several reasons but primarily because there desire to deliver good instruction. This includes the desire to improve student communication, to offer new pedagogical approaches for learning content, to offer students with different learning styles more approaches to meet their needs, to be more flexible for students, to offer students more practice through online assessments, to require more active student participation than a lecture, and to provide "real" world experiences for students (Theroux & Kilbane, 2005; Schweizer et al., 2003; King, 2002; Meyer, 2003; Cottrell & Robinson, 2003; Boyle et al., 2003; Riffell & Sibley, 2004; Cameron, 2003; Bonk & Dennen, 1999; Starenko et al., 2006; Christensen, 2003; MacDonald & McAteer, 2003). The overriding theme seems to be centered on the belief that blended learning will support better student outcomes. Examples of these innovative instructional techniques can be found in Table 1 below.

Table 1. **Blended Learning Pedagogies**

Instructional Technique	Description	Reference
Case Studies	Real-time business case	Theroux & Kilbane (2005)
Small group	Set up online groups & blended groups	Schweizer et al. (2003)
Discussion Critical Thinking	Discussion used to promote critical thinking from students in teacher education	King (2002)
	Coded discussion to show evidence of higher order thinking	Meyer (2003)
	Add instructional variety	Cottrell & Robinson (2003)
Self-assessment	Allows online tests and homework	Boyle et al. (2003); Riffell & Sibley (2004)
Simulation	Graphical representation of material	Cameron (2003)
Role Playing	Students must adopt role and respond in discussion	Bonk & Dennen (1999)
Debate	Tax Policy debates during Presidential election	Starenko et al. (2006)
Learn by Doing	Instructional design	Christensen (2003)
Tutoring Support	Integrated tutoring strategies	MacDonald & McAteer (2003)

Underlying these uses of blended learning and the sources of faculty satisfaction is the desire to help students to comprehend or master learning objectives.

To achieve these instructional outcomes, it is assumed that campuses need to provide better pedagogical support for faculty. This support would likely come from instructional design, information technology support, and faculty exchanges of teaching ideas. Instructional design and teaching support centers are not new but are becoming more pervasive. Higher education remains one of the few enterprises where those in highly skilled front end critical roles like teaching are never taught the best ways to teach. In absence of this kind of required training in graduate school, it seems that some institutions are recognizing a need for supporting teaching through academic support personnel. In many cases, support departments were established for smaller, self-contained distance learning enterprises. Extending these services to more mainstream operations has become a challenge. Arabacz et al. (2003) concluded that many institutions are concerned with delivering the right level of support to users of information technology to faculty and that more colleges indicated that they more often offered technology software and other tool training than instruction on pedagogical techniques.

There is also a movement to align faculty support centers with information technology (Ives & Steinbrenner, 2005). Faculty support centers often try to encourage faculty to get together to exchange ideas. Even if the numbers of academic support personnel are increasing, there still remains the question or problem of how to provide faculty with the time and what the appropriate incentives are to try blended learning. In the early days of online learning it was common to offer faculty release time and/or overload/summer pay for building online courses. While this practice still occurs, several large distance learning providers are beginning to feel that money would be better spent giving faculty more time to exchange ideas with other faculty and meet with instructional design personnel and not in extra pay (Otte, 2005). The rationale behind this is that the time to exchange ideas is more powerful and may have more impact when faculty collaborate with other faculty. Faculty would have more time to exchange ideas and learn from other faculty in their own disciplines if the money were spent to support this effort.

Even though instruction is at the heart of blended learning there are still many other roles as mentioned earlier that faculty must fulfill—does blended learning help or hinder these roles? While research is not required of all faculty, for those who fall under publish or perish rules, blended learning probably helps in offering flexibility in their own schedules to research and write (Monolescu et al., 2004). There is also evidence that the scholarship of teaching has grown to be "real" research (Weimer, 2006). Yet, given the slow to change culture of higher education as well as faculty interests, it seems unlikely that many faculty will be able to make blended learning the main topic of their academic research. Another function faculty are often required to undertake is grantsmanship. While much of this is tied to research, there are grant programs such as the Fund for the Improvement of Post Secondary Education (FIPSE) that are directed to college teaching and learning. Perhaps the single greatest impediment to faculty participation is the promotion and tenure process (Monolescu et al.). Faculty who participate in online learning and blended learning feel as if tenure and promotion committees ignore the work and effort it takes to invest in a blended learning course (Monolescu et al.). Anecdotes are told about mid-tenure faculty avoiding technology enhanced courses because these courses take significant effort and time and are not recognized as important by tenure and promotion committees.

The satisfaction that faculty derive from offering a blended course is tied to student satisfaction and the improved or perceived improvement in learning. This faculty satisfaction appears to be driven by a desire to make instruction more effective. This is not a new goal for faculty. Early research has noted that faculty often change their instructional techniques but that maintaining these changes and getting other faculty to adopt them takes instructional support through technology and personnel (Dziuban, Shea & Arbaugh, 2005). It appears that both blended and fully online learning require universities to support faculty with technology and sharing of pedagogical practices if they want to maintain and disseminate these approaches (Dziuban et al., 2005; Arabacz et al., 2003).

Another tenet of the faculty satisfaction pillar is whether faculty continue to have control of the course and its learning outcomes. Much of the research currently available comes from faculty reporting on their experiences (Boyle et al., 2003; Carroll, 2003; Christensen; 2003; Cottrell & Robinson, 2003; Johnson; 2002; King, 2002; Meyer, 2003; Riffell & Sibley, 2004). In these cases, faculty created the course and designed the evaluation. It is important to recognize that it may be desirable for faculty to share quality control as they do in face to face courses with other faculty.

Other research shares institutional views on the quality of blended learning courses offered by faculty, but generally that research is similar to what institutions expect to be reported on any other courses or programs (Aycock, Garnham, & Kaleta, 2002; Dziuban, et al., 2004). It is important to recognize that faculty may need to share quality control as they do in face to face courses with other faculty or within a department. Most of the Center for Academic Transformation courses started with courses which had documented poor quality outcomes (Twigg, 2004). To receive grant funding, faculty had to be willing to work with other faculty as well as with someone in the administration. The purpose of imposing such a structure was so more people shared in the process and disseminated the techniques for teaching, learning and evaluation (Twigg, 2004).

While less peer-reviewed research is available, it is important to mention other models that are directed by the central administration. For-profit universities typically use this model, although more universities and colleges are beginning to use a development model which includes subject matter experts, typically a group of faculty along with instructional designers, instructional support and technologists (Laster, 2005). The development time and initial costs can be longer but the trade-off is usually that the course can be used by all faculty teaching that course. Undoubtedly, in this model total faculty control of quality is removed. Quality control is shared. However, this model does not seem to be spreading quickly. The Allen and Seaman (2004) data reports that less than 10% of online learning courses is offered by for-profit universities, representing less than 5% of the higher education marketplace. Furthermore in a convenience sample which did not include for-profits, less than 13% of the respondents indicated that they use a team of faculty and staff to design online courses (Vignare, Geith, & Schiffman, in press).

Student Satisfaction

The student satisfaction quality pillar includes student services, technology infrastructure and support, interaction with faculty and other students, learning community and course/learning outcomes which match or exceed expectations (Moore, 2005). The student satisfaction pillar is often closely aligned with student services. Many accreditation bodies, national associations and state higher education regulatory policies recommend or require certain basic student services be met by those who offer online learning. Due to this scrutiny, it is understandable that in some ways there is less debate about student services. The Western Cooperative on Education Technologies (WCET) includes parts of all five Sloan pillars in their recommendations on student services (Shea & Armitage, 2002). While there is some tendency to say all factors in education are part of student satisfaction, even in traditional education we know some factors are more important than others. Beyond just measuring overall course and/or learning satisfaction, student preparation for online learning, communicating sound academic choices, building a student community, access to services, and improving and supporting the learning environment all seem to be critical for student satisfaction (Moore).

For students, satisfaction can be measured globally and individually. While many blended and online learning providers collect data on student satisfaction, the Dziuban, Moskal, and Hartman (2005) collection of nearly 200,000 student surveys over seven years is the most extensive. The volume of surveys combined with the fact that the surveys have been repeated every other year and consistently report similar findings are indicative that high levels of student satisfaction can be achieved (Dziuban et al.). Much smaller scale studies also show that blended learning satisfies students. The larger questions seem to be: How does blended learning satisfy students and what measures should be used to benchmark the attributes that lead to student satisfaction? Even traditional residential programs are still trying to determine what attributes should be measured to determine student satisfaction. Growing in importance are those measuring student engagement and those establishing the timeliness and reliability of student support services. The National Survey on Student Engagement (NSSE) uses questions which measure how much time and involvement students have with coursework, faculty and campus activities to determine how engaged students are in their learning (Klein, Kuh, Chun, Hamilton & Shavelson, 2005). Noel Levitz dichotomizes whether services are used and whether they are important (Low, 2000). More and more campuses are also attempting to align their overall assessment to include student services.

Preparing students to learn online may seem simple but it clearly starts with communication. Online communication consists of keeping websites and course catalogs up to date. While some colleges make it clear in their course schedules that courses are blended, many do not. For example, in cases where faculty are experimenting with blended learning (which happens quite frequently), students begin the course not always knowing that it will be a blended. Minimally, students should receive clear instructions through websites and orientations about the online technologies needed to participate. Access to computers, ability to use the computer, and being prepared for an online experience should be a part of that preparation and unless students know ahead of time that they are enrolling in a blended course, they may be less satisfied with the initial hurdles. The opposite argument could be proffered that if blended learning is considered just another instructional strategy such as small group work, prior notice to students may not be as important. The likely answer to this dilemma lies more with the student population. Given that very few students (less than 30%) are full-time and located on-campus or near campus, it is clear that knowing how time is going to be spent, in class or on your own, would be important information (Oblinger & Oblinger, 2005). On the other hand, once students experience blended learning, they become critical of the way time in the classroom is spent (Kerres & DeWitt, 2004). They develop opinions as to what activities could be done online and what might be done better in person.

If online learning technologies are being used, should student services like orientation, access to online technology support, online library access or online academic support such as tutoring or writing help, which are highly recommended for fully online students, be available? Again the answers will depend on the makeup of the students participating in blended learning. Most of the research thus far on blended has not included studies on student services. The best practices gathered on the value of student services in student satisfaction come from both traditional face to face and fully

49

online programs. In both modalities, we know that only certain students will need services and support. The real question is providing choices for support face to face or online. The nature of the students who enroll in the courses or programs should be considered when making those decisions. There is a growing trend that many student services are offering online support to all students regardless of location. Libraries are converting many card, book, and microform services to electronic database systems which allow all students online access. More and more evidence is surfacing that online tutoring services, once exclusively offered to distance students, are being maximized so they can be offered to most students.

Another recommendation for online learning environments is for students to feel as though they are part of a community. The nature of the community role varies and has different names including communities of learning, inquiry, and practice (Garrison, Anderson & Archer, 2000). Students take on different roles in these communities. There is disagreement as to whether community should be required or only offered to those students interested. Community-building techniques include establishing open student communities (lounges, cafes), allowing chat or discussion boards for sharing information, establishing the same access to services and advice, and providing online student mentors or peers. Online mentors and tutors are often very useful to students who are just starting out, and they serve a role of being an intermediary for faculty and academic support units (Boyle et al., 2003; Chang, 2004).

Technology infrastructure support is also important. In a recent survey on students and technology, 27% of the students expected to need technology support when using a course management system (Kravik & Caruso, 2005). Information technology personnel seem to struggle less with the question of student support than they do with faculty support (Kravik & Caruso; Arabacz et al., 2003). Recommendations vary but many campuses already offer 24x7 technical support. What seems to vary is the amount of pedagogical support for students using online technologies. This may be due in part to what is a natural dividing line—where does a student need instructor help to be successful in the course and where can the technology support center help students without crossing the boundaries into helping the student complete work? Kravik and Caruso conclude that:

> According to survey respondents, the primary benefit of technology (for students) used in courses is convenience, followed by communication with the instructor and other students (connection), management of course activities, and improved student learning. (p.57).

These findings are similar to findings that occur in fully online learning research. Specifically, students choose online for convenience. However, post online course satisfaction surveys find that students value the connection and improved interaction with faculty and other students, perceived learning effectiveness and the ability to control when they learn. (Shea, Swan, Frederickson, & Pickett, 2001). However, the expectations of students continue to change. Younger students, those from the Net Generation, perceive their faculty to be less responsive when technology is used in the course (Dziuban, Moskal, & Hartman, 2005); however, the Zhao et al. (2005) meta-analyses of distance learning effectiveness show students were more likely to be successful in distance learning as long as they had a high school degree. The difference in the two pieces of research may indeed mean that younger students may not have any issues with being successful online but instead they are very different in their expectations of how technology should be integrated into courses.

Access

The access pillar includes technical, academic and administrative services (infrastructure), learning resources, pre-course access and readiness, appropriate program information, and program and course variety. Under technical, academic, and administrative services falls the issue of making sure all students have equal access to online learning. For the most part access is addressed at an institutional level, and it is clear that the mission of the institution impacts its willingness to support access to blended learning (Niemiec & Otte, 2005). There are strategic considerations about whether or not students and faculty need access to alternative modalities such as blended learning (Otte, 2005). In certain universities such as the City University of New York, the University of Illinois Chicago and the University of Central Florida, access to learning is strategic for convenience, for flexibility, and for improved learning. However, the scope of access goes beyond individual institutions and a national consideration remains whether students have access to the programs of their choice (Mayadas, 2001).

Much work has been done in higher education through the Americans with Disabilities Act to support students with disabilities; however, there is no doubt that more needs to be done to make the classroom barrier-free. Burgstahler (2002) provides guidelines and interpretation on how online technologies meet the needs of the students with different types of disabilities. The U.S. Census Bureau tracks the number of individuals with the various types of disabilities and estimates that there are 54 million Americans with disabilities (Waldrop & Stern, 2003). The National Center of Education Statistics provides information at both the K–12 and postsecondary level. In the postsecondary environment there are some 428,280 students with disabilities (Lewis & Farris, 1999). The focus of much of the accessibility literature centers on what the right technologies are for assisting students with disabilities and what the principles of universal design are. Universal design refers to the process of pre-designing instruction so that it meets the needs of all learners. Successful blended learning models recommend planned and integrated use of the classroom and online forums. Universal design could be part of the instructional planning for blended learning.

Burgstahler (2000) shares with us how online distance learning Internet-based communication can be one of the easiest ways to accommodate students with disabilities.

> Text-based, asynchronous resources such as electronic mail, bulletin boards, and listserv distribution lists generally erect no special barriers for students with disabilities. If a prerequisite to a course is for students to have access to electronic mail, individuals with disabilities can choose an accessible e-mail program to use. A student who requires assistive technology to access e-mail will have resolved any access issues before enrolling in the course. His own computer system will provide whatever accommodations he needs. E-mail communication between individual students, course administration staff, the instructor, guest speakers, and other students is accessible to all parties, regardless of disability. (http://www.rit.edu/~easi/itd/itdv08n1/burgstah.htm).

While it is undoubtedly good policy to provide a barrier-free classroom, the issues surrounding accessibility often do not even consider classroom communication (Schenker & Scadden, 2002). One of the pedagogical strengths of online learning is the ability to provide a barrier-free or level playing field for all students in the classroom (Harasim, Hiltz, Teles, & Turroff, 1995). This environment, where communications are open to all, is very conducive to students with disabilities. Blended learning presents the opportunity to meld the two learning environments. Initial evidence seems to support blended learning as a good solution for improving communication in the Deaf and Hard of Hearing student populations (Starenko et al., 2006; Humbert & Vignare, 2004).

Several case studies have also been presented regarding the success of online learning for students with disabilities. At Athabasca University, a fully online distance education university, studies on course completion rates indicate that students with disabilities complete and succeed at lower rates than students without disabilities (Moisey, 2004). This finding of lower success would likely be the same in traditional college courses (Lewis & Farris, 1999). An important finding of the Moisey research is that students with visual and hearing disabilities complete and succeed the best of all students with disabilities. The Open University of the United Kingdom and the National Technological Institute for the Deaf at the Rochester Institute of Technology have also published research on the effectiveness of distance learning for students with hearing disabilities (Richardson, Long & Woodley,

2003, Long & Beil, 2005). In both cases hearing and non-hearing students were shown to be just as successful in the online learning environment. The next step is really finding out whether the opportunity to communicate more regularly with everyone, faculty as well as other students, is important. The Long & Beil and Long, Vignare, Mallory & Rappold (in press) research showed that for the deaf and hard of hearing blended learning significantly improved the quantity and quality of interaction. Further study is needed but if blended learning offers both an easily accessible and more interactive classroom, it could become both a learning and cost effective tool in accommodating the needs of students with disabilities.

Much of the remaining tenets in the access pillar were addressed to an extent in the student satisfaction pillar. There is little research available thus far on learning resources, student readiness or course and program offerings available in blended learning. What can be surmised from the fully online research is that most policy and national association guidelines recommend that there be learning resources and opportunities for students to prepare for online courses.

Cost Effectiveness and Institutional Commitment

The cost effectiveness and institutional commitment quality pillar is the least researched pillar. Information from fully online cost effectiveness research is important to making the case for blended learning (Bishop, 2005). The cost effectiveness pillar includes issues like institutional commitment as evidenced through infrastructure, marketing, business strategies, scalability and partnerships. Within those parameters is an underlying constant that fully online and blended learning continually meet cost effective standards. *Campus Computing* annually publishes information on dispersion of technologies throughout higher education and reports that the purchase of course management software has penetrated 80% of the market (Greene, 2004). The question no longer is whether an online learning technology tool is available but whether it is maximized. Strategically, institutions must align their information technology to ever increasing demands for flexible teaching and learning environments. In an online learning survey, institutions feared they will not keep up with the demand for support from both faculty and students but nonetheless recognized the need to cost effectively invest in the technology and support resources needed (Arabacz et al., 2003).

From a sample of Sloan-C institutions, Schiffman (2005) identified two reasons online learning commenced: to increase access and to increase quality. Increasing access is defined more as providing access to education to non-traditional students and therefore more like the continuing or adult education units of the college. Those institutions that initiated online learning for quality access for on-campus students are exemplified as those trying to address internal problems like student success and improved pedagogical techniques (Schiffman; Twigg, 2004). Arabacz et al. (2003) seemed to align blended learning with increasing quality, but the rise of marketing of blended learning graduate programs may indicate that access and revenues end up being a strong force in the growth of blended learning as well. The differentiation in starting point for on-campus or outreach is useful for understanding the type of business model established. However, it is important to understand that the goal of access does not exclude quality (Greenberg, 2004; Lynch, 2005; Twigg). By far the number of institutions trying to increase access is much larger than those that started online learning to improve quality (Schiffman).

Several case studies of institutions that differ in their starting points reveal significant differences in how online and blended learning operations are set up. Two large public universities that established online learning to improve the quality of the teaching and learning environments were University of Central Florida (UCF) and the City University of New York (CUNY). The operations in each university were established as an integrated and mainstream function (Otte, 2005; Dziuban et al., 2003). The two institutions established the operations and business process units inside of the Information Technology divisions. Support for faculty and students was also coordinated or controlled by this same division. CUNY maintains a two-level approach with a university-wide coordinating level augmented by individual colleges controlling certain aspects of the training, teaching and learning experiences. Examples of universities that initiated online learning to extend access include the University of Maryland University College, University of Massachusetts at Lowell, and the Stevens Institute of Technology (Bishop & SchWeber, 2002; Moloney & Tello, 2004; Ubell, 2004). Organizationally, distance learning was set up as an extension or continuing education operation. While each college applies online learning in unique ways, these colleges are expected to be profitable and still produce quality online learning.

In the 1990s and early 2000s, many questions were raised as to whether online learning, particularly asynchronous learning, was cost effective. Many who were skeptical of ALN demanded economic justification for the investment required to support online learning. Bishop's (2003) synthesis of best practices demonstrates that ALN can indeed be a cost effective investment for the university. Most of the best practices and much of the case study research published by universities also come from universities that identify themselves as self-funded and those that commenced online learning to expand access. Fewer studies can be found from online learning colleges that started with the explicit goal of improving quality. This was probably caused by the fact that there were simply fewer colleges that started online learning to improve instructional quality. The work by the Center for Academic Transformation and the Pew Foundation supports the possibilities of improving quality while reducing costs (Twigg, 2004).

The University of Texas opened a branch campus, the TeleCampus, for the express purpose of providing additional outreach while maintaining and improving quality. It has been able to demonstrate that its costs are not only comparable to face to face courses offered by other branches, but lower in many cases (Robinson, 2005). Since their costs are near the low end of all the UT campuses, the state is now looking into the feasibility of designing online instruction to meet expected increasing enrollment needs to manage capital investments into the campus branches. Cost savings, better use of space, improved learning outcomes and continued growth has also been reported by the UCF (Dziuban, Hartman, Juge, Moskal & Sorg, 2005). The Technology Costing Method (TCM) created in part by the Western Cooperative for Education Technology (WCET) provides colleges with tools to improve their costing of technology expenditures (Johnstone, 2004). Through the use of these tools, colleges have been able to gauge concepts like return on investment through implementation of TCM (Jewett & Henderson, 2004). The clear message being sent here is that today all publicly funded operations must be more accountable (Gandel, Katz & Metros, 2004). While the notion of accountability is grounded in business evaluation methods like return on investment, it is becoming increasingly clear that there will be no turning back from this level of scrutiny with new federal laws like The Sarbanes Oxley Act of 2002. The Sarbanes Oxley Act, which resulted after numerous corporate governance scandals like Enron and WorldCom, also requires non-profit institutions to be publicly accountable and use standard accounting practices for their fiscal operations.

Meyer (2005) demonstrated that not only is there research that supports that cost effectiveness can be linked to improving quality but argues that planning for cost effectiveness is a necessity for online learning. Scarafiotti (2003) recommends that planning for cost-effective student services is an integral part of creating online learning at any institution and was especially true at her own institution, Rio Salado Community College. Rio Salado has experienced tremendous growth and manages to enhance quality while keeping costs in check. Beyond looming new accounting principles are regulatory compliance of accreditation, local, state and federal expectations. Organizations must meet the accreditation guidelines, but further application of business evaluation practices like cost effectiveness helps them yield even higher level results. State and local governments have reduced funding to publicly funded colleges while demanding more accountability. The result is that many colleges must demonstrate greater returns on government investments.

Conclusions and Recommendations

Blended learning may have started after fully online ALN proved to be successful, but it seems to be gaining acceptance at colleges that were very different than many of the early leaders of the online movement. Blended learning research reflects all of the Five Pillars of the Sloan-C framework, but more research is needed, especially in the faculty satisfaction, student satisfaction and access pillars. The nature and application of blended learning may imply that it focuses more on learning effectiveness and cost effectiveness. The summary of what is known seems to show that researchers believe that blended learning will have greater (more widespread) impact than fully online ALN. It is possible that the planned pedagogical integration of face to face and online learning could spark new opportunities for cost effectiveness and sustainable improvement and greater adoption of learner-centered instruction.

The research reveals great potential for introducing new instructional strategies/techniques. Faculty will use these strategies to offer students even more ways to achieve successful course outcomes. For faculty to be innovative and improve blended learning, they will need access to reliable technologies. Technology support, pedagogical support, and faculty time to plan and execute and exchange ideas with other faculty will be critical for success. Students and faculty require similar levels of infrastructure and technological support. Students also perceive that they are better connected, that they can manage their courses better, and that learning improves when technology is added to courses. There are strategic institutional considerations for the access and cost effectiveness pillars. Institutions must decide whether to support access to blended learning for all students or target it to particular students. According to most campus computing or information technology surveys of higher education, the technology support structures are in place for blended learning. While technology can always be improved, the existing hardware and software is capable of doing an effective job. Institutional support on pedagogical techniques can likely be expanded. From a cost effectiveness perspective, it is clear that maximizing resources, maximizing investment (or minimizing costs) while achieving better outcomes is a strategic question. Research mainly from fully online ALNs suggests that to get the most from an investment like blended learning, institutions need to apply more business-like principles and strategically plan for successful implementation.

The blended learning and applicable ALN work is mostly in the form of case studies. There is a need for substantial research to be undertaken at the multiple institution level so the data can be analyzed to see if they are generalizable. There is also a need for researchers to perform meta-analyses on the case study research to attempt to quantify the data. It would also be useful to review this work to attempt to frame effective practices for blended learning much like Sloan-C does for ALN.

References

Allen, I. E. & Seaman, J. (2005). *Growing by degrees: Online education in the United States, 2005*. Needham, MA: Sloan-C.

Allen, I. E. & Seaman, J. (2004). *Entering the mainstream: The quality and extent of online education in the United States, 2003 and 2004*. Needham, MA: Sloan-C.

Arabacz, P. & Baker, M. B. (2003). Evolving campus support models for e-learning. *Educause Center for Applied Research*.

Arabacz, P., Pirani, J. & Fawcett, P. (2003). Supporting e-learning in higher education. *Educause Center for Applied Research*.

Aycock, A., Garnham, C., & Kaleta, R. (2002). Lessons learned from the hybrid course project. *Teaching with Technology Today, 8*(6). Retrieved from http://www.uwsa.edu/ttt/articles/garnham2.htm.

Bishop, T. (2005). Reinventing the university: The business of online education. In J. Bourne & J. Moore (Eds.), *Elements of quality online education: Engaging communities* (pp. 197–205). Needham, MA: Sloan-C.

Bishop, T. (2003). Linking cost-effectiveness with institutional goals: Best practices in online education. In J. Bourne & J. C. Moore (Eds.), *Elements of quality online education: Practice and direction, 4* (pp. 75–86). Needham, MA: Sloan-C.

Bishop, T. & SchWeber, C. (2002). Link cost to quality. In J. Bourne & J. Moore (Eds.), *Elements of quality online education, 3* (pp. 45–58). Needham, MA: Sloan-C.

Bonk, C. & Dennen, V. (1999). Learner issues with WWW-based systems. *International Journal of Educational Telecommunications, 5*(4), 401–417.

Bonk, C. & Graham, C. (2005). *Handbook of blended learning: Global perspectives, local designs*. San Francisco, CA: Pfeiffer Publishing.

Boyle, T., Bradley, C., Chalk, P., Jones, R., & Pickard, P. (2003, October). Using blended learning to improve student success rates in learning to program. *Journal of Educational Media, 28*(2–3), 165–178.

Bransford, J.D., Brown, A.L., & Cocking, R.R. (2000). *How people learn: Brain, mind, experience and school*. National Research Council. Washington, D.C.: National Academy Press.

Burgstahler, S. (2000). *Access to Internet-based instruction for people with disabilities*. Hershey, PA: Idea Group Inc.

Burgstahler, S. (2002). Universal design of distance learning. *Journal of Information Technology and Disabilities, 8*(1), Retrieved May 13, 2005, from http://www.rit.edu/~easi/itd/itdv08n1/burgstah.htm.

Cameron, B. (2003). The effectiveness of simulation in a hybrid and online networking course. *TechTrends, 47*(5), 18–21.

Carroll, B. (2003). Going hybrid: Online course components increase flexibility of on campus courses. *Online Classroom*, 4–7.

Chang, S. (2004). Online learning communities with online mentors (OLCOM): Model of online learning communities. *The Quarterly Review of Distance Education, 5*(2), p. 75–88.

Christensen, T.K. (2003). Finding the balance: Constructivist pedagogy in a blended course. *Quarterly Review of Distance Education, 3(4)*, 235–243.

Cottrell, D.M. & Robinson, R.A. (2003). Blended learning in an accounting course. *The Quarterly Review of Distance Education, 4*(3), 261–269.

Dede, C. (2005). Planning for 'neomillennial' learning styles: Implications for investments in technology and faculty. In D. Oblinger & J. Oblinger (Eds.), *Educating the net generation*, (pp. 15.1–15.22). Boulder, CO: Educause.

Dowling, C., Godfrey, J.M., & Gyles, N. (2003). Do hybrid flexible delivery teaching methods improve accounting students' learning outcomes? *Accounting Education, 12*(4), 373–391.

Dziuban, C.D., Hartman, J., Juge, F., Moskal, P.D., & Sorg, S. (2005). Blended learning enters the mainstream. In C.J. Bonk & C. Graham (Eds.), *Handbook of Blended Learning: Global perspectives, local designs* (pp. 195–208). San Francisco: Pfeiffer.

Dziuban, C., Moskal, P., & Hartman, J. (2005). Higher education, blended learning, and the generations: Knowledge is power--No more. In J. Bourne & J.C. Moore (Eds.), *Elements of quality online education: Engaging communities* (pp. 85–102). Needham, MA: Sloan-C.

Dziuban, C., Hartman, J., Moskal, P., Sorg, S., & Truman, B. (2004). Three ALN modalities: An institutional perspective. In J. Bourne & J.C. Moore (Eds.), *Elements of quality online education: Into the mainstream* (pp. 127–148). Needham, MA: Sloan-C.

Dziuban, C., Moskal, P., Juge, F., Truman-Davis, B., Sorg, S. & Hartman, J. (2003). Developing a web-based instructional program in a metropolitan university. In B. Geibert & S. H. Harvey (Eds.), *Web wise learning: Wisdom from the field*. Philadelphia, PA: Xlibris Publications.

Dziuban, C., Shea, P. & Arbaugh, J. (2005). Faculty roles and satisfaction in asynchronous learning networks. In S.R. Hiltz & R. Goldman (Eds.), *Learning together online: Research on asynchronous learning network* (pp. 169–190). Mahwah, NJ: Lawrence Erlbaum.

Gagne, R. & Driscoll, M.P. (1988). *Essentials of learning of instruction* (2ⁿᵈ ed.). Englewood Cliffs, NJ: Prentice Hall.

Gandel, P., Katz, R., & Metros, S. (2004), The 'weariness of the flesh' reflections on the life of the mind in an era of abundance. *Educause Review*, March/April, 40–51.

Garrison, D. R, Anderson, T. & Archer, W. (2000). Critical inquiry in a text based environment: Computer conferencing in higher education. *The Internet and Higher Education, 2*(2–3), 1–19.

Garrison, D.R & Kanuka, H. (2004). Blended learning: Uncovering its transformative potential in higher education. *The Internet and Higher Education, 7(2)*, 95–105.

Graff, Martin. (2003). Learning from web-based instructional systems and cognitive style. *British Journal of Education Technology, 34(4)*, 407–418.

Graham, C. R. (2005). Blended learning systems: Definition, current trends, and future directions. In C. J. Bonk & C. R. Graham (Eds.), *Handbook of blended learning: Global perspectives, local designs* (pp. 3–21). San Francisco, CA: Pfeiffer Publishing.

Greenberg, M. (2004). A university is not a business (and other fantasies). *Educause Review*, March/April, 10–16.

Greene, K. (2004). *Campus computing 2004: The 15th national survey of computing and information technology in American higher education.* Encino, CA: The Campus Computing Project.

Harasim, L., Hiltz, S.R., Teles, L. & Turroff, M. (1995). *Learning networks: A field guide to teaching and learning online.* Cambridge: MIT Press.

Hartman, J., Moskal, P. & Dziuban, C. (2005). Preparing the academy of today for the learner of tomorrow. In D. Oblinger & J. Oblinger (Eds.), *Educating the net generation* (pp. 6.1–6.15). Denver: Educause.

Hitt, J.C. & Hartman, J.L. (2002). *Distributed learning: New challenges and opportunities for institutional leadership.* Washington, D.C.: American Council on Education, Center for Policy Analysis.

Hiltz, S. R. & Goldman, R. (2005). *Learning together online: Research on asynchronous learning networks.* Mahwah, NJ: Lawrence Erlbaum.

Hiltz, S. R. & Turoff, M. (2005). Education goes digital: The evolution of the online learning and the revolution in higher education. *Communications of the ACM, 48*(10), 59–65.

Howell, S.L., Laws, R. D., & Lindsay, N. K. (2004). Reevaluating course completion in distance education: Avoiding the comparison between apples and oranges. *The Quarterly Review of Distance Education, 5*(4), 243–252.

Hung, D. (2001). Theories of learning and computer-mediated instructional strategies. *Education Media International, 38*(4), 281–287.

Humbert, J. & Vignare, K. (2004). RIT introduces blended learning—successfully!. In J. C. Moore (Ed.), *Elements of quality online education: Engaging communities, wisdom from the Sloan Consortium, volume 2 in the wisdom series.* Needham, MA: Sloan-C.

Ingle, F. (2005). *Student retention and completion rates in a postsecondary online distance learning environment.* (Doctoral Dissertation. Published. Nova Southeastern University, 2005).

Ives, S. & Steinbrenner, K. (2005). Bridging the divide: Combining faculty centers and instructional technology support. *Educause Center for Applied Research, Research Bulletin, 9.* Retrieved from http://www.educause.edu /content.asp?page_id=666&ID=ERB0509&bhcp=1.

Jewett, F. & Henderson, T. (2004). The technology costing methodology project: Collecting and interpreting instructional cost data. *Planning for Higher Education, 32* (1), 15–27.

Johnson, J. (2002). Reflections on teaching a large enrollment course using a hybrid format. *Teaching with Technology Today, 8*(6). Retrieved from http://www.uwsa.edu/ttt/articles/jjohnson.htm.

Johnstone, S. (2004) A policy perspective on learning theory and practice in distance learning. In T. Duffy & J. Kirkley (Eds.), *Learner-centered theory and practice in distance education* (pp. 395–408). Mahwah, NJ: Lawrence Erlbaum Associates.

Karagiorgi, Y. & Symeou, L. (2005). Translating constructivism into instructional design: Potential and Limitations. *Journal of Educational Technology & Society, 8(1),* 17–27.

Kerres, M. & De Witt, C. (2003). A didactical framework for the design of blended learning arrangements. *Journal of Educational Media. 28* (2–3), 101–113.

King, K. (2002). Identifying success in online teacher education and professional development. *Internet and Higher Education, 5,* 231–246.

King, P. & Hildreth, D. (2001). Internet courses: Are they worth the effort? *Journal of College Science Teaching, 31,* 112–115.

Klein, S., Kuh, G., Chun, M., Hamilton, L., & Shavelson, R. (2005). An Approach to measuring cognitive outcomes across higher education institutions. *Research in Education, 46*(3), 251–276.

Kravik, R. & Caruso, J. (2005). ECAR Study of Students and Information Technology 2005: Convenience, Connection, Control and Learning. *Educause Center for Applied Research.* Boulder, CO: Educause.

Laster, S. (2005). Model driven design: Systematically building blended learning experiences. In J. Bourne & J. Moore (Eds.), *Elements of quality online education: Into the mainstream* (pp. 159–175). Needham, MA: Sloan-C.

Lewis L. & Farris, E. (1999). *An institutional perspective on students with disabilities in postsecondary education.* Washington, DC: U.S. Department of Education, National Center for Education Statistics. Retrieved May 4, 2005, from http://nces.ed.gov/pubs99/1999046.pdf.

Lohr, L. L. & Ku, H. (2003). Development of a web-based template for active learning. *The Quarterly Review of Distance Education, 4*(3*),* 213–226.

Long, G. & Beil, D. (2005). The importance of direct communication during continuing education workshops for deaf and hard-of-hearing professionals. *Journal of Postsecondary Education and Disability, 18*(1), 5–11.

Long, Vignare, Mallory, & Rappold. (in press). Access to communication for deaf, hard-of-hearing and ESL students in blended learning courses. *Journal of Postsecondary Education and Disability.*

Low, L. (2000). *Are college students satisfied? A national analysis of changing expectations.* Noel Levitz, USAgroup Foundation, A News Agenda series, 1–35.

Lynch, D. (2005). Success versus value: What do we mean by the business of online education? In J. Bourne & J. C. Moore (Eds.), *Elements of quality online education: Engaging communities, 6* (pp. 183–195). Needham, MA: The Sloan Consortium.

MacDonald, J., & McAteer, E. (2003). New approaches to supporting students: strategies for blended learning in distance and campus based environments. *Journal of Educational Media, 28*(2–3), 129–146.

Mayadas, F. (2001). Testimony to the Kerrey Commission on web-based education. *Journal of Asynchronous Learning Networks, 5*(1*),* 134–138.

McCombs, B. & Vakili, D. (2005). A learner-centered framework for e-learning. *Teachers College Record, 107*, 1582–1600.

Meyer, K. (2005). Planning for cost-efficiencies in online learning. *Planning for Higher Education, 33*(3), 19–30.

Meyer, K. (2003). Face to face versus threaded discussions: The role of time and higher-order thinking. *Journal of Asynchronous Networks, 7*(3*)*, 55–65.

Moisey, S. (2004). Students with disabilities in distance education: Characteristics, course enrollment and completion, and support services. *Journal of Distance Education, 19*(1), 73–91.

Moloney, J. & Tello, S. (2004). Achieving quality and scale in online education through transformative assessment: A case study. In J. Bourne & J. Moore (Eds.), *Elements of quality online education: Into the mainstream, 5* (pp. 199–213). Needham, MA: Sloan-C.

Monolescu, D., Schifter , C., Greenwood, L. (2004). *The distance education evolution: Issues and case studies*. Hershey, PA: Idea Publishing.

Moore, J. C. (2005). A synthesis of Sloan-C effective practices. *Journal of Asynchronous Learning Networks, 9*(3), 55–73.

Moore, J. C. (2002). *Elements of Quality: The Sloan-C framework: Pillar reference manual*. Needham, MA: Sloan-C.

Niemiec, M. & Otte, G. (in press). *Blended learning in higher education: A report from the Sloan-C 2005 Workshop*. Needham, MA: Sloan-C.

Oblinger, D. & Oblinger, J. (2005). *Educating the net generation*. Denver: Educause.

Osguthorpe, R. & Graham, C. (2003). Blended learning environments: Definitions and directions. *The Quarterly Review of Distance Education, 4*(3), 227–233.

Otte, G. (2005). Using blended learning to drive faculty development (and vice versa). In J. Bourne & J. Moore (Eds.), *Elements of quality online education: Engaging communities* (pp. 71–83). Needham, MA: Sloan-C.

Reasons, S., Valadares, K., & Slavkin, M. (2005). Questioning the hybrid model: Student outcomes in different course formats. *Journal of Asynchronous Learning, 9*(1), 83–94.

Richardson, J., Long, G., & Woodley, A. (2003). Academic engagement and perceptions of quality in distance education. *Open Learning, 18*(3), 223–244.

Riffell, S.K., & Sibley, D.F. (2004). Can hybrid course formats increase attendance in undergraduate environmental science courses? *Journal of Natural Resources and Life Sciences Education, 33*, 1–5.

Russell, T. (2001). *The no significant difference phenomenon : A comparative research annotated bibliography on technology for distance education: As reported in 355 research reports, summaries and papers*. Montgomery, AL: International Distance Education Certification Center. Retrieved January 28, 2005, from http://www.nosignificantdifference.org/.

Robinson, R. (2005). The business of online education: Are we cost competitive? In J. Bourne & J. C. Moore (Eds.), *Elements of quality online education:*

Engaging communities, 6 (pp. 173–181). Needham, MA: The Sloan Consortium.

Scarafiotti, C. (2004, Winter). Five important lessons about the costs of e-learning. *New Directions for Community Colleges, 128*, 39–46.

Schenker, K. & Scadden, L. (2002). The design of accessible distance education environments that use collaborative learning. *Journal of Information Technologies and Disabilities. 8*(1). Retrieved May 14, 2005, from http://www.rit.edu/~easi/itd/itdv08n1/scadden.htm.

Schiffman, S. (2005). Business issues in online education. In J. Bourne & J. Moore (Eds.), *Elements of quality online education: Engaging communities* (pp.151–171). Needham, MA: Sloan-C.

Schroeder, R. & Oakley, B. (2005). Adding clicks to bricks: Increasing access to mainstream education. In J. Bourne & J. Moore (Eds.), *Elements of quality online education: Engaging communities* (pp. 101–115). Needham, MA: Sloan-C.

Schweizer, K., Paechter, M., & Weidenmann, B. (2003). Blended learning as a strategy to improve collaborative task performance. *Journal of Educational Media, 28*(2–3), 211–224.

Sener, J. (2004). Escaping the comparison trap: Evaluating online learning on its own terms. *Innovate*, 1(2). Ft. Lauderdale: Nova Southeastern University. Retrieved from http://innovateonline.info/index.php?view=article&id=11.

Shea, P. & Armitage, S. (2002). *WCET LAAP Project beyond the administrative core: Creating web-based student services for online learners*. Retrieved January 3, 2006, from http://www.wcet.info/projects/laap/guidelines /overview.htm.

Shea, P., Pickett, A., & Pelz,W. (2003). A follow up investigation of 'teacher presence' in the SUNY Learning Network. *Journal of Asynchronous Learning Networks, 7*(2), 61–80.

Shea, P. J., Swan, K., Fredericksen, E. E., & Pickett, A. (2001). Student satisfaction and reported learning in the SUNY learning network. *Elements of quality online education, 3* (pp. 145–156). Needham, MA: Sloan-C.

Snyder, T. (2005). *Digest of Education Statistics, 2004*. The National Center for Education Statistics, the Department of Education, United States. Retrieved from http://nces.ed.gov/programs/digest/d04/.

Starenko M., Vignare, K., & Humbert, J. (in press). Enhancing student interaction and sustaining faculty instructional innovations through blended learning. In A. Picciano & C. Dziuban (Eds.), *Blended Learning*. Needham, MA: Sloan-C.

Swan, K. (2005). A constructivist model for thinking about learning online. In J. Bourne & J. Moore (Eds.), *Elements of quality online education: Engaging communities* (pp. 13–30). Needham, MA: Sloan-C.

Tagg, J. (2003). *The learning paradigm*. Bolton, MA: Anker.

Theroux, J. & Kilbane, C. (2005). The real-time case method: The internet creates the potential for new pedagogy. In J. Bourne and J.C. Moore (Eds.), *Elements of quality online education, 3* (pp. 31–40). Needham, MA: Sloan-C.

Twigg, C. (2004). Improving learning and reducing costs: New models for online learning. *Educause Review*, September/October, 28–38.

Ubell, R. (2004). Stevens Institute of Technology: Webcampus. *Journal of Asynchronous Learning Networks, 8*(3), 1–3.

Vaughan, N. & Garrison, D.R (2005). Creating cognitive presence in a blended faculty development community. *Internet and Higher Education, 8*(1), 1–12.

Vignare, K., Geith, C. & Schiffman, S. Business models for online learning: An exploratory survey. *Journal of Asynchronous Learning Networks, 10*(2), 53–67.

Vignare, K. (2002). Longitudinal success measures for online learning students at the Rochester Institute of Technology. In J. Bourne & J. Moore (Eds.), *Elements of quality online education: Practice and direction, 4* (pp. 261–278). Needham, MA: Sloan-C.

Waldrop, J. & Stern, S. (2003). *Disability status: 2000.* U.S. Census Bureau. Washington D.C. Retrieved May 15, 2005, from http://www.census.gov/prod/2003pubs/c2kbr-17.pdf.

Weimer, M. (2006). *Enhancing scholarly work on teaching and learning: Professional literature that makes a difference.* San Francisco: Jossey-Bass.

Weimer, M. (2002). *Learner-center teaching: Five key changes to practice.* San Francisco: Jossey-Bass.

Wu, D. & Hiltz, S. R. (2004). Predicting learning from asynchronous online discussions. *Journal of Asynchronous Learning Networks, 8*(2), 139–151.

Zhao, Y., Lei, J., Lai, B.Y.C., & Tan, H. S. (2005). What makes the difference? A practical analysis of research on the effectiveness of distance education. *Teachers College Record, 107*(8), 1836–1884.

Blending In:
The Extent and Promise of Blended Education in the United States[1]

I. Elaine Allen, Ph.D.
Associate Professor of Statistics & Entrepreneurship
Co-Director, Babson Survey Research Group
Babson College

Jeff Seaman, Ph.D.
Chief Information Officer, Survey Director
The Sloan Consortium
Olin and Babson Colleges
Co-Director, Babson Survey Research Group
Babson College

Introduction

This study builds on the series of annual reports on the state of online education in U.S. Higher Education. Like the previous reports, this study is aimed at answering some of the fundamental questions about the nature and extent of education in the United States. The findings are based on two years of responses from a national sample of over 1,000 colleges and universities.

Both fully online and blended course offerings (i.e., those that combine the elements of an online course with those of face-to-face instruction) have grown dramatically in American higher education in recent years. There is a belief among some that blended courses hold at least as much promise as fully online ones. However, the path of evolution from face-to-face learning to fully online courses is not transparent. It is becoming clear that blended learning is generally not part of an institutional transition strategy from face-to-face to fully online courses, but rather a discrete option which institutions choose on its own merits. In our analyses of survey data on online learning, we reported that U.S. Higher Education has embraced online learning. Some of the evidence presented in these studies to support this conclusion includes:

- Online students, like the overall student body, are overwhelmingly undergraduates.

---

[1] This chapter is extracted from *Blending In: The Extent and Promise of Blended Education in the United States*, Needham, MA: Sloan-C, 2006.

B\line enrollments continue to grow, reaching 3.18 million for fall
)05.

An increasing number of academic leaders say that offering online
courses is critical to their institution's long-term strategy.

A majority of academic leaders believe that the learning outcomes
for online education are now equal to or superior to those for face-to-
face instruction.

What does our survey data say about the growth of blended (or hybrid)
courses and programs relative to fully online ones? What did these academic
leaders think about blended courses, and how did they perceive them as part
of their long-term strategic goals?

Background

For a number of years the Babson Survey Research group has
conducted, and the Sloan Consortium published, annual reports on the state
of online education in U.S. higher education. These reports have examined
both the changing opinions of key academic decision makers as well as
charting the trends in online offerings and enrollments. The intention from
the very beginning was to provide companion reports examining blended (or
hybrid) education. The initial attempt at this, however, quickly encountered a
serious roadblock: Schools were not able to provide accurate reports on their
enrollments in blended courses. Academic leaders told us that they did not
have any reliable means of measuring the number of students enrolled in
blended courses. Unlike fully online courses that make no use of on-campus
classroom facilities, blended courses often appear identically to face-to-face
classes on many institution's reporting systems.

The survey instrument was revised to reflect the inability to
accurately report blended enrollments, concentrating instead on opinion issues
and measuring the extent of blended course and program penetration
(academic leaders did tell us they could accurately report if they offered
blended courses and/or programs, the problem arose when we asked for
counts of students in those courses). This report is based on data collected
from the first three survey years, 2003, 2004, and 2005. It is our intent to
continually expand the number of questions addressing blended learning in
subsequent survey and provide additional, more detailed, reports in the future.

What is Blended Learning?

The focus of this study is blended (sometimes called hybrid)
education. In order to be consistent with previous work, we have applied the
same definitions used in our prior reports of online learning. These

definitions were presented to the respondents at the beginning of the survey and then repeated in the body of individual questions where appropriate.

The primary focus of this study, blended courses and programs, are defined as having between 30% and 79% of the course content delivered online. "Face-to-face" instruction includes those courses in which zero to 29% of the content is delivered online; this category includes both traditional and Web facilitated courses. The remaining alternative, online courses, are defined as having at least 80% of the course content delivered online.

While there is a great deal of diversity among course delivery methods used by individual instructors, the following is presented to illustrate the prototypical course classifications used in this study.

Proportion of Content Delivered Online	Type of Course	Typical Description
0%	Traditional	Course with no online technology used—content is delivered in writing or orally.
1 to 29%	Web Facilitated	Course which uses web-based technology to facilitate what is essentially a face-to-face course. Uses a course management system (CMS) or web pages to post the syllabus and assignments, for example.
30 to 79%	Blended/Hybrid	Course that blends online and face-to-face delivery. Substantial proportion of the content is delivered online, typically uses online discussions, and typically has some face-to-face meetings.
80+%	Online	A course where most or all of the content is delivered online. Typically have no face-to-face meetings.

The definition of an online program or blended program is similar to the definition used for courses; an online program is one where at least 80% of the program content is delivered online and a blended program is one where between 30 and 79% of the program content is delivered online. Institutions have a number of options in how they can choose to structure a blended program—they might, for example, craft a program as a mix of fully online and face-to-face courses. Alternatively, an institution may decide the best option for a particular program is for all the courses to be blended in nature. In this case the program might not contain any fully online or face-to-face courses. Obviously, institutions can mix and match between these two approaches. As long as the proportion of the program content delivered online falls in the 30 to 79% range, the program is classified as blended for purposes of this study.

₁ay offer online or blended learning in a variety of ways.
'espondents to characterize their face-to-face, blended, and
....ıg by the level of the course (undergraduate, graduate,
_..ınuing education, etc.). Likewise, respondents were asked to characterize their face-to-face, blended, and online program offerings for certificate, associate, bachelors, masters, doctoral, and professional programs and by specific discipline.

Detailed Survey Findings

Who Offers Blended Courses?

The latest evidence shows that almost 55% of all institutions offer at least one blended course while 64% offer at least one online course. This single statistic masks considerable variability among different types of institutions; however, for all levels of education, the percentage of schools offering at least one online course is larger than those offering at least one blended course. Of particular interest is the extent to which institutions that provide a particular type of offering in a face-to-face setting also provide the same type of offering in a blended setting. In other words, what proportion of institutions that offer a particular type of face-to-face course or program also provide a blended version of the same type of offering? The following analysis examines the penetration rate for online offerings by course type, program type, and program discipline.

Face-to-face, Online, and Blended Course Offerings — Fall 2004

	Face-to-face	Online	Blended
Undergraduate Level	88.5%	55.3%	45.9%
Graduate Level	39.7%	25.9%	21.9%
Continuing Education	38.6%	21.7%	11.3%

Examining the respective online and blended penetration rates by type of school shows online penetration rates are about 20% higher than blended penetration rates at the undergraduate level and about 13% higher at the graduate level. For Continuing Education courses, online penetration rates are almost double those for blended courses.

Figure 1: Online and Blended Course Penetration Rates - Fall 2004

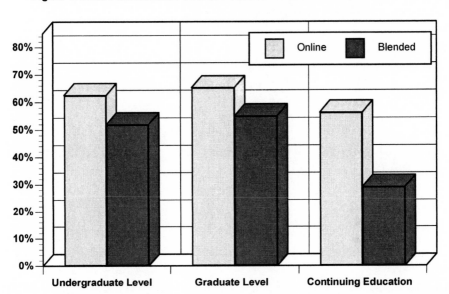

As has been noted in our previous reports on online learning, Public institutions lead other types of schools in offering online education. Similarly, they have a large lead in the provision of blended courses as well, with 79% offering at least one blended course at the undergraduate level. This compares to 32% of Private nonprofits and only 25% among the Private for-profit institutions. It is interesting to note that for Public institutions there is a higher penetration rate for blended courses at the undergraduate level, whereas at Private schools there is a higher penetration rate for blended courses at the Graduate level. The penetration rate for blended courses lags for Continuing Education courses in all types of institutions, perhaps indicating that these are not seen as part of the long term strategy for institutions of this type.

Online and Blended Course Penetration Rates - Fall 2004

	Public		Private, nonprofit		Private, for-profit	
	Online	Blended	Online	Blended	Online	Blended
Undergraduate Level	87.2%	79.4%	36.0%	32.0%	63.5%	25.4%
Graduate Level	77.1%	74.5%	53.2%	45.0%	143.4%	55.3%
Continuing Education	70.0%	35.1%	31.2%	21.2%	359.4%	33.3%

Institution size is also a key factor in determining whether blended and online courses are offered. The smaller the institution, the less likely it is to offer either blended or fully online courses. This pattern holds true for blended courses at all levels; the larger the school, the more likely it is to offer blended courses at the undergraduate level, the graduate level, and for continuing education. In fact, blended course offerings increase dramatically as institutional size increases.

Online and Blended Course Penetration Rates - Fall 2004

| | Under 1500 | | 1500–2999 | | 3000–7499 | | 7500–14999 | | 15000+ | |
	Online	Blended	Online	Blended	Online	Blended	Online	Blended	Online	Blended
Under-graduate Level	46.6%	33.5%	68.3%	57.6%	80.2%	71.8%	89.9%	81.5%	78.3%	76.8%
Graduate Level	55.6%	41.7%	57.6%	48.5%	69.5%	64.0%	84.1%	72.9%	84.2%	79.5%
Continuing Education	39.0%	18.0%	60.5%	29.6%	57.2%	29.5%	79.8%	46.4%	74.7%	48.8%

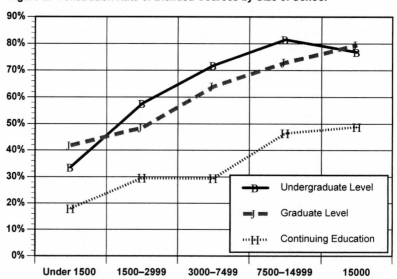

Figure 2: Penetration Rate of Blended Courses by Size of School

The picture is quite different for the small number of schools that offer blended but no online courses, however. Among these institutions the

Specialized schools constitute the largest proportion, with Doctoral/Research and Associates degree-granting institutions making up much smaller proportions as indicated in Figure 3.

Figure 3: Distribution of Schools that Offer Blended but no Online Courses

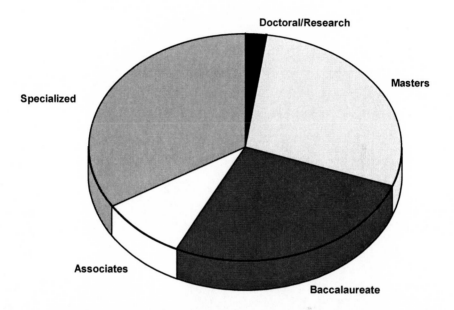

This is an important finding relative to the question of whether blended courses are part of an institutional transition strategy from face-to-face to fully online courses. If blended courses were a universal transition strategy for institutions moving their offerings from only face-to-face to face-to-face and online, the distribution of schools in this stage (having face-to-face and blended, but no online) should be similar to the distribution of those who have completed the transition. However, this is not the case; institutional offerings, and the path they take to get to those offerings, appear to be widely varied. A small number have chosen to add only blended and no online to their offerings, and a much larger number offer both blended and online.

There are dramatic differences in the pattern of online and blended course offerings by Carnegie Class. Among schools that have decided to offer online or blended courses, the most popular choice by far is to offer both. As Figure 4 indicates, 74.8% of Doctoral/Research institutions offer both online and blended courses, compared to only 29.7% of the Baccalaureate institutions. Baccalaureate, and to a lesser extent Specialized schools are the only types of institutions with substantial numbers of schools not offering either blended or online courses.

Among the smaller number of institutions that have elected to offer only one type of online or blended course, there is a slightly higher percentage of both Doctoral/Research and Masters institutions offer only online courses as compared to offering only blended ones, while twice as many Baccalaureate institutions offer only blended courses as compared to offering only online ones. Associates degree granting institutions more closely resemble the Doctoral/Research or Masters institutions.

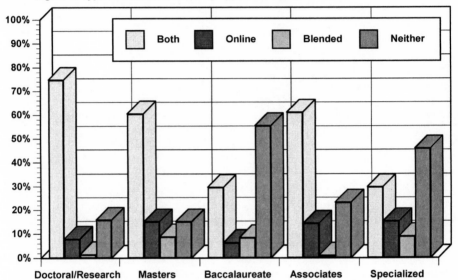

Figure 4: Type of Courses Offered by Type of Institution - Fall 2004

What Percent of All Course Sections are Taught as Blended?

While the percentage of institutions that offer at least one blended course is relatively high, the percentage of reported blended course sections is still quite small. Our previous studies provided some evidence that Chief Academic Officers may not be aware of all blended courses being taught at their institution. Unlike an online course, which is often recorded differently than a face-to-face course, a faculty member may convert a face-to-face course to blended with no change in how the course is recorded by the institution. Because both face-to-face and blended courses require on-campus services such as room assignments and final exam schedules, they are often treated identically by institutions. The actual number of blended courses may, therefore, be higher that what was reported by our respondents. While the overall reported rate of blended courses may be understated, there is no reason to think that this understatement is worse on one year than the next, so year-to-year comparisons can still be made.

**Percent of Course Sections Taught Online -
Fall 2003, 2004, and 2005**

	2003	2004	2005
Mean	6.48%	8.19%	10.86%
Median	2.00%	4.00%	5.00%

In Fall 2005, an average of 5.6% (median = 1%) of all course sections were taught as blended courses compared to 10.6% for online course sections (median = 5%). The percentage of courses taught as blended has shown a steady decline over the three survey years (moving from 6.8% in 2003 to 6.6% in 2004 and 5.6% in 2005). During this same time period the percentage of courses taught as fully online has continued to grow (6.5% in 2003, 8.2% in 2004, and 10.6% in 2005). The median number of courses taught as blended has remained at 1% for all three survey years, while the median for online courses has grown from 2% in 2003 to 5% in 2005.

**Percent of Course Sections Taught as
Blended – Fall 2003, 2004, and 2005**

	2003	2004	2005
Mean	6.81%	6.57%	5.56%
Median	1.00%	1.00%	1.00%

Blended course section offerings showed the greatest overall decline among the largest schools (11.4% to 8.4%); however, the median increased from 2% to 3% for this group, perhaps indicating that it is only a few of the institutions with the largest percentages which have shown the greatest decrease. The largest increase in the percentage of blended courses was among the large mid-size schools (8.0% to 9.9%). When examined by Carnegie Class, Associates institutions are the only type of institution to show an increase in blended course sections over the three year period (4.6% to 5.7%) and Doctoral/Research institutions exhibit the largest decrease (14.3% to 7.9%). Institutions of all sizes and all Carnegie Classes show an increase in the number of course sections offered online from Fall 2003 to Fall 2005.

How Extensive Are Blended Program Offerings?
As previously noted, a blended program can be creat
each course in the program, by mixing face-to-face courses w

73

courses, or by some combination of the two approaches. As long as the end result is that the proportion of the program content delivered online falls between 30 to 79% it is considered a blended program for purposes of this study. An institution that offers a single blended program composed of a mix of fully online and face-to-face courses, for example, would be counted as having online offerings when we are examining *courses*, but treated as having a blended offering when we move to examining programs. Thus we would expect to find penetration rates for blended *programs* to be relatively higher than those for blended *courses*.

While generally smaller than online and face-to-face program offerings, the proportion of programs offered as blended covers a wide spectrum. Overall, 36% of schools offer at least one blended program. The majority of these programs are Associates Degree programs (18%) or Certificate programs (17%) with only a very small number of Doctoral programs (3%). Only Doctoral programs have a larger proportion of blended vs. online program offerings (3% vs. 2%). Penetration rates by type of school show different patterns of blended vs. online program adoption.

Online and Blended Program Penetration Rates - Fall 2004

	Public		Private, nonprofit		Private, for-profit	
	Online	Blended	Online	Blended	Online	Blended
Certificate	45.4%	39.5%	25.8%	11.8%	20.4%	14.1%
Associate	50.7%	47.4%	18.9%	10.1%	43.3%	20.9%
Bachelors	37.6%	36.7%	20.7%	19.5%	64.4%	30.5%
Masters	55.9%	48.7%	34.9%	31.2%	77.5%	60.1%
Doctoral	13.1%	14.9%	9.5%	15.2%	62.5%	62.5%
Professional	27.1%	21.5%	8.1%	6.6%	0.0%	0.0%

Public institutions are in the lead among those offering Certificate, Associates, and Bachelors degree blended programs. Among Private, nonprofit schools, the only blended program that approaches the penetration rate of the online options is for a Masters degree. Although most Private, for-profit institutions do not offer Masters or Doctoral programs, the high penetration rates indicates that both online and blended options are very well received among these schools. Only the Public institutions show strong penetration rates in Certificate and Professional program offerings.

Examining Blended program offerings by institution size shows few discernible patterns or trends. Only Master's program offerings exhibit a early increasing trend as institution size increases. Bachelor degree programs and Profession programs also exhibit this trend, with the exception of the largest schools where the penetration rate for both program types is much smaller.

Figure 5: Penetration Rate of Blended Programs by Type of School

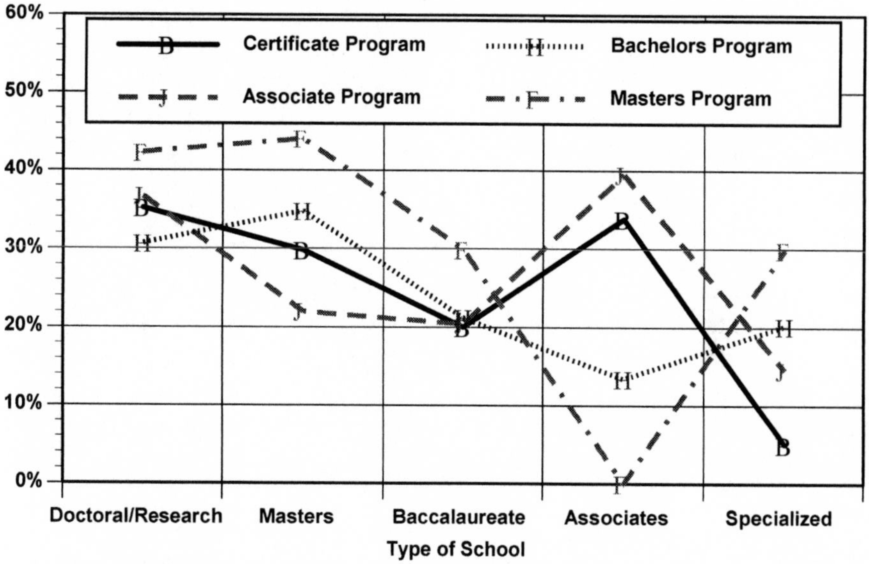

Comparing penetration rates by Carnegie Class shows that blended program offerings are almost identical for Master's and Baccalaureate degree programs but lag behind online Doctoral programs while exhibiting the same pattern of adoption across Carnegie Class.

What Disciplines Offer Blended Programs?

Online and Blended Program Penetration Rates – Fall 2003

	Online	Blended
Business	42.7%	47.9%
Computer and Information Sciences	35.1%	41.5%
Education	24.9%	36.5%
Health Professions and Related Sciences	31.4%	43.5%
Liberal Arts and Sciences, General Studies, Humanities	40.2%	47.8%
Psychology	23.6%	27.1%

Social Sciences and History	28.4%	31.6%
All Other Programs	36.2%	40.1%

As the reported penetration rates indicate, programs which institutions offer face-to-face are somewhat more likely to also be offered as a blended program than as an online program. This suggests that while online course offerings appear to be growing faster than blended courses, it may be easier to move a program from face-to-face to a blended format than it is to move it to fully online.

When examined by type of institution, Public institutions have the most consistent penetration rates, with most discipline areas falling in the 40 to 50% range except for Social Sciences and History (35%) and Liberal Arts and Sciences (60%). Private, nonprofit schools have consistently much lower penetration rates relative to Public institutions, with only one discipline area (Business) having a penetration rate at Private nonprofits of less than 10 percentage points relative to Publics (43.6% vs. 49.8%). Private, for-profit institutions show the most variability in penetration rates ranging from very high (84% in Business; 92% in Education) to relatively low (e.g., 28% in Psychology and 35% in Social Sciences and History).

It is unclear how respondents considered courses that were taken before an individual declared a major. At many four-year institutions, for example, students often select from a wide range of courses from different departments during their first two years before concentrating on courses related to their major during their final two years. If such preliminary courses are considered part of the particular program, then according to the definitions provided to the respondents, they should have been considered in determining if the program met the definition of blended or not. If, on the other hand, the particular program requirements were merely to have a minimum number of credits before beginning the study of a particular major, the initial courses would not have been considered as part of the specific program.

Who Teaches Blended Courses?
The most recent report on online education in the United States found that the majority of institutions were using primarily core faculty to teach their online courses (*Growing by Degrees: Online Education in the United States 2005*, The Sloan Consortium, www.sloan-c.org). Survey respondents were asked to categorize their use of core or adjunct faculty to teach online, blended, and face-to-face courses as "Exclusively" one type or the other, "Mostly" one type or the other, or a "Roughly equal mix of core and adjunct faculty." Respondents indicate that core faculty are used to teach online courses about as

frequently as they are used to teach face-to-face courses. The percent of institutions reporting that core faculty are teaching blended courses is larger than the percent reporting that core faculty are teaching face-to-face courses.

Who Teaches Face-to-face, Online, and Blended Courses - Fall 2004

	Face-to-face	Online	Blended
Core Faculty	61.6%	64.7%	67.4%
Split	24.7%	16.4%	16.0%
Adjunct Faculty	13.0%	18.1%	14.8%

Fewer than 50% (45%) of Private, for-profit institutions report that core faculty are teaching blended courses, which is comparable to the percentage saying core faculty teach online courses (48%) and higher than the percentage saying core faculty are teaching their face-to-face courses (38%)

Figure 6: Percentage of Institutions Reporting Their Courses are Taught by Core Faculty

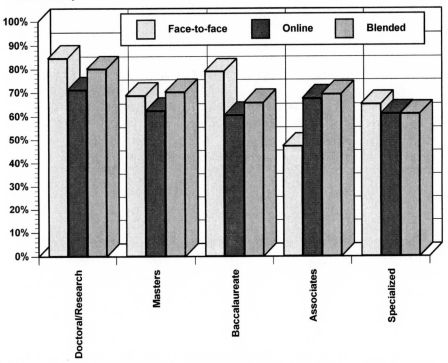

Somewhat surprising is that the largest schools (15000+ students) report the highest percent of core faculty teaching blended courses (78%) and the smallest schools (under 5000) report the smallest percent (56%). By

Carnegie Class, differences exist between Doctoral/Research institutions, where 80% report that their blended courses are taught by core faculty, and all the other classifications, where between 60% and 70% report their courses are taught by core faculty. With the exception of Specialized institutions, the percentage of institutions reporting that blended courses are taught by core faculty is slightly larger than the percent reporting that core faculty teach their online courses. Perhaps this is because online courses can be taught by faculty not on the physical campus but blended courses require at least part-time residence on-campus.

Do Blended Courses Hold More Promise than Fully Online?

Academic leaders were asked to rate their degree of agreement with the statement "In my judgment, blended courses (those that combine online with classroom) hold more promise than fully online courses" on a seven point scale. The Likert scale ranged from "1" for "Strongly Disagree", "4" for "Neutral", to "7" for "Strongly Agree." There was no strong level of agreement or disagreement with this statement among the survey respondents; over half (55%) were neutral in 2004, up from 47% in 2003. This change mirrors the increasing rate of offerings of online courses and the relatively unchanged percentage of blended courses. Only the small number of schools which offer blended but no online courses were more likely to agree with this statement (69% in 2004), while schools offering online but no blended courses were the least likely to agree (22% in 2004).

While there were some differences noted by type of institution, the overall pattern is similar for Public, Private nonprofit, and Private for-profit institutions with a majority of all types of schools rating blended and online courses equally. There was slightly greater and stronger agreement among the smaller, private, nonprofit institutions.

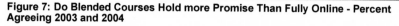

Figure 7: Do Blended Courses Hold more Promise Than Fully Online - Percent Agreeing 2003 and 2004

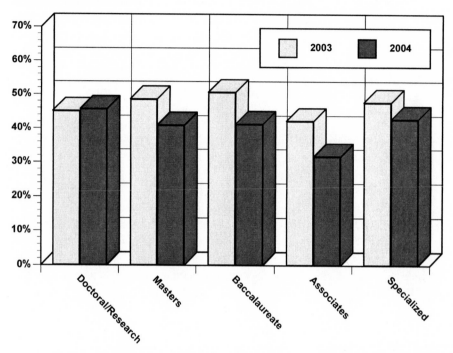

When examined by Carnegie Class, size of school, and type of offering, it is the smaller, private, Baccalaureate institutions that agree most strongly with this statement but the majority of these schools are still neutral. Within Carnegie Class, all types of institutions show a decrease in the percent agreeing with this statement between 2003 and 2004 with the exception of a 0.6% increase among Doctoral institutions.

Survey Support and Methodology

The sample for the analysis is composed of all active, degree-granting institutions of higher education in the United States that are open to the Public. An email with a link to a web-based survey form was sent to Chief Academic Officers at these institutions. If there was no designated Chief Academic Officer, the survey was sent to the President of the institution. In some cases, the survey team was notified by the recipient of another, more appropriate, recipient and the survey was forwarded to this individual.

Institutional descriptive data come from Nation Center for Educational Statistics' IPEDS database, described on their web site as:

> *"The Integrated Postsecondary Education Data System
> (IPEDS), ..., is a system of surveys designed to collect data
> from all primary providers of postsecondary education. IPEDS
> is a single, comprehensive system designed to encompass all
> institutions and educational organizations whose primary
> purpose is to provide postsecondary education."* See
> http://nces.ed.gov/ipeds/ for more information.

All sample schools were sent an invitation email and two reminders, inviting their participation and assuring them that no individual responses would be released. All survey respondents were promised that they would be notified when the report was released and would receive a free copy. Of 3216 surveys sent, 1025 responses were received, representing a 31.9% overall response rate. These responses were merged with the data from the previous survey year (1170 responses in 2004) for examination of changes over time. A stricter definition of "agree" and "disagree" for questions dealing with the level of agreement with particular statements was used in 2005; data from the previous year used for comparison have been recoded to match the new definition.

After the data were compiled and linked to the IPEDS database, the responders and nonresponders were compared to create weights, if necessary, to ensure that the survey results reflected the characteristics of the entire population of schools. The variables used for producing probability weights included size of the institution, region of the country, public/private, nonprofit/for-profit, and Carnegie class of school (Doctoral/Research, Masters, Baccalaureate, Associates, and Specialized). These weights provided a small adjustment to the results allowing for inferences to be made about the entire population of active, degree-granting institutions of higher education in the United States.

The Research Chapters

Realizing the Transformational Potential of Blended Learning: Comparing Cases of Transforming Blends and Enhancing Blends in Higher Education

Charles R. Graham and Reid Robison
Brigham Young University

Rapid technological innovation over the past decade has dramatically increased the variety of ways that teaching and learning can occur. Learning environments that were once limited by space and time now no longer have the same constraints. We have also seen a trend towards the *hybridization* of the university in which the boundaries between distributed services and on-campus services are increasingly blurred (Cookson, 2002; Kappel, Lehmann, & Loeper, 2002; Lewis, 2002; Waddoups & Howell, 2002). Blended learning environments are at these crossroads;they integrate distributed (or technology-mediated) instruction with traditional face-to-face instruction (Graham, 2005; Graham & Allen, 2005; Graham, Allen, & Ure, 2005). There is a growing awareness of the use of blended approaches in higher education. John Bourne, editor of *The Journal of Asynchronous Learning Networks*, has predicted a dramatic increase in the number of hybrid (i.e., blended) courses to include as many as 80-90% of the range of courses (Young, 2002), while de Boer (2002) claims that "blended learning . . . is already the norm" in many European countries (p. 29).

Despite these trends, it is surprising how little we understand about the nature of blended learning systems. Bonk and Graham (2005) recently co-edited *The Handbook of Blended Learning: Global Perspectives, Local Designs,* which contains descriptions of almost forty cases and models of blended learning from around the world. This publication highlights how rich and simultaneously complex the concept of blended learning currently is. For example, blending can occur at several different levels: the institutional level, the program level, the course level, or the activity level (Graham, 2005). The salient research issues at each of these levels can be quite different. Additionally, there is a wide range of blends possible intended to meet a wide range of very different needs. At one end of the spectrum there is instruction that is mostly online with minimal face-to-face contact and at the other end there is instruction which is predominantly face-to-face, supplemented with minimal online resources and activities.

The research presented in this chapter explores the use of blended learning at a traditional undergraduate university campus. The chapter explores the prevalence of blended learning as well as how blended learning approaches are currently impacting instructional practices at traditional universities.

Context

This study was conducted at the Brigham Young University (BYU) Provo, Utah campus. BYU has a strong commitment to supporting traditional on-campus learning environments as well as distance learning through its Independent Study program. BYU is one of the largest private universities in the U.S., with approximately 1600 faculty and an enrollment cap of 30,000 students. BYU's primary commitment is to providing students with a quality undergraduate education. In addition, the university enrolls approximately 3,000 post baccalaureate students in graduate programs, giving it the Carnegie classification of Doctoral/Research University Extensive (McCormick, 2001). BYU's Division of Continuing Education is also known for its extensive Independent Study program. In 2004 the Independent Study outreach effort resulted in 27,218 university course enrollments and 83,341 high school enrollments. Over the past several years an increasing number of Independent Study courses have been offered and taken in an online format. For university level courses there are currently 182 offered in an online format and 270 in a paper format. For high school courses 222 are available online compared to 214 in paper format. Overall, 61% of the enrollments are for online courses and 39% for paper courses.

The practice of blending traditional face-to-face and technology-mediated learning has received considerable attention at BYU. BYU's Center for Instructional Design (CID), was created in 1999 by combining three related organizations. The CID facilitates large scale course development projects that involve the use of technology as well as providing faculty-specific technology integration support and consulting. Early experiments with blended learning entailed the creation of "semester online" courses that involved online media-rich general education courses in the areas of Physics, Chemistry, Physical Education, and English Writing. These courses generally involved students completing a number of online learning modules and reduced the required number of face-to-face meeting times (Waddoups & Howell, 2002).

Since 2003, the University has adopted Blackboard™ as the primary platform for the delivery of technology outside of the classroom. This online course management tool assists instructors in their organization of course materials, while providing the technology to perform online assessment, class collaboration, and communication. By the end of that year, approximately 2,000 of the 6,000 course sections offered each semester at BYU were using Blackboard.

During the last decade BYU has provided its faculty with an unprecedented level of resources and support to innovate with technology in their teaching. While there are many individually documented exemplary cases of blended learning at BYU, this paper attempts to establish a broader picture of faculty use of blended learning across the entire BYU campus.

Literature Review

The potential for technology to act as a catalyst in the tr.
of traditional approaches to teaching is a concept that has been w.
for some time (Reigeluth & Joseph, 2002; West & Graham, 2005) ...rison
and Kanuka (2004) have recently written about the potential for blended
learning to transform higher education: "The real test of blended learning is
the effective integration of the two main components (face-to-face and
Internet technology) such that we are not just adding on to the existing
dominant approach or method" (p. 97). In reviewing chapters for the
Handbook of Blended Learning Graham noticed that some blends seemed to
transform the instruction while other blends just seemed to *enhance* existing
instructional practices (Bonk & Graham, 2005).

There are many reasons why technological innovations have had
limited impact on transforming educational practices. Salomon (2002)
describes three major barriers, one of which "results from the consistent
tendency of the educational system to preserve itself and its practices by the
assimilation of new technologies into existing instructional practices." (p.
71). He elaborates, "A most powerful and innovative technology is taken and
is domesticated, or if you want—trivialized, such that it does more or less
what its predecessors have done, only it does it a bit faster and a bit
nicer . . ." (p. 72).

What is currently happening with blended learning in higher
education? Is it helping instructors to change their teaching paradigms or is it
just making current practices easier? Today in higher education much of
teaching and learning is still focused on the "transmission" model with the
lecture used by 83% of higher education instructors as the predominant
teaching strategy (U.S. Department of Education, 2001). In distance
education, there is often a similar problem of focusing on "transmissive"
rather than "interactive" learning strategies (Waddoups & Howell, 2002).
The possibilities available through blended learning have the potential to
help instructors re-conceptualize the teaching and learning relationship and
transform their teaching practices away from a transmission model to a more
active learning centered model. Alternatively, blended learning may be used
only as a way to perpetuate current practices by increasing the productivity
or convenience of instructors and students. For example, *Newsweek* recently
reported on a trend called "course casting" which allows students to
download weekly lectures onto their iPods and skip attending face-to-face
lectures all together (Tyre, 2005). It is important for us to understand the
nature of blended learning practices in higher education so that we can
develop strategies and instructional models for harnessing its
transformational potential.

Methodology

This chapter attempts to shed light on the prevalence of blended learning as well as the nature of faculty practice when it comes to implementing blended learning at BYU. This research addresses the following two research questions:

1. How prevalent is blended learning at BYU?
2. How is blended learning changing instructional practices at BYU?

The first question is answered primarily through a faculty survey distributed to all BYU faculty in 2004. The second question is addressed though the analysis of 72 faculty interviews specifically related to integration of technology into their teaching practice.

Data Collection

The research draws on four distinct sources of data to help understand the current state of blended learning at BYU. These sources of data were collected over a 2 year time frame by multiple researchers. For all data used, participants provided consent for their interviews to be used by the researchers. The first data source is quantitative in nature while the other three data sources provide a more detailed, qualitative case study look into faculty use of technology in their teaching. All data sources represent attempts to better understand how technology is impacting teaching and learning at BYU. A description of the data sources is included below.

Faculty Survey on Blended Learning

In early 2004, as part of a doctoral dissertation, a survey was conducted (by the second author) to determine the extent that blended learning was being implemented by BYU faculty as well as to better understand faculty attitudes towards blended learning at BYU (Robison, 2004). The survey was sent both electronically and via a paper mailer to each of the 1,600+ faculty members employed at BYU. A total of 471 (28.5%) responses from the survey contained answers to the question "Have you ever taught a blended learning course?" Of these respondents, 180 (38.2%) responded positively to the question and 291 (61.8%) responded negatively. There were some anomalies with the data collection. Electronic and paper versions of the survey were sent to each potential respondent. Responses came from 225 (47.8%) electronic submissions and 246 (52.2%) paper submissions. Although the term blended learning was defined for participants on the first page of the survey, fifty-seven of the electronic responders and eight of the paper responders put in the open ended comments that they did not know what blended learning was. (We assume that participants responding online were less careful about reading the introductory material to the survey.) All 65 respondents who were confused about the definition of blended learning responded negatively to the question of whether they had taught a blended learning course before, even though a few made mention of their use of online learning in their courses. This means that the percentage of faculty that implement blended learning may be under represented by the survey data.

Faculty Case Interviews

Three sources of faculty interview data (for a total of 72 interviews with 70 faculty) were included in this research. The faculty interviews represent perspectives from 12 of 13 colleges across the BYU campus. The faculty interviews were all related to how technology was being used by faculty in their instructional practice. Table 1 provides a summary of the interview sources and shows the distribution of interviews across the BYU colleges. The subsequent sections describe each of the interview data sources.

Table 1. **Sources of Faculty Interview Data**

College	Dissertation Interviews (N=10)	Innovative Technology Users (N=37)	Blackboard Users (N=25)	Total (N=72)
Biology and Agriculture	1	0	5	6
Business	3	2	3	8
Education	2	6	0	8
Engineering & Technology	0	2	3	5
Family, Home, and Social Sciences	0	1	5	6
Fine Arts and Communications	0	4	2	6
Health and Human Performance	0	4	2	6
Humanities	1	7	2	10
International Studies	0	0	0	0
Law	0	2	0	2
Nursing	1*	2*	1	4
Physical & Mathematical Sciences	2*	5*	1	8
Religious Education	0	2	1	3

* A faculty member appeared as a case in two separate studies

Ten Dissertation Interviews

The first source of interview data comes from a series of ten interviews conducted as part of the Robison (2004) dissertation study mentioned earlier. Each interview was conducted with a faculty member who was recommended to the researcher multiple times because of his/her experience and passion for blended learning. Interview questions explored each instructor's use of and experience with blended learning.

Thirty-seven Interviews with Innovative Technology Users
The second source of faculty interviews came from a study conducted in 2004 that looked at innovative faculty uses of technology in teaching across the BYU campus (West & Graham, 2005). To identify the "innovative" users of technology in teaching, referrals were requested from every department Chair on campus and from the instructional designers at BYU's Center for Instructional Design. A list of 135 instructors was generated. Recommended faculty were contacted by the researchers to request their participation in an interview. Thirty-seven faculty instructors agreed to participate. The participating faculty provided representation from 11 out of 13 colleges across campus. Interviews with these faculty members explored how the faculty were using technology in their teaching.

Twenty-seven Interviews with Faculty Using Blackboard
The third source of interview data came from an evaluation conducted in conjunction with the CID in 2005 (West, Waddoups, & Graham, in review; West, Waddoups, Graham, & Kennedy, in review). The goal of the evaluation was to understand how faculty at BYU were using the Blackboard™ course management tool in their courses. This evaluation used excerpts from fourteen of the West & Graham (2005) interviews (cases in which faculty members discussed using Blackboard™ in their courses). Other interviews were solicited from the BYU community. Initially, invitations to participate were extended to two randomly selected faculty members in each departmental unit across campus. This initial invitation resulted in approximately twenty interviews. Additional interviews were then solicited based on recommendations from departmental secretaries and faculty peers. Some faculty were willing to participate in interviews for the evaluation but weren't willing to provide informed consent for their interviews to be used in research. In all, twenty-five new faculty interviews with informed consent were able to be included in the analysis.

Data Analysis

To address the first question regarding the prevalence of blended learning at BYU, we present descriptive statistics from the faculty survey on blended learning. Faculty adoption of blended learning is compared based on several demographic variables such as age, rank and status, and gender. Analysis was conducted to understand if certain demographics are more or less likely to implement blended learning strategies.

The analysis of the qualitative case interviews uses a framework described by Graham (2005) to identify examples of transforming blends, enhancing blends, and enabling blends. Exemplars for each of these categories were drawn from the seventy-two faculty interviews described previously. Three main criteria were considered when selecting the case vignettes to present in this chapter: (1) the scope of the blend, (2) the purpose of the blend, and (3) the nature of the blend.

Scope of the Blend

The scope of the blend has to do with the question of how significant the blend is in the context of the course being considered. As a rough measure, one can look at the percentage of the course that is impacted by the blend. At one end of the continuum, a very small percentage of the course activity is impacted by the blend while at the other end of the spectrum the entire course is impacted by the blend. Because there is such a wide range of possible blends the scope is not easy to measure precisely. For example, some courses have a fixed blend (e.g., a percentage of their face-to-face contact time is replaced by online activities), while other courses only have certain activities during the semester that are blended. It is possible for a course to have a very well designed blended activity that only takes place during one week of the semester. In this case the scope or potential impact of the blend on the entire course would be relatively small.

In the scope dimension, transforming blends need to impact a significant portion of the course activities. For us this meant that the blend was viewed as impacting the course and not just a particular activity or assignment within the course. Case vignettes were selected to highlight major differences in scope between transforming and enhancing blends rather than to define a specific point at which a case changes from one category to another.

Purpose of the Blend

We attended to how the instructors talked about the purposes for the instructional interventions that they were implementing. We looked for evidence of a focus on improved pedagogy, increased productivity (or cost effectiveness), and improved convenience or access. While the goals aren't mutually exclusive, it was often evident what the primary goal was. A strong focus on improved pedagogy was a requirement for identifying transforming blends.

Nature of the Blend

The nature of the blend refers to how the blend is being used in a particular educational context. Salomon (2002) writes, "It is not the computer per se that makes a difference, for it only offers affordances and opportunities; it is the pedagogical way in which it is used that makes the difference" (p.75). In analyzing the nature of the blends, we looked at affordances of the technology being used and how the blends attempt to take advantage of the strengths of the computer-mediated environment as well as the strengths of the face-to-face environment.

A strategy for understanding the nature of the blend is to ask the question: What learner activity does the technology allow that would be difficult or impossible without the use of the technology? If the primary answer to this question has to do with increased access and convenience for the students then we have an enabling blend. If the answer has to do with increasing instructor or student productivity (e.g., increasing the amount of information students are able to cover or increasing the richness of the material covered) then we are dealing with an enhancing blend. If the answer has to do with facilitating an improvement in pedagogy by moving from a more information transmission focused pedagogy to a more active learning pedagogy then we likely have a transforming blend. Roschelle et al. (2000) identify four fundamental characteristics of effective learning environments that we drew on to help identify improvements in pedagogy: (1) active engagement, (2) participation in groups, (3) frequent interaction and feedback, and (4) connections to real world contexts.

Table 2 shows how scope, purpose and nature were used to identify cases of transforming, enhancing and enabling blends.

Table 2. **General Description of Blend Categories by Scope, Purpose, and Nature**

Transforming Blend	Enhancing Blend	Enabling Blend
A. Scope: large (course level or many activity level blends) **Purpose:** improved pedagogy **Nature:** affordances of environment used for a move towards active learning	**B. Scope:** small (activity level) **Purpose:** improved pedagogy **Nature:** affordances of environment used for a move towards active learning **C. Scope:** any size **Purpose:** increased productivity **Nature:** affordances of environment used for increasing instructor or learner productivity	**D. Scope:** any size **Purpose:** access/ convenience **Nature:** affordances of environment used for increased access/ convenience

Each of these cases implicitly assumes that affordances in the environment were used to improve the instruction in some way. Not represented in this chapter are the cases in which change does not result in improved pedagogy, increased productivity, or increased access/ convenience. In those cases there is often a mismatch between the purpose for the blend and the nature of the blend. For example, a practice that was intended to save students time may actually require more time of the students.

Researcher Bias

The three categories of blended learning identified by Graham (2005) follow patterns that were originally observed in the dozens of cases documented in the Handbook of Blended Learning: Global Perspectives, Local Designs. These patterns generally follow the primary purposes for implementing a blended learning environment: (1) improved pedagogy, (2) increased cost-effectiveness, and (3) improved access/convenience. While we acknowledge the importance of all three of these goals, we have a clear bias towards the preeminence of the first goal of improved pedagogy. We agree with Garrison (2004) that blended learning should be primarily about "rethinking and redesigning the teaching and learning relationship" with efficiency and convenience as possible secondary benefits (p. 99). The case comparisons between the transforming blends and the enhancing blends are intended to accentuate differences between blends that focus dominantly on the use of technology to transform pedagogy and those that do not.

Findings

Prevalence of Blended Learning

To determine how extensive the use of blended learning was across the BYU campus, a survey was both e-mailed and mailed to each of the 1,600+ faculty members employed at BYU during the winter of 2004. In the survey blended learning was defined as, "Blended learning instruction combines elements of online instruction with elements of face-to-face instruction." A total of 471 respondents answered the question: "Have you ever taught a blended learning course?" The respondents matched the demographics of the university population well. Of the respondents, 180 (38.2%) responded affirmatively and 291 (61.8%) responded negatively. Figures 1–3 show that implementers of blended learning come from a broad range of demographic backgrounds. One might expect that younger faculty might be more likely to implement blended learning because they are from a more "tech savvy" generation. Alternatively, one might predict that faculty with higher rank might be more likely to implement blended learning because untenured faculty have to focus on research rather than innovative teaching.

Our data (see Table 1 and 2) did not show any big differences in these areas except that adjunct professors were more than three times as likely to uses blended learning as a strategy than not. Interestingly, female faculty were more likely to use blended learning than not while male faculty were slightly less likely to use blended learning strategies (see Figure 3).

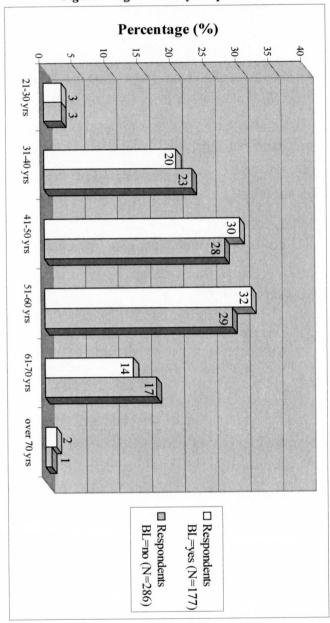

Figure 1. Age of Survey Respondents

Figure 2. **Rank and Status of Survey Respondents**

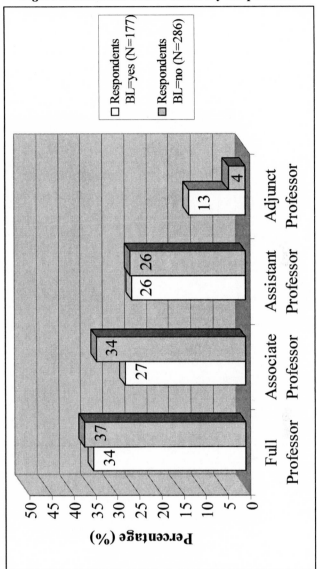

Figure 3. Gender of Survey Respondents

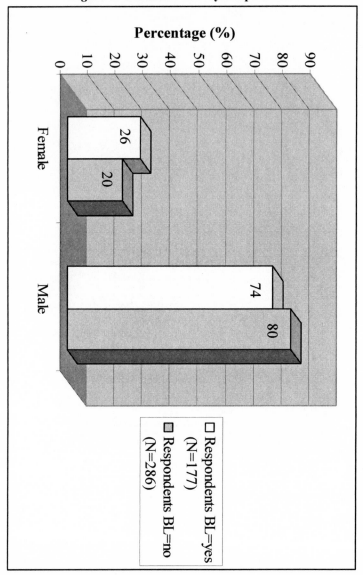

The respondents who had taught a blended learning course were asked to indicate the scope of the blend by articulating the percentage of online versus face-to-face instruction in their course. Figure 4 shows that the clear majority of faculty are substituting very little online instruction for face-to-face instruction in their implementation of blended learning.

Figure 4. Survey Response to the Question: How Much Technology Enhanced
Online Instruction was Used in Your Class? (N=162)

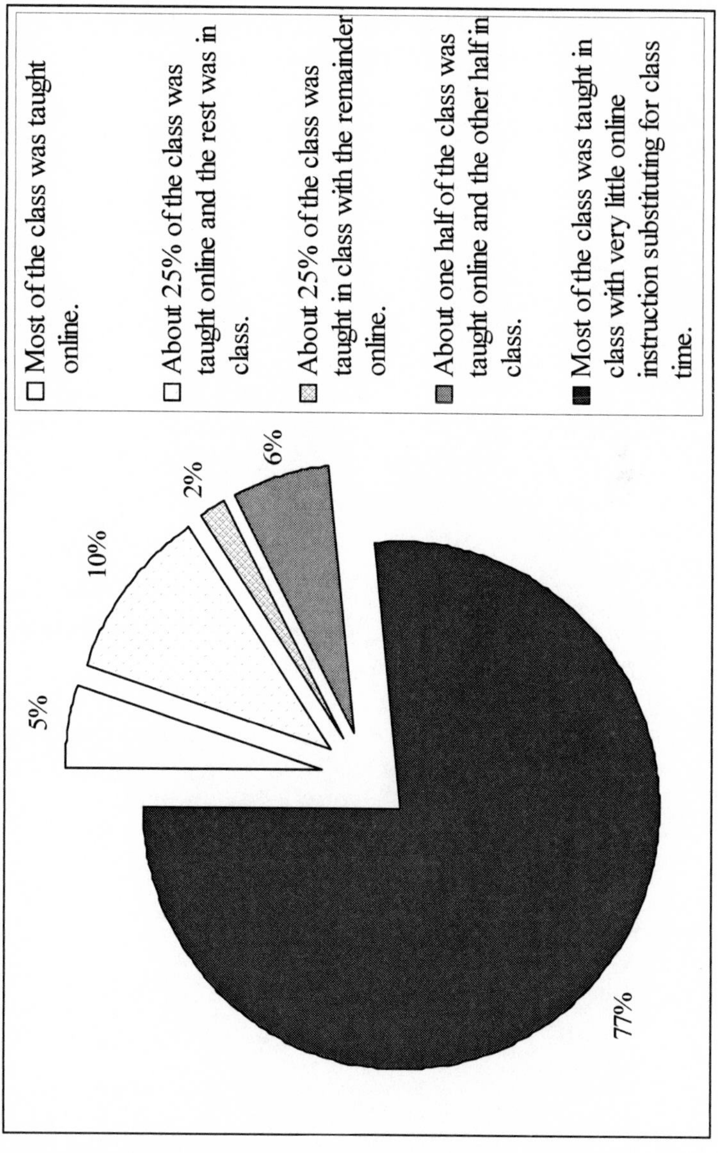

Cases of Blended Learning

In this study we did not categorize each of the seventy cases as
transforming, enhancing, or enabling. This would have been a very difficult
task because each case doesn't neatly fit into one of the categories. Instead,
the categories represent archetypes of blends that we have widely observed.
Exemplar vignettes were drawn from the case interviews to accentuate the

three categories of blends and to provide the practitioner with a way of thinking about his/her own instruction. Anecdotally, the researchers observed a much greater prevalence of enhancing blends than transforming blends among the cases. This data corroborates with the survey data in Figure 4 showing that the scope of a majority of the blends is likely small. It remains to be seen if the multitude of enhancing blends are really transforming blends in embryo.

Transforming Blends

The criteria we looked for in cases of transforming blends were (1) the scope had to be large, (2) the primary purpose for the blend had to be improved pedagogy, and (3) the nature of the blend had to take advantages of affordances of the blended environment to move towards a more active learning pedagogy (see A in Table 2). Case A1 shares two examples of instructional simulations that have dramatically changed how faculty teach as well as how and what students learn. Case A2 shares an example of a faculty member who has used multiple technologies and strategies to increased active engagement, participation in groups, and interaction and feedback in his course.

Case A1: Instructional Simulations—Virtual Audiometer & Virtual ChemLab

Two prominent cases on campus involve the use of instructional simulations in transforming the teaching and learning environment. In both cases, the simulations are used as tools for both in-class and out-of-class work. The first is the Virtual Audiometer (see Figure 5) which is used in the Audiology and Speech Language Pathology department. The second is the Virtual ChemLab (See Figure 6) which is used in undergraduate chemistry classes. In both cases, the use of instructional simulations has changed the nature of teaching and learning in the courses where they were used.

Figure 5. **Virtual Audiometer**

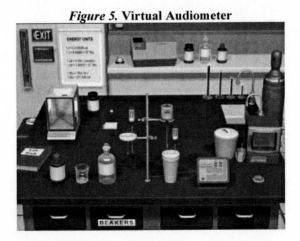

Figure 6. Virtual ChemLab

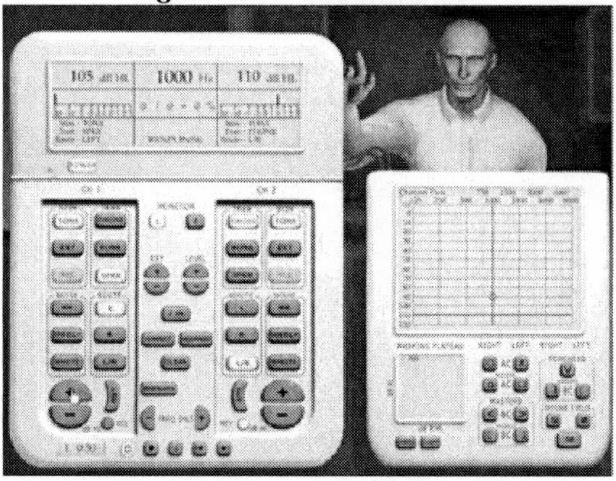

In the Audiology course, one of the major challenges that faculty faced was being able to provide the sixty students a semester with the quality and quantity of practice they needed to become proficient at doing a range of clinical hearing tests. The instructor explains some of the challenges in this way:

> We had a series of portable hearing testing equipment which the class would be assigned so many laboratories a term and they would check equipment out and test each other's hearing. And also we'd have them get ear plugs and somewhat simulate someone with a hearing loss, but you really can't do that effectively with ear plugs, but all of this was better than doing nothing, and obviously they would turn in their labs and there was no way of me checking for accuracy, no way of me posing more and more, stepping up the problem, making them more challenging or more complex. That just couldn't be done.

Using real patients wasn't a logistically feasible option either because "you're not going to get half a dozen patients that are going to be tested by sixty students." Even if they were able to, the instructor would have to test each patient himself to know if the student diagnosis were accurate. The virtual audiometer simulates both the patient and the expensive testing equipment. The instructor is able "simulate all sorts of problems and patients." Instead of having a class that is focused primarily on conveying information, the class can be centered around working problems and discussing student misconceptions. Because the instructor can adjust the hearing impairment of the simulated patient, the instructor is able to provide layered scaffolding from extreme procedures to less extreme textbook examples. The students were able to practice more (and at their own convenience) and the instructor was also able to provide more detailed and timely feedback. Since using Virtual Audiometer, the instructor has seen big improvements in the student performance on exams.

In the second instructional simulation case, the course instructors were interested in developing students that "think like chemists." This involved moving from memorizing and conducting cookbook solutions to "problem-solving, creative-based activities." This was a challenge, because in the physical chemistry laboratory "what really happens is that because of cost, time, safety issues, liability issues, students when they get into the lab, they don't apply what they have learned, they cookbook, they follow their directions because you can't give them no directions . . . it would be unsafe, it would cost too much, it would have too much liability, so we have to tell them exactly what to do."

The use of Virtual ChemLab in the course doesn't replace the hands-on experience they get in the lab. Rather, it provides a safe lab environment where they can be given open-ended problems to solve. "We're simulating the cognitive processes, the creative abilities, the problem solving aspects of laboratory . . . when you want to simulate that, then all of the simulations have to open-ended and very flexible, based on what the teacher wants to do, so you have to go very easy to very hard." They can experiment with different lab equipment and see the realistic effects (like the change of a solution's color or an explosion) of combining different chemicals without the physical risks involved. They also use the affordances of the technology to allow students to speed up the time required to conduct certain experiments. "Instead of taking 20 minutes to centrifuge something, you click a button and it does it, instead of doing a flame test, a flame test takes 10 seconds." This allows students to focus more on the problem solving than on the technical procedural knowledge.

The instructor who uses and helped to design Virtual ChemLab has thought very carefully about the use of technology and how it specifically helps him to reach his goal of helping students to engage in a different type of learning:

> So in your big picture of technology in the classroom, you've got to know what are you trying to do with the technology. What are you trying to teach with it? If you're trying to just demonstrate a concept, that's very different than trying to do a different type of learning [like problem solving].

Case A2: Just-in-Time Teaching—Physical Science 100

Dr. Tuckett teaches Physical Science 100. This course is a large enrollment course with about three hundred students per section and about five to six thousand enrollments a year. Dr. Tuckett has taught both

Independent Study (completely online) and traditional sections of the course. He describes himself as a "lecturer at heart." He views an important part of his role as "helping students maybe capture, but at least understand, some of [his] passion [for the subject matter]." Dr. Tuckett is very thoughtful about the strategies he uses in his teaching and how he blends the face-to-face with the technology-mediated aspects of the course. When considering the use of technological tools he tries "to use each of the modes of instruction and learning for what they're good at." He did not want to replicate online what was done in class just because a different media was available; He said, "We wanted to do online the things that we could never do in a class."

Dr. Tuckett used strategies that involved a host of different technologies to enhance performance in his class. He calls one of his teaching strategies "just-in-time teaching" because the integration between the online and face-to-face strategies allows him to provide instruction that is targeted immediately and directly to student needs and misconceptions. Through the use of Blackboard, he gives online quizzes on the reading material that are due an hour before class. About 95% of his students come to class having already read the assigned readings. He then uses the responses from the quizzes to "shape" the discussion and learning activities for that day in class. Dr. Tuckett commented:

> For the large classes especially, you want to engage them. It's easy to sit in the back of the room and get lost, but if they're seeing their answer come up and were talking about something they just addressed themselves, and they've had a personal connection to it, they seem to be much more involved, their questions are better . . . now we're trying to fix some misconceptions rather than just getting it the first time.

Dr. Tuckett also uses an in-class electronic response system. The system consists of transmitters purchased by each of the students and a receiver used by the faculty. The response system allows the instructor to present questions in class that every student has to respond to. The instructor can then look at the responses in the class and dynamically adjust the discussion to address class needs. Dr. Tuckett says:

> I could get to see where they were, in the middle of the instruction, I could say ... tell me why you thought that ... and usually after they discuss a little bit, they'd do better having got it, sometimes it would be just to make sure you are with me. Sometimes students zone out if it gets too hard, so I'd say, I'm going to have a quiz on this. Does anyone have any questions before I ask your quiz question ... and all of a sudden these students who had been quite passive became quite active wanting to make sure they understood the concept before they were tested on it, so you get a chance

for real-time interaction in a class in a way, in a small class I can usually do it, if there's only three of you, I'm going to call on you next and you're going to go up to the board and show me what's there, but classes of three hundred, when a third of them are zoned out, that's a technique I was using when I was teaching to engage them... and a lot of times I'd have them vote, and check with your partner, and now let's vote again. It was helpful in making the learning environment more active than it was before.

Dr. Tuckett also uses online interactive animations and simulations to help students visualize relationships that may be difficult to understand. Dr. Tuckett worries that some in the "video game generation" might not associate the simulations they are doing online with the real world. So he often includes activities that involve the physical and tactile senses like standing on a scale as you ride up an elevator. He commented:

We thought it was valuable to ... let them know this is a simulation but this is how things really work, and also involve more senses, they can touch it, they can see it, we wanted to make that connection in places where we could, but for those for whom it wasn't available, we thought the simulations would be second best.

Dr. Tuckett uses lots of interventions throughout his course. His blending of the technology-mediated and the face-to-face environments has been carefully thought out. In fact, some interventions, such as the use of asynchronous discussions, he tried and didn't use because it didn't meet his goals. He has used strengths of both environments to increase student engagement, collaboration, and his ability to provide timely feedback to students.

Enhancing Blends

There are two types of enhancing blends represented in this section. The first is very similar to a transforming blend with the exception that the scope is small (see B in Table 2). The second type of enhancing blend entails blends of small or large scopes that primarily focus on improving instruction by increasing student and faculty productivity (see C in Table 2). By productivity, we mean that there has not been a paradigm shift from a pedagogy focused on information transfer to active learning, but rather, the blend has created improvements in the efficiency and/or effectiveness with which learning occurs in the traditional paradigm.

Case B1: Asynchronous Discussion Activity

Dr. Jones teaches History of Civilization with over 100 students per class. She has started to use one asynchronous discussion assignment a semester as a way to increase engagement in the class. "I've started using the discussion board for a major assignment in each of my classes and it's been really fruitful, because students who will not say a word all semester will write tons of stuff and respond and get very enthusiastic about discussing things in a different format." She elaborates, "With 120 people in a classroom, not very many people talk. The same 15–20 talk, the other 100 sit there. So, this gives them a chance, everybody is required to do it, so it gives them a chance to say stuff."

Dr. Jones divides her class up into discussion groups of twenty five or less, so that students are not overwhelmed with the number of posts in the forum. She does not make comments on the discussion until the discussion time is over. Then she prints and takes notes on the discussion. Then during class time she gives oral feedback to everyone based on the discussion ideas that were presented.

She feels that not only do students like the assignment "because it is something that they can do at home at midnight" but also because "your face isn't there, you can compose your thoughts before you post them. You get a chance to read what everybody else has said." She also believes that the assignment has helped improve student learning in part because it helps them to think about the class topics and interact with class members outside of the limited lecture time. She says, "I think they have to be learning more because they're thinking more. It's not like, class is over, I stop thinking about it and go home. Class is over and I keep thinking about it because I know that I have to go to Blackboard™ and I have to think of something to say."

Case C1: Small Scope Enhancements

The majority instructors who are blending face-to-face with computer-mediated instruction across campus are doing it on a small scale. Often the purpose is improved productivity. Consider three common practices:

1. Providing more content — "[Blackboard™] allows us to post additional things that we don't get to in class. We say, oh that's a really interesting topic. Check Blackboard™ this afternoon and we'll have more information for you. So, it allows for expanded learning."

2. Increased communication — "[Technology] allows me to communicate with the students more quickly, and things of greater volume." Faculty communicating more with students electronically. Technology facilitates student faculty contact outside of regular class time that wasn't easily possible before.

3. Saving class time — Many interviewees mentioned how the university course management system helps them to save time. Some of the most prevalent ways are (a) moving exams and quizzes online so that they take place outside of face-to-face class time and (b) providing access to course content, grades, frequently asked questions, and announcements in one place so that face-to-face class time doesn't have to be taken up with administrative logistics. One faculty actually decreases a two hour class block by a half hour because of the time savings. Another instructor said, "We like to write up as many announcements as possible at the beginning of the semester and set specific dates for them to come up so that the system can take care of it from there."

One irony mentioned in the interviews was the idea that sometimes faculty inadvertently decrease student productivity in their attempt in increase it:

I've become very comfortable now with finding a website that explains a particular principle and making a quick link and off they go. That's something that otherwise would require me to print out a copy, and email everybody and Xerox the thing. That literally could save me 10, 15, 20 minutes in some cases. I think also, though, there's another side that isn't quite bad ... that it gives me reasons to do more things than I otherwise would, even though the things are not all that essential. For example, do the students really need to see this [paper]? Would I be fine if I just described it briefly in class? . . . Probably, but what am I going to do, I'm going to try and upload the thing. Just knowing that I can do that makes me, gives me that option now, and what I'm finding a lot of students talk about is that faculty can't stop themselves, they start uploading the kitchen sink, everything in the world. Instead of syllabi with 10 or 15 articles, now all of a sudden faculty are giving 300 articles because it is so darn convenient. Students sometimes I think are confused and overwhelmed and not quite knowing for sure what is essential and what is just spur of the moment fun. . . . It can become addictive, it can make the students very inefficient because I think there is a temptation with the faculty to just overload them, and not to be very discriminating about what is essential and what is superfluous. But that's up to the faculty member to have a little self-discipline.

Case C2: Face-to-face Seat-time Reduction in Accounting

It has become quite popular of late in the School of Business for faculty to video record a series of thoughtfully crafted lectures. The videos are then combined with presentation materials. Typically, the final product includes a small frame with the faculty delivering the lecture combined with a larger frame containing visuals, demonstration problems, etc. that the instructor is explaining. The instructional package is burned onto CDs and purchased by students at the beginning of the semester. Then during the semester, instead of attending a face-to-face lecture session twice a week, they might only be required to attend once a week.

Dr. Cormick is one of several faculty members in the School of Business who has successfully used this approach. He adopted the practice in his undergraduate class because "The bottom line is I believe it is better for the students." He explains, "Undergraduate classes that I teach in Accounting tend to be a little more heavily computational, strictly information, how the numbers come together, how the formulas work, so it is more of a technical information transfer as opposed to an analytical and discussion that builds on that." He explains his frustration with trying to teach the technical material in a traditional lecture:

> I found it very frustrating as an instructor to have 50 students in the room knowing that some are with me and some are not. They come with different backgrounds and different aptitudes . . . when I take a piece of chalk or an overhead projector and I whip through some very technical material, I would find out of a group of 50, my best guess is maybe 10 were with me, 10 were close enough that they would raise their hands and ask questions, and hopefully they stayed with me throughout. But maybe I had another 30 that either they were so far out of sync that they did not dare ask questions. Or maybe there is a personality issue and they are just not comfortable in a group of 50 peers raising their hand and asking for a clarification on a point or two.

With the blended approach, students are able to go through the technical material at their own pace. They are able "to isolate on the sections that were confusing to them and to hear that over and over again." It also allows his students "to have access to my chalkboard discussion, if that is what you want to call it, 24X7 . . . I feel it was a way for me to give detailed explanation to all of the material I felt they needed to understand for my class and then let the students kind of customize and match that discussion to their learning needs."

Ideally class time is spent in doing application and discussion. The mastering of the technical material is a prerequisite for being able to do that effectively. An important goal, especially as they move into upper division classes, is to go beyond the technical material to judgment, decision making, and application. Dr. Cormick acknowledges some of the challenges with achieving this in the face-to-face lecture:

> How can I design [the course] so that students are able to get what I hope they can get outside of classroom and how can I build on that when I am in the classroom. So it was a different challenge to instructors, because I think many including myself who spent a lot of time in the old method going over answers to problems in the text. If that is the only thing we are doing in the classroom, then in my opinion we are not capitalizing on our opportunities in the classroom. . . . I think the biggest challenge is back to the instructor on the design and to force yourself to do something different. Instead of going over homework in the class, what if they came in understanding the homework. What could you do differently in the classroom?

Enabling Blends

Enabling blends are blends that focus primarily on providing access and convenience to students (see D in Table 2). One example is provided below.

Case D1:Online Course with Optional Face-to-face Sessions

In the nursing program at BYU, undergraduate students take a class that familiarizes them with research in the field. The class is scheduled during a semester when the students "are in heavy clinical rotations where they spend 12–16 hours a week onsite in hospitals for clinics." This poses real logistical challenges for the department as well as the students; there are some rotations in the morning and others in the evening so it is difficult to find a time when over 50 students could all physically meet during a two hour block for class. The instructor explored using a predominantly online approach for the class. The instructor goals for the class were "to expose the students to research and to have them be able to understand it as clearly and as well as if they were sitting in a traditional classroom." She further explains her reasoning for doing the majority of the class online, "For the convenience of the students . . . They are in hospitals two full days a week, it's really difficult to pull them up to campus an extra day. I thought it'd be convenient for the students—user friendly."

The course was designed to be predominantly self-paced. "Once the calendar is set, they can go as fast as they can. Some of them have finished in half the time, and that's wonderful." However, there are deadlines set throughout the semester to prevent the procrastinating of work to the very end. In the course students read a text book and take online quizzes in Blackboard from a databank with randomized questions. They also read journal articles and critique them in an asynchronous discussion forum. The instructor commented on an advantage of the discussion forum: "I can hear every student, whereas in a traditional class, I may not. Because I can monitor who and who does not contribute to the discussion . . . it does force them to say something . . . it requires more participation." The instructor is careful to respond to all postings in the forum during the semester. The instructor believes that with this instructional approach "they are getting it because it requires them to read the text. They can't sit and daydream in class."

Some students complained that they felt they would learn much better in a classroom setting. So, the option for coming to a face-to-face lecture session was provided to the class on an ongoing basis. "However, no student has ever come in." The instructor comments, "When it comes right down to 3 o'clock on Monday afternoon and they've been in clinicals or wherever they've been, they don't come in, so my assumption is the convenience is working for them."

The convenience afforded by the course format extends to the instructor as well as to the students. One level of convenience comes from being able to provide feedback to students at any time of the day or night, "if I want to get up and grade papers at 2:00 in the morning I could do that. Not that I would." Another benefit comes from being able to communicate with the class while out of town at professional conferences. "I ran a class from Chicago because I was at a conference. . . . it was nice, so students didn't miss a beat."

There has been an evolution in the course to make it even more convenient for the students. This has typically entailed eliminating required face-to-face sessions while leaving the optional face-to-face sessions. In the first iteration of the course, students met face-to-face for an orientation on the first day of class and also on the last day of class to present their work. Since then, meeting the last day of class has been eliminated because students are finishing the course work at different times throughout the semester. An online module has also been created to orient the students without the need to attend class on the first day.

Discussion

With the possible exception of case C1 all of the cases represent instructors who have been innovators in constructing blended learning environments for their students. Cases A1, A2, and B1 highlight instructors who have integrated the use of technology with face-to-face instruction in a way that moves away from the traditional "information transmission" paradigm. In the two cases of extensive simulation use (transforming blends), faculty focused more on active inquiry and problem solving skills and dramatically increased student opportunities for practice and feedback. In case A2 (a transforming blend), a large enrollment, lecture oriented class was turned into a class with a high level of interactivity not previously possible. Case B1 (an enhancing blend) used asynchronous discussion to increase the interactivity and engagement between students. This case was classified as an enhancing blend primarily because the scope was limited to one assignment only during an entire semester.

Case C2 (an enhancing blend) is an example of an innovative approach of using a blend to more efficiently disseminate information to learners. While the information transmission paradigm was kept intact in the course, students were able to increase their productivity through 24X7 access to the content and the ability to selectively review content they were struggling with. The instructor in case C2 is obviously thinking about things that he might do to "capitalize on the opportunities of the classroom" by "doing something different" with face-to-face class time. The scenarios presented in Case C1 (enhancing blends) were the most prevalent blends found in the interviews. They consisted of small scale course enhancements that often had minimal overall pedagogical impact on the learners.

Case D1 (an enabling blend) exemplifies a focus on increasing access and convenience for the students. The goal in this case was not necessarily to go beyond what could be done in the traditional classroom but to match the outcomes in a more time and space convenient way.

As blended learning becomes more prevalent in higher education contexts, it is important to consider how to foster blends that promote improved learning. This can either be achieved through systemic change or through a more graduated series of changes. The Center for Academic Transformation has promoted systemic change by funding 30 large enrollment course redesign projects at universities across the United States. Almost all of the course redesigns involved the use of blended learning (Graham & Allen, 2005), and a majority of the projects reported both improvements in achievement as well as reductions in cost (Twigg, 2003). In contrast, the Center for Higher Education Policy Studies did a multi-national study looking at information and communication technology (ICT) usage in higher education and found a gradual "stretching the mold" scenario to be the predominant approach to integrating technology into teaching (Collis & van der Wende, 2002).

There are several barriers to achieving the kind of change blended learning can offer. Three of these barriers are (1) the proliferation of superficial blends, (2) a focus on the scope of blends, and (3) a focus on efficiency and productivity.

Barrier 1: The Proliferation of Superficial Blends

In many cases we observed superficial blends, meaning that the blended approach wasn't adding anything significant to the instruction. While these cases may not be the most interesting from a research perspective, they represent evidence of a growing willingness among both instructors and administrators to step outside the traditional instructional boundaries and experiment with blended learning. The risk comes in the fact the time costs for a implementing a superficial blend can easily outweigh the instructional benefits. This could discourage faculty from exploring further adoption of blended learning approaches. It remains to be seen if the more superficial blends become stepping stones on the path towards adoption of more transformational pedagogical practices or if they are "final destinations" for faculty integrating technology into their teaching.

Barrier 2: A Focus on the Scope of a Blend

Sometimes when talking about blended learning environments, the temptation is to focus predominantly on the scope of the blend (e.g., something like 25% online and 75% face-to-face, or a reduction in X% of the seat time). We agree with Jay Cross (2005) that these are not useful descriptions of a blended learning environment. While the scope is important, the purpose and nature of the blend should be the most important defining characteristics. This has interesting implications for educational administrators because typically the thing most easily controlled by administrators is the scope of a blend. For example, administrators might be tempted to specify that blended courses will replace half of the face-to-face "seat time" with online activities without considering pedagogical implications or providing support for taking advantage of the strengths of the two environments.

Barrier 3: A Focus on Efficiency and Productivity

Efficiency and productivity are both noteworthy goals. However, it is easy for these goals to take precedence over the goal of effective pedagogy. The enticement of using technology to disseminate information more efficiently may distract many from considering blended options that could change their pedagogical paradigm. One perspective is that technology can be used exclusively to increase productivity and that this in turn frees up time and energy for the faculty or student to dedicate to more active and innovative face-to-face experiences. The logic of this argument is hard to counter. It would be interesting to investigate how frequently energy saved through technological efficiencies is actually put back into improving the face-to-face portion of a course. The authors believe that for blended learning to achieve its transformational potential, the primary goal needs to be rethinking the teaching and learning relationship and secondarily efficiency or productivity (Garrison & Kanuka, 2004).

From Enhancing to Transforming Blends

Is there a clear path to help faculty who have implemented enhancing blends to move towards more transformational blends? Case B1 is an example of an instructor that is heading that direction. She began using

107

asynchronous discussions for one assignment in one course. That quickly evolved to using asynchronous discussions in her other courses on a limited basis. She mentioned in her interview that in one of her courses, she is "up to four [online discussions] now" and in her graduate course they are up to doing one a week. Case A2 is an example of a course that has evolved over time to include the use of a variety of different technologies in the innovative ways described. In both of these cases the enhancing blends started out small but still seemed to be focused on improved pedagogy. It is less clear whether other small scale blends with a focus on productivity as represented by the scenarios in Case C1 will eventually lead to pedagogical transformations.

One challenge to effectuating change is that most faculty do not have ready access to effective mental models of blended learning. Most aren't even aware of what the possibilities are. Most have grown up and taught in environments without technology or where technology has been primarily a tool for accessing and disseminating information rather for purposes articulated by Roschelle et al. (2000) such as (1) active engagement, (2) participation in groups, (3) frequent interaction and feedback, and (4) connections to real world contexts. A good beginning point for facilitating change will be to develop well articulated examples, cases, and models of how blended learning can work in a variety of different contexts.

Conclusion

In this chapter we have looked at the prevalence of blended learning at Brigham Young University. We found that there has been widespread adoption of blended learning across the campus. However, we also discovered that much of the blended learning on campus has not dramatically changed the pedagogical strategies being used in the class but rather is being implemented as enhancement to the traditional on-campus, lecture oriented pedagogy. It remains to be seen whether there is an evolution from smaller scale enhancing blends to more transformative blends. We also found several practical yet innovative blends that have dramatically changed the nature of the courses where the blends are being implemented.

For there to be greater adoption of transforming blends among faculty, we believe that there needs to be a greater focus on developing cases and models that can help faculty to see what the possibilities are and how to achieve those possibilities within the resource constraints of their institutions. While systemic changes mandated through administrative channels will surely account for some change, the majority of change is likely to come more slowly from faculty "stretching the mold" with their use of technology in their teaching (Collis & van der Wende, 2002). Faculty are still the primary decision-makers when it comes to pedagogy, so it is critical for them to be able to see effective models of blended learning and believe that it is within their reach.

References

Bonk, C. J., & Graham, C. R. (Eds.). (2005). *Handbook of blended learning: Global perspectives, local designs*. San Francisco, CA: Pfeiffer Publishing.

Collis, B., & van der Wende, M. (2002). *Models of technology and change in higher education: An international comparative survey on the current and future use of ICT in higher education*. Enschede, NL: Center for Higher Education Policy Studies, University of Twente.

Cookson, P. (2002). The hybridization of higher education: Cross-national perspectives. *International Review of Research in Open and Distance Learning, 2*(2).

Cross, J. (2005). Foreword. In C. J. Bonk & C. R. Graham (Eds.), *Handbook of blended learning: Global perspectives, local designs* (pp. xvii-xxii). San Francisco, CA: Pfeiffer Publishing.

de Boer, W. (2002). ICT in teaching and learning: Part of a blend. In B. Collis & M. van der Wende (Eds.), *Models of technology and change in higher education: An international comparative survey on the current and future use of ICT in higher education*. Enschede, NL: Center for Higher Education Policy Studies, University of Twente.

Garrison, D. R., & Kanuka, H. (2004). Blended learning: Uncovering its transformative potential in higher education. *The Internet and Higher Education, 7*(2), 95–105.

Graham, C. R. (2005). Blended learning systems: Definition, current trends, and future directions. In C. J. Bonk & C. R. Graham (Eds.), *Handbook of blended learning: Global perspectives, local designs* (pp. 3-21). San Francisco, CA: Pfeiffer Publishing.

Graham, C. R., & Allen, S. (2005). Blended learning evironments. In C. Howard & J. V. Boettecher & L. Justice & K. D. Schenk & P. L. Rogers & G. A. Berg (Eds.), *Encyclopedia of Distance Learning* (pp. 172-179). Hershey, PA: Idea Group Inc.

Graham, C. R., Allen, S., & Ure, D. (2005). Benefits and challenges of blended learning environments. In M. Khosrow-Pour (Ed.), *Encyclopedia of Information Science and Technology* (pp. 253–259). Hershey, PA: Idea Group Inc.

Kappel, H.-H., Lehmann, B., & Loeper, J. (2002). Distance education at conventional universities in Germany. *International Review of Research in Open and Distance Learning, 2*(2).

Lewis, R. (2002). The hybridization of conventional higher education: UK perspective. *International Review of Research in Open and Distance Learning, 2*(2).

McCormick, A. C. (2001). *The Carnegie classification of institutions of higher education 2000 edition*. Menlo Park, CA: The Carnegie Foundation for the Advancement of Teaching.

Reigeluth, C. M., & Joseph, R. (2002). Beyond technology integration: The case for technology transformation. *Educational Technology, 42*(4), 9–13.

Robison, R. A. (2004). *Selected faculty experiences in designing and teaching blended learning courses at Brigham Young University.* Unpublished doctoral dissertation, The University of Nebraska - Lincoln, Lincoln, NE.

Roschelle, J. M., Pea, R. D., Hoadley, C. M., Gordin, D. N., & Means, B. M. (2000). Changing how and what children learn in school with computer-based technologies. *Children and computer technology, 10*(2), 76–101.

Salomon, G. (2002). Technology and pedagogy: Why don't we see the promised revolution? *Educational Technology, 42*(2), 71–75.

Twigg, C. A. (2003). Improving learning and reducing costs: New models for online learning. *Educause Review, 38*(5), 28–38.

Tyre, P. (2005, November 28). Professor in your pocket. *NewsWeek,* 46–47.

U.S. Department of Education. (2001). *The condition of education 2001* (2001-072). Washington, DC: National Center for Educational Statistics.

Waddoups, G., & Howell, S. (2002). Bringing online learning to campus: The hybridization of teaching and learning at Brigham Young University. *International Review of Research in Open and Distance Learning, 2*(2).

West, R. E., & Graham, C. R. (2005). Five powerful ways technology can enhance teaching and learning in higher education. *Educational Technology, 45*(3), 20–27.

West, R. E., Waddoups, G., & Graham, C. R. (in review). Understanding the experiences of instructors as they adopt a course management system.

West, R. E., Waddoups, G., Graham, C. R., & Kennedy, M. (in review). Weighing costs versus benefits; Evaluating the impact from implementing a course management system.

Young, J. R. (2002, March 22). 'Hybrid' teaching seeks to end the divide between traditional and online instruction. *Chronicle of Higher Education,* pp. A33.

Discovering, Designing, and Delivering Hybrid Courses

Robert Kaleta, Karen Skibba, and Tanya Joosten
University of Wisconsin-Milwaukee

Hybrid courses are becoming increasingly popular with faculty, students, and institutions. Thus, it is important to investigate why faculty adopt the hybrid course model and how to best prepare faculty for teaching hybrid courses. This chapter presents the results of a qualitative research study that focused on the hybrid teaching experiences of 10 faculty from three universities. The study was conducted by the University of Wisconsin-Milwaukee's Learning Technology Center, one of the pioneers in developing the hybrid course model. The opportunities, challenges, and advice offered by the faculty in this study have been consolidated with extensive previous hybrid course development experiences to create a set of practical and essential recommendations for fostering interest in hybrid teaching and for supporting faculty in their efforts to teach hybrid courses. These recommendations can serve as a guide for institutions developing hybrid course initiatives, as a foundation for faculty developers charged with preparing faculty for hybrid teaching, and as advice for faculty teaching hybrid courses.

Developing a hybrid course for the first time is challenging for any instructor. Hybrid courses are substantially different from wholly face to face or online courses. They require faculty to develop new teaching skills and to learn how to design hybrid courses. Although effective hybrid courses can result in a number of benefits for faculty, students, and institutions, poorly designed and taught courses can be disastrous. Thus, some busy faculty who are secure in their current teaching styles and reluctant to take risks, especially in front of students, need encouragement to try the hybrid model. The major goal of this study is to use the experiences of faculty to help guide institutions in their efforts to develop faculty interest in hybrid teaching and to prepare faculty to design and teach successful hybrid courses.

Opportunities and Challenges of the Hybrid Course Model

To teach a hybrid course an instructor reduces in-person classroom meetings and replaces a significant amount of that instructional time with online learning activities (Garnham & Kaleta, 2002; Swenson & Evans, 2003). There are many potential benefits for students, faculty, and institutions associated with the hybrid course model. This is primarily because hybrid courses can incorporate the best instructional methods from both traditional and virtual environments. Hybrid courses that effectively integrate pedagogical strategies in both the face to face and online environments have "the potential to increase student learning outcomes" (Dziuban, Hartman, & Moskal, 2004, p. 6). Garnham and Kaleta (2002) reported that instructors "almost universally believe their students learned more in a hybrid format than they did in the traditional class sections" (p. 2). This potential to improve learning has led many institutions to adopt a "hybrid" solution (Skill & Young, 2002).

In addition to increased student learning, other benefits of hybrid courses include making courses more accessible and learning more convenient for students, providing faculty with greater flexibility in how they structure their time, and increasing classroom space for institutions to serve more students without building more classrooms (Bonk, Olson, Wisher, & Orvis, 2002). Because of these potential benefits, an increasing number of institutions are interested in developing hybrid courses, programs, and degrees. Bonk, Kim, and Zeng (2006) conclude that "blended learning is proliferating across college and university campus, and this trend will increase" (p. 553). In 2002, the editor of the *Journal of Asynchronous Learning Networks* (2002) predicted that 80% to 90% of all courses will eventually become part online and part face to face (cited in Young, 2002).

To reap the benefits of the hybrid course model, institutions are faced with two major implementation issues: 1) how to foster faculty awareness and interest in hybrid teaching, and 2) how best to prepare faculty to teach hybrid courses. Therefore, it is important to understand how faculty discover the hybrid instructional model and how they design, and deliver hybrid courses.

Faculty Adoption of Hybrid Courses

Although much has been written regarding faculty adoption of distance education (Carr, 1999; Christo-Baker, 2004; Keller, 2005; Simonson, Smaldino, Albright, & Zvacek, 2000), little has been published regarding faculty adoption of hybrid teaching. There are a number of studies that cite the reasons why faculty like hybrid courses and continue to teach them (Dziuban, Hartman, & Moskal, 2004; Johnson, 2002; Martyn 2003; Skibba, 2005), but there is little information about what prompted faculty to initially try the hybrid course model, why they adopted this format, and how they designed and taught these courses. One of the major goals of this study is to understand why faculty adopt and implement the hybrid instructional model.

Everett Rogers' (1962, 1995) theory on the Diffusion of Innovation (see Figure 1) provides a useful framework for examining why and how faculty adopt the hybrid course model. According to Rogers, the decision to adopt an innovation, the innovation-decision process, is a progression that involves five stages and is influenced by many factors. A person's decision to adopt an innovation occurs over time and progresses "from first knowledge of the innovation" [Knowledge Stage], "to forming an attitude toward the innovation" [Persuasion Stage], "to a decision to adopt or reject" [Decision Stage], "to implementation of the new idea" [Implementation Stage], and "to confirmation of this decision" [Confirmation Stage] (p. 161).

Figure 1. Stages of Rogers' (1995) Innovation-Decision Process

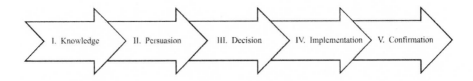

Figure 1. During the Innovation-Decision Process, a person's decision to adopt an innovation progresses from the Knowledge Stage when the innovation is discovered to the Persuasion Stage when an attitude about the innovation is formed to the Decision Stage when the innovation is adopted or rejected to the Implementation Stage when the innovation is implemented and finally to the Confirmation Stage when the decision to continue to use the innovation is confirmed or reversed (Rogers, 1995). Adapted from *Diffusion of Innovations* (4th ed.) (p. 163), by E. M. Rogers, 1995, New York: Free Press.

The first three stages,Knowledge, Persuasion, and Decision,are particularly important in understanding why someone tries an innovation for the first time and are used in this study to analyze and understand faculty responses adoption of hybrid courses. Using this model as a framework provides information regarding how faculty first heard about hybrid courses, what persuaded them to take a closer look at hybrid courses, and what ultimately led them to decide to try to teach a hybrid course. The fourth stage, Implementation, provides a context for examining faculty experiences as they design and teach hybrid courses, which is the second major focus of this study. The fifth stage, Confirmation, addresses the issue of why instructors decide to continue or not continue to teach hybrid courses.

Instructor Roles Are Transformed

Most of the literature on faculty experiences teaching hybrid courses describes specific hybrid courses and the perceived benefits of the hybrid course model (Aycock, Garnham, & Kaleta, 2002; Johnson, 2002; Martyn, 2003; Skibba, 2005). What is lacking is a more detailed examination of how instructors' experiences change when they design and teach hybrid courses. The second major goal of this study is to do precisely this, and to discuss within the context of these roles the challenges encountered and lessons learned by faculty. Furthermore, the examination of these experiences provides valuable information that faculty developers can use to develop and improve efforts to prepare faculty for hybrid teaching. Implementing a hybrid course for the first time is a complex process. To transform a course from a face to face format to a hybrid format, an instructor must re-examine course goals, develop new online and face to face learning activities, utilize new types of assessment, integrate face to face and online learning activities, and interact with students in new ways. As Bonk, Kim, and Zeng (2006) note, "Blended learning highlights the need for instructional skills in multiple teaching and learning environments" (p. 564). Thus, designing an effective hybrid course and learning to teach in new ways involves significant pedagogical changes that require instructors to gain new skills and assume multiple roles.

In order to organize, analyze, and understand faculty experiences designing and teaching hybrid courses during the implementation stage, this study utilized a framework developed by Berge (1995) for enhancing online courses. This framework describes the pedagogical, social, managerial, and technological roles that online instructors assume when they teach online. These roles translate well in the hybrid environment, which incorporates both online and face to face instruction. Following is a brief description of the four roles modified for the hybrid learning environment (Berge, 1995).

Pedagogical Role. This role includes both the design and the delivery of instructional learning activities for the in-person and online environments. Instructors design the course structure and assignments and assume the roles of facilitator and teacher, asking questions, offering feedback, summarizing student comments, providing instructions, presenting information, and giving advice. In the case of hybrid instructions, this includes in-class and online learning activities.

Social Role. This involves creating a friendly and nurturing environment that supports a community of learners. The social role also involves communication between the instructor and students and among students within the course. Actions include personalizing communication, incorporating humor, and displaying empathy to create a sense of community and humanize instructor-student and student-student interactions.

Managerial Role. The managerial role relates to overseeing course structure and tasks. Managing a hybrid course requires balancing the organization of both the online and face to face environments. This includes all aspects of coordinating a course, including scheduling online and in-person interaction, setting due dates, and managing assignments, discussions, assessments, and student roles.

Technological Role. According to Berge (1995), "The facilitator must make participants comfortable with the system and the software" required by the course (p. 3). Technical knowledge includes instructors easily utilizing a course management system to organize course content and assisting students with user or system technology issues.

In the hybrid course model these roles change significantly from a traditional course. Therefore, faculty need to learn how to teach in new ways, such as facilitating online interaction and integrating the online and face to face environments. The potential for improving teaching and learning through hybrid courses has created the need for faculty development programs.

Preparing Faculty for Hybrid Teaching

To help faculty make the transition to hybrid teaching, institutions are creating faculty development programs to guide faculty as they redesign their courses and get ready to teach courses that are partially online and partially face to face. This is necessary because successful hybrid teaching requires a significant course transformation. Faculty must rethink and redesign their course, create new learning activities, and integrate online and face to face course components. Most faculty also have to learn new teaching skills in order to successfully manage online interaction, incorporate new methods of assessment, and effectively use the interactive and organizational tools found in course management systems.

Some institutions such as the University of Central Florida (UCF) and the University of Wisconsin-Milwaukee (UWM) offer extensive faculty development programs that are taught in the hybrid format and cover a number of instructional design and pedagogical topics. (Dziuban, Hartman, Juge, Moskal, & Sorg, 2006; Learning Technology Center, University of Wisconsin-Milwaukee, 2006). Preparing faculty to teach hybrid courses is a complex process. Research is needed to understand the opportunities and challenges hybrid instructors face and to determine which elements of hybrid course faculty development programs are most useful, which need to be emphasized more, and which new topics should be incorporated.

Research Questions

The purpose of this qualitative research study was to understand the experiences of instructors as they learned about, designed, and taught hybrid courses, and to use this information to better prepare instructors for hybrid teaching. The study's overarching question asked, *What are faculty experiences while discovering, designing and delivering a hybrid course?* To probe the instructors' processes while they discovered this instructional model, a sub-question asked, W*hy did instructors choose to adopt the hybrid model?* Rogers' Innovation-Decision process provided the framework to understand these questions about how faculty first became aware of the hybrid course model, what factors persuaded them to consider this method for their courses, and what finally encouraged them to decide to try this new mode of instruction.

To understand the instructors' processes as they implemented the design and delivery of their courses, another sub-question asked, *How did instructors' roles change as they implemented the hybrid model?* Berge's (1995) instructor role framework was used to investigate the pedagogical, social, managerial, and technical roles that instructors must assume as they teach hybrid courses. Faculty observations and advice, along with the extensive experiences of UWM's Learning Technology Center, were used to answer the final sub-question, *What are the implications for hybrid faculty development programs?*

Methodology

In order to understand why faculty choose to adopt the hybrid instructional model and to gain an in-depth understanding of faculty hybrid teaching experience, this study employed a basic qualitative interpretive approach (Merriam, 2002). The qualitative method was used to provide a rich descriptive of understanding, meaning, and process (Denzin & Lincoln, 2003). According to Merriam (2002), researchers conducting a basic interpretive study seek to "understand how people make sense of their lives and their experiences" (p. 38). The basic interpretive method was used to allow the participants to explain in their own words their experiences with the hybrid instructional model.

Sample

The 10 interview participants were recommended by faculty developers at three participating institutions selected by the director of UWM's Learning Technology Center. Criteria for participant selection required that they (a) taught in higher education, (b) taught a hybrid course in the last year, and (c) participated in a hybrid course faculty development program based upon the model program created by UWM's Learning Technology Center. Study participants consisted of three males and seven females who ranged in age from 35 to 66. Three were full professors, four were associate professors, two were assistant professors, and one was teaching academic staff. Although participants had experience teaching from one to five hybrid courses, the majority (60%) had taught only one or two hybrid courses. Sixty percent had over 10 years' teaching experience in higher education while 40% had four to nine years of experience.

The three higher education institutions included a two-year associate degree granting college, one comprehensive university offering bachelor's and master's degrees, and one Ph.D. granting institution. In order to obtain a more diverse perspective on the hybrid course model, faculty from the University of Wisconsin-Milwaukee (UWM) were not included in this study. The authors were already very familiar with faculty hybrid teaching experiences at UWM and wanted to learn more about the hybrid teaching experiences of instructors at other institutions. The participants taught in a variety of disciplines, including English, music, education, interior architecture, kinesiology, and family and consumer sciences. Nine of the courses were undergraduate courses and one was a graduate course. The courses taught by these instructors had a diverse ratio of online to face to face learning activities, with about 33% to 80% of the courses online. However, for the majority of the participants, 40% to 60% of their course learning activities were online.

Data Collection

The primary method of data collection was in-depth, semi-structured telephone interviews that lasted anywhere from one and a half to two hours. An interview guide was used to ask questions that focused on the innovation-decision process of adopting the hybrid course format, on participants' faculty development experiences, and on participants' perceptions of how their pedagogical, social, managerial, and technical roles changed when they taught a hybrid course. The interviews were audiotaped and transcribed. Prior to the interviews, a Web-based 34-item survey was administered to gather demographic data, information on the participants' hybrid teaching experience, and information on their preparation for hybrid teaching.

Data Analysis

Data were analyzed throughout the study using an inductive analytic process incorporating many of the procedures of the constant comparative method to conduct theoretical sampling (Patton, 2001). This method was used to extract themes from the Rogers and Berge frameworks without imposing preexisting expectations on the data (Patton, 2001). The data analysis process consisted of three steps. First, a computerized data analysis system (Nvivo) was used to code the data based on Rogers' (1995) innovation-decision process and Berge's (1995) pedagogical, social, managerial, and technological roles. Second, researchers analyzed each individual interview for key themes based on these frameworks. Third, the researchers compared data together to further distill the themes. These themes were also examined using matrices developed from the survey data, making it possible to look at similarities and differences related to demographic and other survey variables.

Quality control measures included member checks and peer reviews (Lincoln & Guba, 1985). During the interview process, member checks (Guba & Lincoln, 1989) were used to assure the researchers' understanding of the participants' discussion, and transcripts of the interviews were sent to the participants to ensure understanding. Peer reviews took place as the three researchers double-checked coding and verified the themes throughout the study.

Findings Summary

Willingness and ability to change is critical for faculty who choose to decide to teach hybrid courses. In general, findings indicated that the hybrid model requires that faculty modify familiar roles and learn new ones, such as facilitator, instructional designer, community builder, time-manager, and even technology "troubleshooter." Examining these roles carefully, and learning what aspects of the different roles are particularly problematic for faculty, will help faculty developers design more effective and successful programs to prepare instructors to teach hybrid courses. Similarly, because faculty enjoy learning from their colleagues, these findings—derived from faculty experiences—will be especially useful and welcome to faculty who are contemplating teaching a hybrid course.

Faculty Experiences: Adoption of Hybrid Courses

An individual's decision about an innovation occurs over time and is influenced by many factors. Rogers' (1995) innovation-decision process provides a useful framework to understand faculty experiences adopting and implementing the hybrid instructional model.

Innovation-Decision Process: Knowledge Stage

The innovation process begins when an individual "is exposed to an innovation's existence and gains some understanding of how it functions" (Rogers, 1995, p. 162). According to Rogers (1995), a change agent is often involved in creating awareness and motivation to adopt an innovation. Prior to this study, only one of the faculty was specifically aware of the hybrid model because she had "positive" experiences with a hybrid course when she was a graduate student. Half of the instructors had limited knowledge of the hybrid format from colleagues and conferences. Instructors who heard about hybrid previously had reservations about trying it. Some noted that they "thought it was interesting," but didn't think that the hybrid format would work for their courses. "I had no interest in doing it myself because I teach lab science courses and couldn't really see how to do labs in that format." Another noted, "I wasn't sure that my activities really fit into the description that was listed [about hybrid]."

The change agent for the research participants was an institutional initiative that provided information on the hybrid courses model and offered to provide faculty with support as they designed and taught their first hybrid course. The invitation to participate in a hybrid course faculty development program included a description of hybrid courses and their potential benefits. It was this invitation that generated an awareness and basic understanding of the hybrid model.

Innovation-Decision Process: Persuasion Stage

During the Persuasion Stage of the innovation-decision process, the individual "forms a favorable or unfavorable attitude toward the innovation" (Rogers, 1995, p. 168). The instructors in this study received grant funds or stipends as incentives to be part of a faculty development program for teaching hybrid courses. The grant provided the incentive and the "structure and schedule" some of the instructors needed to make the decision to learn more about the hybrid model. However, some instructors said that the stipend was only part of the motivation to learn more about hybrid courses. The more critical factors that persuaded the research participants to seriously consider teaching hybrid courses were the teaching and learning benefits described in the communication accompanying the invitation to participate in training. These benefits included increased student learning and the potential to "get students to work independently" and become "more responsible for their own learning." Others wanted to find "ways of engaging students" by reducing in-class lectures, adding online interactive activities, and taking advantage of the strengths of both online and face to face environments. One noted, "When I read about it, I thought it was something that was worth it for me because I thought it fit into a lot of the things that I believe in as far as student learning."

In addition to the stipend and the potential for improved teaching and learning, the instructors cited the "flexibility" and "convenience" for their students and themselves as important factors in electing to learn more about hybrid courses. Some instructors were interested in including online activities, which they felt were important since "computers are important to reach this generation." A detailed presentation and discussion about the benefits of the hybrid-learning model was part of the first session in the faculty development program. Research participants made it clear that the presentations at the faculty development workshop and the exchanges in the workshops with experienced hybrid instructors, who also talked about the advantages of the hybrid course model, convinced them that the student learning benefits were real. The perceived and expected teaching and learning benefits were major factors persuading them to seriously consider the hybrid course model.

Innovation-Decision Process: Decision Stage

Next in the innovation-decision process, Rogers (1995) describes the Decision Stage, which takes place when a person "engages in activities that lead to a choice to adopt or reject an innovation" (p. 171). Instructors in this study initially had concerns about using the hybrid model because of the substantial time commitment required and the fear of losing "connection" with students in a non-traditional course format. Rogers (1995) explains, "One way to cope with the inherent uncertainty about an innovation's consequences is to try out the new idea on a partial basis" (p. 171). All the research participants attended a hybrid faculty development program that provided in-depth information on the hybrid course model and, more importantly, guided them through the course redesign process.

The faculty development programs were based on the UWM model and included presentations, demonstrations, group discussions, face to face small group work, course redesign assignments, online small group work, and facilitator and peer feedback on assignments. The instructional design and pedagogical topics covered include sessions focused on rethinking course goals and objectives, creating online and face to face activities to achieve those goals, integrating face to face and online components of the course, developing and managing effective online discussions, facilitating online small group work, using template rubrics, managing student expectations, effectively using technology, considering multiple approaches to assessment, and managing a hybrid course. During this program, instructors not only learn more about the hybrid course model, but also actually start to design and develop their first hybrid course. Faculty leave the program with materials they can use in designing and teaching their first hybrid course, including a course redesign plan, draft syllabus, learning activities, discussion assignments, and the start of an assessment plan.

According to Kaleta and Garnham (2001), "It is important for faculty who are going to teach Hybrid courses to experience Hybrid courses as students do" (p. 2). Consequently, the UWM program is taught in the hybrid format and involves multiple face to face classes interspersed and integrated with online learning activities. As a result, faculty experience a hybrid course as students and are exposed to good examples of hybrid course design and teaching practices. As part of the faculty program, instructors have the opportunity to work and interact with experienced hybrid instructors. Many of the research participants emphasized that what helped them the most was learning from other faculty who have gone through the process of redesigning courses into hybrids, and hearing about what worked, what didn't work, and why. "The examples provided and the interaction of the group in the training sessions showed many different ways to approach the hybrid course."

The research participants explained how the faculty development experience was critical to creating their hybrid course. One instructor said, "The workshop prepared me intellectually to expect a variety of things." Another exclaimed, "I could never have done it without the training!" However, there was a lot for participants to learn. One instructor described the training in this way: "It was vital; however, there was so much to learn when it was all new, it was quite overwhelming at first." Other participants said that they would have preferred an extended program that provided them with more guidance and information. One instructor commented: "I think it would have been good to have been forced to actually develop the complete course during the training."

The three instructors who had already taught online felt the hybrid training was not as critical to their success, yet it was important for instructors who were converting a traditional course into a hybrid for the first time. The instructors with online experience would have preferred a more "accelerated" training program. However, for the majority of the instructors, the training program was essential to guide them to the implementation stage of designing and teaching an effective hybrid course. One instructor summarized:

> I think being selected for the training and doing the training
> showed me that there were all sorts of interesting things that
> could happen [in a hybrid course] and that would be a more
> effective way of presenting a class. I think the training itself
> persuaded me to actually start doing hybrid courses.

The findings also indicated that a comprehensive faculty development program not only provides faculty with the skills to create and teach a hybrid course, but also provides the structure, dedicated time, and motivation to try this new learning model. The research participants felt that the faculty development experience benefited them in many ways. They left the program with a better understanding of hybrid learning, a partially redesigned course, and the enthusiasm to move ahead. All of these factors played a role in the decision to move to the Implementation Stage of the Innovation-Decision Process.

Innovation-Decision Process: Implementation Stage

Implementation occurs when an individual puts an innovation into practice (Rogers, 1995). "A certain degree of uncertainty still exists for the individual at the Implementation Stage, even though the decision to adopt has been made previously" (Rogers, 1995, p. 173). When the participants launched their hybrid courses, more challenges surfaced. One commented, "When I actually taught the course I encountered situations that the training didn't cover." Despite extensive training, one person noted that he still learned a lot about the hybrid format "through trial and error." This is typical in the Implementation Stage as the individual continues to "re-invent" the innovation (Rogers, 1995, 174). The importance of experience is reflected in the comments of several instructors who said that the best way to learn about the hybrid instructional model is to "seek out people who have done it and done it well." Following are faculty experiences during the Implementation Stage when they designed and taught their hybrid course and assumed the multiple roles required of a hybrid instructor.

121

Hybrid Instructors Assume Multiple Roles

During the implementation of their hybrid courses, instructors not only assumed new roles, but multiple roles as well (see Table 1). For example, they may have lectured or led group discussions in the classroom one day, and the next day they may have facilitated online discussions, activities, and assessments or even solved technology issues (Swenson & Evans, 2003). Thus, the hybrid instructors' roles changed week to week as they traverse the in-person and online environments. Additionally, hybrid courses require more decisions about which instructional strategies work best for course goals, both in the face to face and online teaching environments. When the 10 hybrid instructors in this study were asked how their role as a teacher in a hybrid course compared to or differed from their role in the traditional classroom, their answers reflected the diverse pedagogical, social, managerial, and technical roles described in Berge's (1995) framework. To understand what occurred during implementation, the next section will discuss the participants' experiences using Berge's classifications of 'instructor roles' and offer advice for faculty preparation.

Table 1. **Summary of Instructor Roles: Hybrid instructors engage in all four instructor roles in both the online and face to face environments.**

Instructor Roles	Description	Components
1. Pedagogical	Design and teach the course	Design the course structure, create learning activities, integrate face to face and online activities, facilitate discussion, provide content and resources, offer guidance and constructive criticism, ask questions, conduct assessments
2. Social	Develop a collaborative community of learners	Personalize communication, provide timely feedback, build a climate of trust, provide confidentiality guidelines, display empathy, humanize instructor-student and student-student interactions, use humor
3. Managerial	Oversee course structure and coordinate tasks	Schedule activities and class meetings, set due dates, coordinate assignments, assign group and student roles, present clear expectations and instructions, manage grading, and clarify course policies
4. Technological	Manage and support course technology	Utilize a course management system to organize course content and learning activities, assist students with technology issues, orient students to course technology

Note. Based on Berge (1995) and adapted from "Summary of the Pedagogical, Social, Managerial, and Technological Roles of the Online Instructor" (Bonk & Dennen, 2003, p. 339).

Pedagogical Role

In order to create interesting and interactive hybrid courses, Swenson and Evans (2003) cautioned that hybrid instructors "must be more than information suppliers," since students can easily access information. Many faculty need to change significantly the way they teach, as students "want instructors who are guides" who can navigate the various technologies available to "foster broader student engagement through more complex classroom interactions than are typical in a traditional instructional setting" (p. 29). In addition, instructors need to significantly redesign courses for hybrid learning, taking advantage of the strengths of the online and face to face teaching environments to facilitate student learning and to achieve course goals and objectives. Thus, there are two related but distinct aspects to the pedagogical role: instructional design and teaching style. As the research participants described next, both are very important for instructors as they transition to the hybrid-teaching model.

Teaching Transformed

All the instructors interviewed agreed that their role as teacher changed significantly when they began teaching hybrid courses. One instructor said this format "may challenge you in a whole new way of teaching." All the participants voiced how teaching a hybrid course transforms the teacher-student relationship to be "more centered on the student" (Swenson & Evans, p. 68). All described their role as a "facilitator" and several as a "cheerleader." Many also talked about how the hybrid format helped them to be a "guide on the side" of student learning instead of being a "sage on the stage." Learner-centered instruction requires that faculty give students some control over their learning (Weimer, 2002). In a hybrid course, both students and teachers faced challenges in renegotiating teacher-learner relationships.

Teacher-Learner Relationships

Many instructors cautioned that the learner-centered nature of the hybrid environment is not an easy transition because both faculty and students need to make significant adjustments. The research participants explained that they had to be willing to give more control to students. One participant noted that the facilitative role "really drives the dialogue between students—and that is what I want." The facilitative role was easier for the instructors who had previously taught online and more difficult for those transitioning from traditional lecture courses. For example, the instructor who taught his first hybrid freshmen seminar course said he desperately wanted to show the same "enthusiasm" in the online environment that he demonstrated in his traditional courses. "It is difficult to get that same excitement when you write it." Another first-time hybrid instructor said she needed to work on not having her online content and discussions be so "static" and learn "how to get people to interact." Research participants found that even though they had many years of teaching experience, they had to learn new ways of teaching when using the hybrid course model.

The instructors also reported that many of the undergraduate students had difficulty taking responsibility for their own learning. The participants said some students enrolled in a hybrid course because it was a three-credit class that only met face to face once a week. As one stated, "They think it is going to be easy." Another added, "One challenge is for students to accept responsibility that they are not just taking half a class." The graduate instructor and those who had previous online and hybrid teaching experience did not have these issues. However, these instructors also said that they set clear expectations for both learning environments.

Advice for Faculty Preparation

In order to successfully transition to the role of facilitator in hybrid courses, instructors must know how to effectively facilitate and manage both online and face to face discussion and interaction. Based on years of experience in the classroom, most instructors felt comfortable managing interaction in the face to face environment. All but three of the participants, however, had no experience managing and facilitating online interaction. The ability to facilitate effective online discussions is cited in the literature as the most important skill for online instructors (Anderson, Rourke, Garrison, & Archer, 2001). The research participants concurred and emphasized this as an important ability in the hybrid environment.

Even though this was a topic covered and practiced in the faculty development programs, the newer hybrid instructors struggled with maintaining or even starting productive online discussions. The more experienced hybrid instructors or those who had taught online previously had already mastered the techniques and skills needed to make discussions meaningful and to ensure participation of the entire class. For example, several instructors emphasized the importance of integrating discussion assignments into the course assessment plan and assigning points for participation so students understand the importance of participating in the online discussions, as well as in the face to face sessions. "You have to require posting and responding, otherwise it isn't going to happen." Another addressed the importance of using discussion rubrics and added that you need to "be very, very specific and very detailed about what it is that you expect."

One research participant explained that instructors need to "evolve to understand that facilitating is also teaching." This requires that faculty development programs provide new teaching strategies that are more learner-centered, facilitative, and promote meaningful, interactive discussions and activities that connect learners online and face to face. One instructor who had taught five hybrid courses offered the following cautionary advice for successfully teaching a hybrid course:

> One thing would be to frequently remind yourself of what your goal was for doing the hybrid....You are used to the way you taught in the face to face. It is very easy to slip back into the way you used to do it [teach] because it is a habit. The hybrid design really kind of demands that you are very conscious about doing things differently.

Faculty who are preparing to teach hybrid courses must be made aware of the importance of making the transition from acting as a presenter of content to becoming a facilitator of student learning. Because hybrid courses are more student-centered and incorporate more student assignments and learning activities, instructors must be prepared to devote more effort toward guiding, supporting, and encouraging students in their work.

Instructional Re-design is Critical

When asked which activities consumed the most time when making the transition from a traditional face to face course to a hybrid course, the most frequent responses focused on instructional design issues including reflecting on goals and objectives, and creating online learning activities, assessments, and discussion forum assignments. It was difficult for the research participants to estimate, but they guessed it took from 25% to 300% longer to prepare a hybrid course compared to the same course taught in a traditional classroom. Many said it was impossible to guess because "they were still refining." In order to convert a traditional course to the hybrid format, instructors had to become instructional designers, and they found it time-consuming to totally redesign their courses. Findings indicate that instructors struggled most with re-examining course goals and objectives, selecting the best activities for the online and face to face environments, and succumbing to the tendency to have too much content and activities designed into the course. UWM's Learning Technology Center coined the term "the course and a half syndrome" to describe the latter difficulty.

Re-examining Course Goals and Objectives

When designing their hybrid courses, the research participants emphasized the importance of critically re-examining course goals and learning objectives, even if they had taught the same course previously in the traditional format. One said she was a "believer" in focusing on course goals: "What do you want them to learn and how do you want them to learn it?" The hybrid format demanded even more reflection because two learning "spaces" needed to be considered. One research participant said you can't just "divide it [the course] in half" and another elaborated on this part of the course redesign process:

125

> I went through and really thought about what are the learning goals of the course, what are the things that we do to lead to those goals, and then what are the best ways would each of those mini-goals best be facilitated, online or face to face.

Another instructor summarized, "Goals and objectives must come first in developing any course...I feel that connecting the online and face to face activities needed attention because they need coordination in order to be integrated into a unified whole." When discussing course design, instructors concurred that it was "time consuming" but essential "because it is a conscious decision-making process" of deciding which lesson plans work best online or face to face. Findings indicate that faculty found that the process of reexamining their learning goals and objectives was critical to developing a successful hybrid course.

Online or Face to face

Redesigning a traditional course into a hybrid course compelled faculty to think through how best to use two learning spaces instead of just one. "I really just had to reconfigure the class to include, or to sort through, what I was going to do online and what I was going to do face to face." After reflecting on their goals, the research participants used a variety of methods to decide which environment to use for which learning activities.

Instructors tended to use the online environment for work that students could do "on their own," such as assessments, tutorials, readings, and quizzes. Some of the instructors who were new to hybrid teaching felt that it would be a "waste of face to face class time" to do these things in the classroom. Other instructors saved activities for the in-person class that required "interaction" and to address "issues or misconceptions that popped up in the online discussion." For example, one instructor used the face to face environment to introduce a complex essay critique assignment. Then she followed up online by reading the students' essays, answering critical reading questions, and drafting a summary. Face to face was also used to present visual information like film clips, provide demonstrations, conduct hands-on activities like labs, conduct group activities and student presentations, give lectures, answer questions, and give exams. Findings indicate that the majority of instructors used the face to face environment to present information needing context and interpretations to facilitate better student understanding. In contrast, the online environment was used for information that was independent in nature or was clearly conveyed and easily facilitated in the online environment.

However, the more experienced hybrid instructors, and those who taught online previously, included more critical reflection and interactive discussions online, and then they continued those discussions in class. These experienced instructors said that online discussions provide more time for "deeper thinking than face to face where shy people don't talk or it is just the initial knee-jerk responses." Others indicated that the online component of hybrid courses provides opportunities for accommodating different "learning styles." Findings suggested that as faculty become more experienced, they are better able to integrate and extend student learning in both environments.

The Course and a Half Syndrome

UWM defines the "course and a half syndrome" as the tendency for faculty to be unable to give up any material from their face to face course and simply add additional online content and activities to an existing course when they transition to the hybrid model (Aycock, Garnham, & Kaleta, 2002; Skibba, 2005). A number of the research participants succumbed to the "course and a half syndrome" and said that they felt they were "teaching two classes." Although the dangers of this "syndrome" were stressed often throughout the faculty development training program, many instructors still got "carried away with activities." Another instructor commented similarly and admitted, "Something that I am probably guilty of ... is packing in too much." A common finding was that the study participants tended to overload their courses with activities and needed to rethink the amount of work they assigned students and, consequently, themselves.

Advice for Faculty Preparation

As the participants pointed out, the process of "reflecting on goals and objectives" in the faculty development program was critical to determining which activities worked best for each of the face to face and online environments. Instructors felt that the structure provided by the faculty development program helped them to really "think through everything." A faculty development program should help instructors examine course goals and how they can be met in the dual environments of the hybrid format.

According to Skill and Young (2002), "The integrated hybrid course is carefully redesigned so as to best leverage powerful in-class, face to face teaching and learner opportunities with the content richness and interactivity of electronic learning experiences" (p. 25). Findings indicated that some of the hybrid instructors were not utilizing both environments to their full potential. While the online environment can be used for collaboration and rich interactive learning and higher-level learning, many of the first-time hybrid instructors used the online environment for lower-level activities. All the participants wanted to learn how to create more "meaningful learning experiences." Faculty development programs should help instructors realize the potential of both environments to create an integrated and rich learning experience.

Finally, when instructors were asked what advice they would share, many said "not to do too much" and "start small and you can build it one step at a time." Another said that it helped when he asked his former students for advice on what would work online from the traditional course. Research participants also suggested getting feedback and ideas from other instructors who have designed hybrid courses. Despite the fact that the faculty development program warned faculty of the pitfalls of the course and half syndrome, it is clear from participants' experiences that more emphasis needs to be placed on how to streamline hybrid courses and how to integrate the online component without overloading the course. Instructors need to determine what content is really necessary. One said she is always asking, "Do I really have to do these things?" Activities that are not necessary to reach the learning goals can be removed. In addition, many of the instructors wanted to learn how to create more interactive online activities that would provide "choices" of learning opportunities for students. Findings also indicated the importance of helping faculty develop strong links between the activities that are conducted online and face to face must be emphasized, so instructors do not end up teaching two parallel but unconnected courses.

Finally, a faculty development program should stress the importance of setting aside a significant amount of time prior to the start of the course for instructional design. One instructor stated, "The development part of it is definitely more effort." Another added, "One thing about a hybrid class, all the work comes on the front end. You have a lot of work and a lot of involvement in terms of the development and putting the course together." Based on the findings, faculty development programs should help instructors get an early start on course redesign and use their time wisely to reflect on course goals, determine which activities are best online or in-person, limit course content and activities, and integrate online and face to face activities.

Social Role

Many of the instructors talked about the importance of creating a "community of learners," which is a well-known challenge in online education (Brufee, 1999; Harasim, Hiltz, Teles, & Turoff, 1998). To create this community, the research participants shared their experiences of establishing "social presence," also known as a feeling of connection and community among individuals (Short, Williams, & Christie, 1976). One instructor summed up what many discovered:

> A lot of people are afraid that replacing seat time with online is going to diminish the quality of the relationship—whether it is teacher-student or student-student. And actually I have to say from my experience it is contrary to that... I get more quality interactions and feedback from the students ... which then helps increase my connection to them.

Study findings indicate that when a positive climate is created, hybrid environments have the potential to increase and extend connectivity and to build relationships even more so than in traditional or online courses.

Connectivity Challenges

The biggest concern instructors feared when converting their traditional courses to the hybrid environment was the potential of losing the connection they had with students. One instructor who taught a freshman seminar explained that he had "withdrawals" from not being able to meet personally with each of his students as often as he did when he taught the same course face to face. Another undergraduate lecturer felt a sense of "panic at first" because she also was concerned about the lack of social interaction. Both instructors admitted that they needed more experience creating interactive discussions, particularly with freshmen who needed more attention. These instructors also noted that students seemed to "disengage" from discussions if they were given too much work. Others noted that "sometimes students disappear" online and that it can be tricky to get some students to participate. However, experienced hybrid instructors and faculty with online teaching experience were more at ease "encouraging people to ask questions of each other online" and getting students to share ideas. These instructors also found that their students were excited about logging in to see what people said. So while many felt it was important to "have some physical contact with an instructor," they also were able to build connections through online discussions in between in-person meetings. When these connections were created, most felt that the communication increased in a hybrid course compared to traditional courses.

Community Building

Although some of the instructors were concerned about losing the personal touch with students, others related how they were able to get to know their students even better in a hybrid course. The majority of the instructors said students were more conversational "and more open" online than they were in the classroom. Plus, students who normally did not speak up in class participated online. For example, when talking about personal subjects like dating, religion, and sexuality, the psychology instructor was surprised how "comfortable" students were sharing personal information. Many of the instructors also explained how these frank conversations started online and carried over into the classrooms where strong "friendships formed." In addition, students "were more willing to participate in class" because they were "warmed up by the fact that they have already been contributing to the discussions online." The three instructors who incorporated group work in their hybrid courses said that a sense of community also carried over when group members worked together, either face to face or online, and enhanced the interactions and productivity of the groups.

Advice for Faculty Preparation

Many of the inexperienced hybrid instructors were concerned about a "loss" of personal connection with students when they moved to the hybrid format because of less time spent face to face. Therefore, faculty developers should guide faculty on how to increase communication and personal connections using the combination of online and face to face environments. Some of the instructors were able to create a positive learning community by building a comfort level for students to share information online. One instructor commented, "It is all about building a climate of trust." Several suggested providing guidelines for "maintaining confidentiality" and "respecting" classmates' opinions. The most common advice that the faculty shared was to create a positive hybrid learning community by being "flexible," "available," and "accommodating."

Another important element in building trust in an online and hybrid environment involves fostering "immediacy" of responses (Short et al., 1976). One instructor stressed that students want quick responses to their questions and sometimes they "panic" until they get answers. To increase connectivity with the students, some of the instructors noted that they plan to increase the number of in-person class meetings between the online sessions or provide places online for students to share personal information. Other instructors indicated that using a "conversational" tone and incorporating active listening and questioning techniques were also important in encouraging students to participate more, both online and face to face.

The advice from the research participants and supporting literature revealed that online communication can provide more socially intimate communication than sometimes can be achieved in "parallel face to face situations" (Walther, 1996). This requires that faculty know how to create "respectful and meaningful" online discussions that provide a "safe" place to share ideas. While these skills take experience, faculty developers can offer guidance on how to use the hybrid format to extend personal relationship from both environments to create an integrated and positive community of learners.

Managerial Role

Findings indicate that managing hybrid courses forced instructors and students to become "more organized" and "prepared" than they had to be in a traditional course. The hybrid environment also added additional scheduling challenges as courses meet both online and face to face. Although both faculty and students enjoyed the "flexibility" and the increased "personal contact," navigating these dual-learning spaces did cause some challenges and confusion. As one instructor said, it can be hard "to keep straight" when the class is meeting in person or online. To create one seamless course, the hybrid instructor's role needs to expand to include unique scheduling and organizational tasks (Sands, 2002). The following are the major faculty and student benefits and challenges of the managerial role as shared by the research participants; they involve course scheduling, course organization, and student time management.

Course Scheduling

A major decision for faculty was the frequency and pattern of scheduling for face to face and virtual activities. Some faculty still met with their students weekly, while others only met face to face a few times in a semester. When asked how they decided when to meet as a class, reasons varied, including "it depended on the content," the need to schedule around other obligations and courses, and a desire to give students an opportunity to work on a project online between classes. The frequency and pattern of course meetings varied greatly for the study participants. For some instructors, the class meeting schedule "was different every week" while others convened on a regular schedule every week equaling half of the original course time. While both faculty and students appreciated not having to meet in person as often, many instructors commented that it was often difficult to manage the online workload. Comments included "there is so much to read" and "it was difficult for me everyday to get online because of my busy schedule." Faculty explained that it is important to set aside time to focus on the online components. One instructor explained, "It is a matter of self-discipline, to sit down and just read it or do it or set a time block aside where I am going to read posts and be committed to it." Despite these initial challenges, as instructors gained more experience, these scheduling issues diminished over the semester.

Course Organization

While the time commitment was a concern, many of the instructors raved about how the course management system increased their efficiency because of its ability to organize the course and automate some of the activities such as quizzes, grading, and surveys. Three of the instructors had no prior experience using a course management system, while four had only used this system previously for posting course materials. Once they started to use the course management system extensively, they were very impressed with the organization and managerial benefits it provided. One instructor summarized, "The main benefit is that everything is all laid out...well organized...it is all right there.... there shouldn't be any mystery" because all the discussion threads, course documents, announcements, and grades are easy to find, refer to, and print if necessary. Instructors liked that they "didn't have a lot of papers to shuffle." Although the course management system led to a more efficient course due to automated processes and its organizational benefits, instructors said that managing a hybrid course was still "more time consuming" than a traditional course.

Student Time Management

Student benefits and challenges mirrored those of the faculty. Several instructors noted that hybrid offers "flexibility for over-burdened students" and for those with family and job responsibilities. However, like faculty, students had more difficulty committing time to online work than they did for "those 50 minutes in class." Some students viewed only the face to face portions as the real class, and "ignore the responsibility of doing all the other work." One instructor noted that students "have twice as many opportunities to miss an assignment" because they are responsible for both in-class and online activities. "They [students] have a lot of things to keep track of." Others put a positive spin on this challenge and felt that the hybrid format should go beyond teaching students content to teaching "important life skills" of time management, self-discipline, and organization. One instructor said, "A challenge and benefit for students is that they needed to learn to better manage their time." Instructors said it is important to clarify that it is the student's responsibility to "check the course page" for weekly announcements and assignments.

In addition to helping students better manage their time, instructors noted how working online also made the face to face time "more serious and more valuable." One instructor noted how prepared students were for the face to face class after participating online: "When they came into class on Tuesday nights, they were really focused.... I think it [the hybrid format] made that time more productive." Scheduling flexibility and time management were the benefits as well as the challenges for students.

Advice for Faculty Preparation

Faculty appreciated how the hybrid format forced them to get organized in advance of the first day of class. One instructor cautioned, "Don't wait until the last minute." The faculty in this study realized the importance of planning, scheduling, and being flexible in managing their hybrid courses. Also, they discovered the importance of the course management system in organizing online components as well as increasing the efficiency of certain tasks due to the automated features of the technology. A faculty development program needs to demonstrate how course management software can help organize and manage the many hybrid activities. This point was unexpectedly emphasized by several of the instructors trying the hybrid format for the first time.

Further, faculty need assistance in determining how to carefully manage their online tasks and the time involved. Many commented, "My biggest thing is I learned personally I probably did too much." Others noted it was too much to "read all the messages." Faculty should consider the time they will set aside each week to read online comments and assignments. Some instructors suggested using what was previously scheduled face to face time that was no longer needed, because of the hybrid format, to manage online activities. "I just had to make sure to schedule the time and keep that as my class period." Other instructors scheduled time each week when they would complete their online responsibilities. Without the requirement of meeting weekly face to face, some instructors found themselves falling behind in their online tasks due to busy schedules or lack of scheduling "online time." That is why all noted how important it is "to manage your time" and to not "burn out."

Many of the faculty who taught hybrid for the first time tended to be the "gung-ho new hybrid teacher," as one said, and tried to do more than was humanly possible. The previously discussed "course and a half syndrome" manifested by several of the instructors resulted in too many student assignments and, consequently, significant additional work for instructors. This had the result of significantly compounding the time management challenges that these new hybrid instructors encountered.

A faculty development program should provide guidance with regard to managing both the online and in-class workloads. Faculty also need to know the importance of providing students with "clear expectations," tips, and reminders for managing both the in-person and online requirements. For instance, one instructor stated, "I think for students [scheduling] is also an issue to make sure that they are scheduling themselves time to be in the online course." The research participants expressed the importance of being "flexible in scheduling" assignment due dates, but also expressed the need to follow the schedule outlined in the syllabus in order to stay on track. Managing a hybrid course has many challenges as well as rewards that need to be clearly explained in faculty development training.

Technological Role

In addition to the anticipated teaching and learning benefits, some of the instructors also adopted the hybrid format because they felt it was a good way to "get on the technology bandwagon," "reach this generation" of students, and "instill excitement into education by using more 'interactive' activities." While some instructors had high expectations for incorporating technology, many did not anticipate just how significant the impact of technology would be on them. Their role expanded to include being a technical expert and "troubleshooter." Study participants who had not previously taught using technology became "stressed" with learning how to use the technology themselves and then dealing with student technology issues and "fears." In some cases the instructors' and students' lack of familiarity with technology, accompanied by the unreliability of technology affected the instructors' ability to teach.

Familiarity with Technology

A number of the faculty members commented on their discomfort with technology and expressed the need to learn more. Several admitted to their newness and being "apprehensive" with courseware systems and technology in general, explaining "I had to learn a whole new language" and "I never considered myself particularly computer literate." One instructor was concerned about how students would perceive and react to his lack of expertise in using technology. He said it was important to continue to become more familiar with technology beyond the initial training because "students smell fear." In addition to learning new technology themselves, many study participants pointed out that instructors "cannot assume" that students are familiar or proficient with using computers. Even though the course catalog stated that "technology is required," some students who sign up "have no clue about technology" including how to open an attachment or use a courseware system. One instructor stated, "I thought that the kids coming out of today's schools are very computer savvy and I found out they are not." Students' discomfort and frustration with technology not only negatively affected their course learning experience but it also adversely affected some faculty because of the additional challenges and responsibilities it placed on the instructors.

Reliability of Technology

The majority of the instructors felt they "were getting good training" and technology support on their campuses, but did not always feel that students were receiving the same kind of support. Instructors were chagrined that many students preferred to ask or "complain" to the instructor instead of seeking campus assistance. When discussing their technology role, many instructors described technical failures as "upsetting" for both instructors and students, such as when the courseware would go down for long or short periods of time. Instructors also noted high occurrences of students playing the "blame game" of giving numerous technical excuses for not getting online work completed and "trying to pass off their own lack of timeliness and blaming it on the system." This study's participants concurred with Hollingshead, McGrath, and O'Connor (1993) suggestion that newness of the medium led to poorer task performance for some computer users. In order for the hybrid course format to be effective, instructors emphasized the importance of personally gaining familiarity with the technology, in addition to providing opportunities for students to gain the same technology familiarity.

Advice for Faculty Preparation

Instructors in this study who were concerned with their own lack of ease with the courseware product as well as other software and hardware issues suggested that new hybrid course instructors "start small," and don't try to incorporate too much technology all at once. "If it is not done properly, the students aren't going to benefit from it." Berge (1995) points out that when the technology is transparent, then the focus can be on learning. Faculty development programs should help instructors to seek out a support system for using new technology. Participants suggested providing opportunities for collegial support with other instructors who participated in the hybrid course faculty development program. Similarly, some suggested that faculty "find their champion" or "find a partner" that can assist and encourage them while they continue to learn how to use the technology. Other participants recommended creating an e-mail listserv and regularly scheduled face to face meetings to help deal with technical issues and questions. Beyond collegial support, instructors recommended that faculty new to technology should find technical support on campus for themselves and for their students.

Instructors in this study also emphasized the need to understand that "technology can and will fail" so it is important to "always have plan B." One instructor recommended having a backup copy of files on a home computer so an instructor can always e-mail important information to students. If students have computer failures, one instructor asked: "What accommodations are you willing to make? Some things are not negotiable but other things may be, so what are those things of which you are willing to negotiate?" Other instructors expressed the need "to stay calm," "flexible," "positive," and "teach them [students] to be proactive." A faculty development program should guide instructors as they consider and develop plans for times when technology fails.

Also, instructors in this study were very concerned with their students' lack of proficiency with the technologies required for them to succeed in the course. For students to become more comfortable with the technology, instructors need to design activities that orient the students to the technology such as "scavenger hunts" during the first class meeting that will "lead the students through the technology," and provide them with documentation and help sheets on how to use the courseware system. Faculty development programs should help instructors identify and create activities and materials that familiarize students with the technology, thus ensuring that the hybrid course is a rewarding and less "stressful" learning experience.

Innovation-Decision Process: Confirmation Stage

Rogers (1995) states "a decision to adopt or reject is often not the terminal stage in the innovation-decision process" (p. 180). It is at the

Confirmation Stage that the adopter "seeks reinforcement of the innovation-decision already made or reverses a previous decision to adopt or reject the innovation if exposed to conflicting messages about the innovation" (Rogers, 1995, p. 181). Called "re-invention" by Rogers (1995), instructors were always assessing, questioning, and self-reflecting on how to better use the hybrid format and if it was right for their course. After teaching their first, second, and even fifth hybrid course, all of the research participants shared that they had plans to rework, modify, or add to their hybrid courses based on their experiences or students' comments. "I like to think of it as work in progress."

All of the instructors in this study planned to continue teaching hybrid courses. One of the participants pointed out that not all courses work well with the hybrid format and that she was changing one of her graduate courses back to the face to face format. A few others planned to include more in-person activities. The research participants, however, all agreed that incorporating technology into the classroom is the way of the future. As one instructor said, "The university demands it, students want it, and this is the way education is going." Instructors in this study did say that hybrid "is the best of both worlds." Finally, one instructor said, "Give it a try once. I think people owe it to their educational mission of being a teacher and instructor to try one hybrid course."

Conclusions and Recommendations

The wealth of information in this study provides valuable insights into the processes that faculty go through as they discover, design, and develop hybrid courses. This information is also a source of lessons learned that can be used to inform institutional hybrid course initiatives to foster faculty interest in the hybrid course model and prepare them to teach hybrid courses. This chapter concludes by sharing these insights and uses the lessons learned to develop recommendations for the adoption and teaching of hybrid courses.

Encouraging Adoption of Hybrid Courses

Most of the participants in this study first learned about and became interested in teaching hybrid courses as a result of an organized institutional effort designed to encourage hybrid teaching. Faculty decided to try the hybrid model because of the many teaching and learning benefits that were promoted by the institutions and their colleagues, including the ability to provide more "active learning" and "engage" students by using technology. While they were interested in these benefits, they didn't have the motivation or opportunity to try the hybrid format until they received institutional assistance in the form of funding and training. The faculty development program provided the skills and courage to overcome the instructors' initial fears about how their teaching style or course would translate to the new model. The training helped faculty "actually start" and finally adopt the hybrid instructional model. Based upon the results of this study and the experiences of the Learning Technology Center at the University of Wisconsin-Milwaukee, the authors recommend that institutions do the following in order to encourage faculty adoption of the hybrid course model.

1. Launch a hybrid course initiative that informs faculty about the teaching and learning benefits of hybrid courses and encourages adopting this model.
2. Create a faculty development program that provides detailed information on hybrid and prepares instructors to design and teach this type of course.
3. Offer a stipend to attract and compensate faculty for the challenging effort required to learn about and redesign hybrid courses.
4. Ensure that ongoing pedagogical and technical consultation is available to support ongoing faculty course hybrid redesign and teaching.

All of these initiatives and activities positively affected the decision by participants in this study to become hybrid teachers. These suggestions can be adopted by other institutions wishing to encourage hybrid course development and teaching.

Preparing Faculty for Hybrid Teaching

The study also investigated the changing roles that faulty encountered as they moved from a traditional format to a hybrid course format. In all cases, faculty teaching roles were transformed. Those faculty who embraced the traditional role of a teacher as lecturer had the most difficulties in the transition. Thus, instructors who adopt the hybrid format need to be prepared to leave their previous constructs of what a teacher is behind and to anticipate how the new model redefines them, their course, and their students. Instructors are no longer just "teaching"; they are facilitators of the learning process, functioning in multiple roles. Findings indicated that instructors' roles expanded in the hybrid format to include pedagogical, social, managerial, and technical challenges and opportunities.

Once faculty make the commitment to try hybrid teaching and begin the implementation process, they almost immediately encounter significant challenges as they start to redesign and teach their courses for the first time. Therefore, faculty preparation for hybrid teaching should address the challenges and opportunities presented in their new pedagogical, social, managerial, and technological roles. As faculty developers build a program to guide faculty through the course design process and prepare faculty for the teaching transitions they will encounter, the developers must realize that structure, format, and types of activities are as important as the topics covered. The authors recommend faculty developers incorporate the following features into their efforts to prepare faculty for hybrid teaching.

1. Start the faculty development program at least six months prior to the time instructors will be teaching their first hybrid courses because of the significant time required to redesign hybrid courses.
2. Use the hybrid format to teach the faculty development program so that faculty directly experience the advantages and challenges of the hybrid course model.
3. Include extensive opportunities for participants to interact with experienced hybrid instructors and see that hybrid courses work and the benefits are real.
4. Ensure that participants leave with the start of their hybrid course and with a plan for continuing the redesign process.
5. Provide ample opportunities to learn and practice the new teaching skills needed for hybrid instruction.
6. Have faculty work in small collaborative groups as they deal with course redesign issues to develop confidence and foster ongoing collegial support.

The faculty experiences reported in this chapter suggest a myriad of topics that could be covered in a hybrid course faculty development program. Typically, faculty have to modify their approach to teaching, manage their own and students' expectations regarding hybrid learning, integrate face to face and online teaching environments, learn new communication skills, master new technologies, and much more. A list of all the possible topics for an effective faculty development program would be very long. However, based upon this study's data and the hybrid course experiences of the UWM Learning Technology Center, the following is a short list of a dozen primary issues and topics, which should form the core of any program preparing faculty for hybrid teaching. This list is written for faculty developers but it can also be a helpful guide for faculty who are preparing to design and teach their first hybrid course.

1. Begin the course redesign process by re-examining course goals and objectives and by considering how they can best be achieved in the hybrid environment.
2. Develop new learning activities that capitalize on the strengths of the online and face to face learning environments.
3. Integrate face to face and online learning activities to avoid teaching two parallel and unconnected courses.
4. Learn to make the transition from a lecture-centered teaching approach to a more learner-centered teaching focus.

5. Avoid the common tendency to cover too much material and include too many activities in the redesigned course that result in a "course and a half."
6. Acquire and practice the skills needed to effectively manage and facilitate online discussion and interaction.
7. Learn to create an online community of learners by providing an inclusive, positive, and friendly learning environment where students feel safe sharing ideas.
8. Keep technology use simple in order to avoid turning the course into a support nightmare and gradually add more advanced technology.
9. Develop a plan for conducting course activities when technology fails.
10. Manage student expectations regarding the hybrid format and course workload.
11. Identify and develop plans, materials, and activities to help students with the technology and time management challenges many encounter.
12. Use the tools in the course management system to get organized and stay organized when teaching hybrid courses.

A successful hybrid course initiative requires substantial efforts from institutions, faculty developers, and faculty. This study's recommendations, which are designed to be both effective and practical, are grounded in data derived from actual experiences. Furthermore, the recommendations can be readily adopted by others, as they strive to help faculty discover, design, and implement their hybrid courses.

Implications of the Hybrid Model

Faculty, students, and even institutions, like hybrid courses. The benefits of improving student learning, providing time flexibility for students and instructors, and offering scheduling and classroom space flexibility for institutions are compelling. However, what might be one of the more significant benefits of the hybrid course model may be classified as an example of "unintended good consequences"—learning to teach hybrid courses appears to transform faculty's teaching in all their courses.

A number of the research participants said that the hybrid course experience has caused them to reconsider and improve how they teach their other courses. This is consistent with what the authors have observed as they have worked with hybrid instructors over several years. Faculty appear to be changing their approach to teaching and learning, primarily by taking a more learner-centered approach. Learning to teach hybrid courses accomplished what faculty often resisted in other faculty development programs that were designed to introduce them to learner-centered activities and to wean them from an exclusively lecture format. As a result, the hybrid course experience may be transforming higher education by making it more learner-centered. Additional research is needed to verify these observations and to obtain a better understanding of the impact of the hybrid teaching experience on the overall pedagogical philosophy of instructors.

A second observation that merits additional study is related to the type of prior teaching experiences that instructors bring with them to a hybrid course faculty development program. Faculty who had previous online teaching experience felt that parts of the faculty development program were rather basic and that the program could be accelerated. These instructors were already familiar and experienced with utilizing online discussion forums and effectively managing online interaction. However, the experienced online faculty might need sessions that focus on different topics and challenges. Some online instructors have little or no experience in the face to face classroom and would benefit from sessions that focus on how to effectively use the classroom time in a hybrid course and how to facilitate advantageous face to face interaction. Further research is needed to identify the needs of faculty whose prior teaching experience is primarily online in order to construct faculty development experiences that would most benefit them. Given the increasing number of instructors whose primary teaching experience is with fully online courses, it is important that programs be designed to meet their unique needs.

Another unexpected observation that emerged in this study relates to the technology experience of the faculty in this study. As mentioned earlier, 70% of the research participants had no or limited experience using technology for teaching. One admitted, "My idea of getting into technology was a new piece of chalk each semester." Rogers (1995) would characterize these individuals as "late adopters." These are individuals who are in the last group to adopt an innovation and do so only after the benefits have been clearly demonstrated.

It appears that the benefits associated with the hybrid course model not only caused these "late adopter" instructors to try these courses but also provided them with the motivation to acquire the necessary technology skills to effectively teach them. A number of the instructors commented that it was the perceived benefits of hybrid teaching that made them finally take the leap and learn more about instructional technology. Thus, it appears that the hybrid course model can be an important factor in getting late majority faculty to adopt instructional technology and incorporate it into their teaching. Additional research is necessary to explore the influence of the hybrid course model on the willingness of late majority faculty to learn about and adopt instructional technology. Hybrid courses may play a significant role in further integrating technology into the curriculum because of their ability to motivate late adopter faculty to incorporate it into their courses.

Investigating these three issues will not only enable institutions to better prepare their faculty for teaching hybrid courses but will also provide insight into the broader impact of these courses. Hybrid courses may be having a more transformational effect on teaching and learning than ever anticipated.

References

Anderson, T., Rourke, L., Garrison, D. L., & Archer, W. (2001). Assessing teaching presence in a computer conference context. *Journal of Asynchronous Learning Networks, 5*(2). Available: http://www.sloan-c.org /publications/jaln/v5n2/v5n2_anderson.asp.

Aycock, A., Garnham, C., & Kaleta, R. (2002). Lessons learned from the hybrid course project. *Teaching with Technology Today, 8*(6). Retrieved February 13, 2006 from http://www.uwsa.edu/ttt/articles/garnham2.htm.

Berge, Z. L. (1995). Facilitating computer conferencing: Recommendations from the field. Educational Technology, 35(1), 22–30.

Bonk, C., Kim, K. J., & Zeng, T. (2006). Future directions of blended learning in higher education and workplace learning settings. In C. Bonk & C. Graham (Eds.), *The handbook of blended learning: Global perspectives local designs* (pp. 550–567). San Francisco: Pfeiffer.

Bonk, C. & Dennen, V. (2003). Frameworks for Research, Design, Benchmarks, Training, and Pedagogy in Web-Based Distance Education. In M.G. Moore & W.G. Anderson (Eds.), *Handbook of distance education* (pp. 331–348). New Jersey: Lawrence Erlbaum Associates, Inc.

Bonk, C. J., Olson, T. M., Wisher, R. A., & Orvis, K. L. (2002). *Reflections on blended distributed learning: The armor captains' career course.* (Research Note 2003-06). Alexandria, VA: U.S. Army Research Institute for the Social and Behavioral Sciences.

Brufee, K. A. (1999). *Collaborative learning: Higher education, interdependence, and the authority of knowledge* (2nd ed.). Baltimore: John Hopkins University Press.

Carr, V. (1999). Technology adoption and diffusion. In E. Ullmer (Ed.), *An online sourcebook.* ERIC Document Reproduction Service No. ED453360.

Christo-Baker, E. (2004). Distance education leadership in higher education institutions: Explored within theoretical frameworks of organizational change and Diffusion of Innovations Theory. *World Conference on Educational Multimedia, Hypermedia and Telecommunications 2004 (1),* 251–156. Available: http://dl.aace.org/15407.

Denzin, N., & Lincoln, Y. S. (2003). *Collecting and interpreting qualitative materials.* Thousand Oaks, CA: Sage Publications.

Dziuban, C. D., Hartman, J. L., & Moskal, P. D. (2004). *Blended Learning* (Research Bulletin 7). Boulder, CO: EDUCAUSE Center for Applied Research.

Dziuban, C. D., Hartman, J. L., Juge, F., Moskal, P., & Sorg, S. (2006). Blended learning enters the mainstream. In C. Bonk & C. Graham (Eds.), *The handbook of blended learning: Global perspectives local designs* (pp. 195–208). San Francisco: Pfeiffer.

Garnham, C., & Kaleta, R. (2002, March). Introduction to hybrid courses. *Teaching with Technology Today, 8*(10). Retrieved May 9, 2005 from http://www.uwsa.edu/ttt/ articles/garnham.htm.

Guba, E. G., & Lincoln, Y.S. (1989). *Fourth generation evaluation.* Thousand Oaks, CA: Sage Publications.

Harasim, L., Hiltz, S. R., Teles, L., & Turoff, M. (1998). *Learning networks: A field guide to teaching and learning online.* Cambridge, MA: The MIT Press.

Hollingshead, A. B., McGrath, J. E., & O'Connor, K. M. (1993). Group task performance and communication technology: A longitudinal study of computer-mediated versus face to face work groups. Small Group Research, 24, 307–333.

Johnson, J. (2002). *Reflections on teaching a large enrollment course using a hybrid format.* Retrieved February 8, 2006 from the Teaching with Technology Today Web site: http://www.uwsa.edu/ttt/articles/jjohnson.htm.

Kaleta, R., & Garnham, C. (2001). Hybrid I: UW System Hybrid Course Project– Overview, Faculty Development, Student Resources. *Proceedings of the 17th Annual Conference on Distance Teaching and Learning,* University of Wisconsin-Madison.

Keller, C. (2005). Virtual learning environments: Three implementation perspectives. *Learning, Media & Technology, 30*(3), 299–311.

Learning Technology Center, University of Wisconsin-Milwaukee (2006). Hybrid Course Web site. Available: http://www.uwm.edu/Dept/LTC/hybrid/.

Lincoln, Y. S., & Guba, E. G. (1985). *Naturalistic inquiry.* London: Sage Publications.

Martyn, M. (2003). The hybrid online model: Good practice. *EDUCAUSE Quarterly, 26*(1), 18–23.

Merriam, S. B., & Associates (2002). *Qualitative research in practice: Examples for discussion and analysis.* San Francisco: Jossey-Bass.

Patton, M. (2001). *Qualitative Research and Evaluation Methods.* (3rd ed.). Thousand Oaks, CA: Sage Publications.

Rogers, E. M. (1962). *Diffusion of innovations.* New York: Free Press.

Rogers, E. M. (1995). *Diffusion of innovations* (4th ed.). New York: Free Press.

Sands, K. (2002). Inside outside, upside downside: Strategies for connecting online and face to face instruction in hybrid courses. *Teaching with Technology Today, 8*(6). Retrieved February 13, 2006 from http://www.uwsa.edu/ttt/articles/sands2.htm.

Short, J., Williams, E., & Christie, B. (1976). *The social psychology of telecommunications.* London: John Wiley & Sons.

Simonson, M., Smaldino, S., Albright, M., & Zvacek, S. (2000). *Teaching and learning at a distance: Foundations of distance education.* Upper Saddle River, NJ: Prentice Hall.

Skibba, K. (2005). How faculty use hybrid courses to facilitate adult learning. *Proceedings of the 24th Annual Midwest Research-to-Practice Conference in*

Adult, Continuing, and Community Education, University of Wisconsin-Milwaukee.

Skill, T. D., & Young, B. A. (2002). Embracing the hybrid model: Working at the intersections of virtual and physical learning spaces. *New Directions for Teaching and Learning, 92*, 23–32.

Swenson, P. W., & Evans, M. (2003). Hybrid courses as learning communities. In S. Reisman, J. G. Flores, & D. Edge (Eds.), *Electronic learning communities: Issues and practices* (pp. 27–71). Greenwich, CT: Information Age Publishing.

Walther, J. B. (1996). Computer-mediated communication: Impersonal, interpersonal, and hyper-personal interaction. *Communication Research, 23*, 3–43.

Weimer, M. (2002). Learner-centered teaching: Five key changes to practice. San Francisco: Jossey-Bass.

Young, J. R. (2002, March 22). Hybrid teaching seeks to end the divide between traditional and online instruction. *The Chronicle of Higher Education*, p. A33.

The authors would like to thank Professor Barbara Daly for her advice on the design of the research project and Carla Garnham for her help with the preparation of the final draft of this chapter.

Student Perceptions of Assessment Efficacy in Online and Blended Classes

Gary Brown
Washington State University
Tamara Smith
University of Nebraska, Kearny
Tom Henderson
Central Washington University

The evidence that learning requires a lifelong commitment is apparent in the changing demographics of higher education. The traditional 18 to 24 year old now makes up just one quarter of all degree-seeking undergraduates in the U.S. (Zernike, 2002). Increasingly the backgrounds and experiences of students, even younger students often identified as "traditional," are changing in dramatic ways. More students now represent ethnic minorities. More are female. More arrive more variously prepared to meet the requirements of successful matriculation. And more students, regardless of demographics, are technology savvy, and consequently more place-bound or time-constrained students are enrolling in blended or asynchronous courses accessible all or in part through the Internet (Wilgoren, 1999).

In addition to changing demographics, the need for lifelong learning is amplified by the growing complexity of the global society and the subsequent and increasingly urgent need to implement pedagogies that are more responsive to students and society, and that best reflect our most current understanding about how people learn. Educators can do more, in other words, to provide students with deep, authentic, and responsive learning opportunities (Wildman, 2005). They can do more to help students become more facile and flexible learners, or, as Paul and Elder (1996) frame it, to help students develop more sophisticated ways of thinking.

To begin to address this confluence of changing student demographics, technology, and different pedagogies, the study reported here examines students' perceptions of the efficacy in different learning contexts, focusing particularly on different ways students are assessed or graded in online and in blended courses. Different assessment strategies are central in shaping students' learning experiences (Angelo & Cross, 1993). "If we want people to gain control of important habits of standards and habits of mind," Wiggens (1993) argues, "then they have to know, *perhaps first of all*, how to accurately view those things…" (p. 54). Further, the way a learner perceives the learning task defines the strategies they employ to perform that task (Bereiter & Scardamalia, 1993).

This study reports on the way students perceive different assessment strategies or tasks and their perceptions of the efficacy of those assessment strategies in blended and online environments. In particular, this study examined the way those perceptions differ between students with more and less experience. The practical focus of this study is to help explain how assessment, particularly in online and blended learning environments, might be deployed more effectively to meet and shape learners' expectations and experiences to help them "gain control" of "important standards and habits of mind."

Review of Literature

The extent to which students believe an assessment or test accurately reflects what they understand assumes some degree of self-knowledge or metacognition as well as some understanding of the way knowledge is structured within a domain. Though experts within different disciplines hold different and often competing views of the way knowledge is understood in their disciplines (Donald, 2002), they rarely contest the notion that as students gain understanding and experience, they should also gain an increasing sophistication in their thinking as well as a more comprehensive and appreciative understanding of the complexity of knowledge within a discipline (Perry, 1981; Paul, 1993; Donald). Further, as Wiggens (1993) and Paul point out, good habits-of-mind require learners to effectively monitor and assess their own and each others' learning in order to attain even foundational knowledge and to learn essential facts as well as to apply learning meaningfully, the ultimate measure of learning. Noting the common if misguided tendency to accept Bloom's Taxonomy (Bloom, 1964) "as a chronology for teaching" (p. 54), Wiggens argues that to think critically, to understand even foundational knowledge as well as to develop higher order skills, learners should not be dependent upon a single authority to "correct" their learning. One implicit goal of an academic endeavor, therefore, is to help students increase their independence as learners if they are to attain admittance into a larger discourse community.

It is that larger community that Bruffee (1984) called the broader "conversation" as it pertains to the social dimension of learning. Bruffee contends that for learning to be authentic and engaging, students have to realize that learning is reduced when it is relegated exclusively to the dyadic relationship of teacher to student and contingent upon the authority traditionally imbued to that dyadic relationship. Bruffee argues, further, that more sophisticated and meaningful learning and deeper understanding is necessarily social.

Wildman (2005) extends the implications of the point when he notes that "one of the key points of contention with respect to social learning theory is that school learning is usually not a replication of the authentic practice of the discipline under study" (p. 21).

This discussion suggests two lines of inquiry—student perception of and engagement in their own and each others' learning, and the efficacy of the assessments we use to promote and determine their engagement and subsequent learning.

The efficacy of the assessment strategy is a critical variable in understanding (and therefore improving) student learning. Different assessment strategies reveal a different picture of student learning. Picciano (2002) found, for instance, that students' perception of social presence, a sense of belonging to a group related to online interaction, associates with significantly better performance on essay examinations; however, students in the same study demonstrated no such association between presence and performance when performance was assessed using a multiple choice examination. The author speculates that the difference perhaps indicates that students distinguish between an activity that is "expressive" and one that is "impersonal" (p. 33). More pointedly, the distinction suggests implications of the efficacy of various assessment strategies for ascertaining what it is educators might or should value.

Clearly, students' perceptions of the efficacy of an assessment will alter their performance. When a test matters to them, they will perform better. Paxson and Tarnai (2005) found, for instance, that business students' exam performance varies significantly on standardized professionally developed exams when students are provided with financial incentives for improving their performance. It appears, in other words, that the incentive adds to students' perception of the efficacy of the examination task, or, conversely, that efficacy diminishes proportionate to a learner's perception of an examination's relevance.

More recently and directly related to online and blended learning environments, innumerable researchers have argued that social interaction—especially in online environments—is not just an add-on but an essential requisite for effective online learning (Meyer, 2003; Swan, 2002). "The quality of academic production emerges significantly from purposeful social interaction" (LeBaron and Santos, 2005, p. 1). Alternately, Johns and Swales (2002) identify learning tasks that are characterized as isolated and recognizable to the extent that the purpose of the assessment or task will be assessed solely by a teacher, sans all social interaction. They call those exercises "pseudocommunicative" or "school" tasks. Furthermore, to the extent that quality interaction may be essential for rich learning, it is not necessarily the case that "school" tasks like traditional forced or multiple choice exams, or even "pseudocommunicative" essays, measure the essential attributes associated with or gained from collaborative or "community" interactions. Or, as Wildman notes (2005), "We now know that it makes a great difference where and how we look to understand learning" (p. 18). An

147

important study by Wright, Millar, Kosciuk, and Penberthy (1998) illustrated this point when they reported that a comparison between a well-received lecture course and an alternate collaborative learning based course in mostly traditional entry level science courses yielded similarly positive student evaluations and test results. However, students from both groups were assessed orally by faculty from sequel science courses who found that the students who participated in the collaborative learning groups had a much more thorough understanding of the material and were much more facile at applying the information to new questions and circumstances. The findings suggest, first, that traditional tests and student evaluations are not particularly sensitive measures for assessing what educators value most and, second and not incidentally, that even novice learners in socially rich collaborative or "community" learning contexts are capable of deeper, more meaningful learning than their counterparts in traditional "school" entry level courses when the measures used to assess that learning are appropriately calibrated. Finally, and also not incidentally, it is important to recognize that traditional entry level students, like the faculty involved in the Wright study, may not have been adequately prepared to recognize the critical distinctions and implications that characterize and extend from traditional and collaborative learning-based pedagogies.

In this study, we have tried to update, narrow and focus on particular aspects of these issues in the context of online and blended learning and, specifically, determine how different assessment strategies that reflect "school" and "community" assumptions are perceived by students in predominantly online environments and how those perceptions might vary across different populations. The hypothesis was that students' views of socially isolated forced-choice assessment measures like multiple choice, fill-in-the-blank, and true-false exams usually associated with "school" tasks will be perceived with diminishing value as learners gain cognitive maturity commonly associated with experience and age.

Method

To assess students' perceptions of assessment efficacy, the present study used data gathered from The Center for Teaching, Learning, and Technology (CTLT) at Washington State University (WSU) as part of an ongoing assessment process developed to systematically evaluate the use and impact of innovative teaching practices. In collaboration with several WSU faculty and other educational professionals, WSU's CTLT developed a series of surveys (available on request) that have focused on faculty and student learning goals, activities, and practices (GAPs). The surveys were distributed online via a survey generator (CTLSilhouette) developed by the CTLT. All individuals using the centrally supported online learning technologies at

WSU, including those teaching fully online courses or those who taught blended courses, were invited to participate in the GAPs survey process.

GAPS consisted of two surveys: one for the instructors and one for students. The instructor survey focused on instructors' course goals and the activities and practices they use to accomplish those goals and to assess students' work. The student survey asked questions based largely on the Seven Principles of Good Practice in Undergraduate Education (Chickering & Gamson, 1987). Additional questions focused on constructs such as the alignment of goals, perceived efficacy of teaching and learning practices, and teaching goals (Angelo & Cross, 1993). The construct of principle focus in this study was the question that focused on the activities and assessments that students felt best provided evidence of their learning.

Data for this research was gathered from student responses to the GAPS student surveys over a two year period, specifically from Fall 2002 and Fall 2003 terms to provide some control for participation. The survey announcement and links were included in the two web-based course management systems used by the institution. Student responses to the survey were gathered from 41 different classes in Fall 2002 and 34 classes in the fall of 2003. Twenty of the classes in Fall 2002 were from blended courses; twenty-one were from fully online courses offered by the WSU distance degree program. In the Fall 2003 courses, eleven were drawn from blended courses; twenty-three were from fully online courses. The responses reflected a convenience sample drawn from both blended and fully online courses from various disciplines and with students from different ages and sexes.

The GAPs survey is administered mid-semester and is intended to provide formative assessment for faculty who teach using WSU's online environments. Angelo and Cross (1993) sum up the spirit of GAPs when they note the distinction between classroom research for accountability and assessment for improvement. Since the survey is offered in 75 different classes, incentives for student participation varied from no and little faculty encouragement to respond to pronounced faculty enthusiasm, or, as one faculty member described her effort,"*I was a cybernag.*"

Analysis for this study has been focused on the following open-ended question: *Which method of assessing your work is most likely to reflect what you are learning in this course?*

Analysis of the qualitative responses was correlated with students' age, sex and race, as well as the number of college courses students had taken since high school. Two individuals independently coded responses for this question into subcategories including: Exams (general), multiple choice exams, essay exams, individual projects, term papers, discussions, peer assessment, group work (projects), self assessment, portfolios, and simulations. Although inter-rater reliability of the coding process was high (89%), there were remaining inconsistencies. These subcategories were then

149

sorted into two larger pre-established categories suggested by Johns and Swales (2000): school tasks or community learning. "School" tasks are characterized by the exclusive audience of the resulting performance—the instructor who rates or grades the work. "Community" reflects some degree of participation or review of the student work or performance, regardless of the formal assessment criteria, by peers or other professional or para-professionals. (Some of the online courses included feedback from designated peer-facilitators or invited faculty and professionals from various occupations.) The responses pertaining to homework were eliminated from this analysis because the independence or social aspects of various assignments across multiple courses could not be determined. Percentages in each category were compared with results for age, sex, and number of college course taken. (The analysis of sex has not been included in this report for reasons of space and scope, though the research merits additional attention).

The sample was determined by convenience commonly associated with field research. Over 200 faculty members were invited to participate in the instructor survey each term, and only the students of the instructors who took the instructor survey were offered the student survey. Only response rates from classes that exceeded 20% were included in the analysis.

Initially, data from Fall 2002 and Fall 2003 were analyzed separately to control for population variance and to increase the magnitude of the findings. In fact, findings from the different terms and from fully online and blended courses were consistent so combining data was appropriate.

Student age was parsed into 1 of 3 categories. Category 1: 18–20 years of age; category 2: 21–23; category 3: 24 and over. Because the two separate semesters were similar we also analyzed the combined dataset providing a dataset of 783 students.

Qualitative data from students' many open-ended comments were necessarily coded into more than one category, which resulted in more responses than the total number of students who completed the GAPS survey. The total number of discrete comments was used in the analysis. The open-ended responses were assessed qualitatively and sorted into either the "community" or "school" constructs. Two quantitative procedures were used to determine and verify statistical significance. Both the Cox and Snell and the Nagelkerke logistical regression procedures estimate the regression coefficient in logistic regression where R2 is problematized by the binary categorical (*community and school*) constraints. Samples of the qualitative student comments are included in the following sections of this study to amplify the quantitative findings and to further clarify the constructs. The quantitative data is presented in tables and figures in the findings section of this report.

Additional analysis of the aggregate data further suggests the sample is representative of students using web-based course management systems in both blended and fully online courses, which is the population to which the results of the study may be generalized. It may be reasonable to extend the findings further to include other online text-rich environments such as wikis and blogs, particularly given the expanded audiences of those tools which, complementing the findings of this study, often are implemented with the intent to transcend classroom boundaries.

Finally, there is sufficient distribution within and between each 'group' in the sample to confirm that no group was over or under represented relative to the target population. In other words, responses provide a good depiction of the overall population. Results from this sample can be reasonably generalized to the institution's student population who use web-based course technologies.

Results

Response Rates

The students taking the survey were from 41 different classes in Fall 2002 and 34 in Fall 2003. There were 488 students who responded to the survey in Fall 2002, 424 of whom provided information about age and answered the question about assessment. There were 412 students responding in fall 2003, 359 of whom provided information necessary to complete the analysis based on age. The total number of students responding to the surveys totaled 900 student surveys. Sixty four percent of the students were female and 36% were male.

These response rates support research that suggests females are more likely than males to respond to online surveys (Underwood, Kim, & Matier, 2000). The students taking the survey were predominantly white (84.975%). The high percentage of participation from distributed students (46%) reflects the support the study received from WSU's Distance Degree Program.

The response rate also corresponds with other research findings that suggest that distributed students who tend to be older, with more web access, are more likely to respond (NCES 1999–2000; Carnevale, 2002).

Perceptions of Assessment Efficacy

1. In both blended and fully online courses, novice or less experienced learners reported greater confidence in all methods of assessment.
2. Novice learners (67.9% for Fall 2002, 70.9% for Fall 2003, 69.3% overall) reported that "school" activities, predominantly multiple choice exams and customary term papers, better reflected their learning than did "community" assessment activities.
3. Novice learners (18–20 years) were more likely than older students to report that multiple-choice questions best reflected their learning.
4. Novice learners also reported more confidence in essays and other assessment strategies including simulations, homework, and term

papers performed primarily as an individual activity associated with "school."

5. Conversely, more experienced or older students reported that "community" assessment activities better reflected their learning than did "school" assessment activities, and their comments illuminate the implications of the richness of a learning experience that extends beyond traditional "school" boundaries.

6. Activities such as peer assessments and peer (threaded) discussions were reported as significantly more efficacious assessments by more experienced learners: novice learners at 23.9% compared with experienced learners at 47.9% (see Table 1).

7. There is a statistically significant relationship between age and the "community/school" variable. For every increase in age category, there is an approximately 50% chance reduction in preference for "school" (see Table 1).

Table 1. **Effect of Age**

	B	S.E.	Significance
Age	-.467	.075	>.0001
Constant	1.338	.179	>.0001
Cox & Snell R Squared=.038 Nagelkerke R Squared=.051			

Dependent variable is preference for school or community

8. There is a statistically significant relationship between "course experiences" and the "community/school" variable. For every categorical increase in "course experiences," blended and fully online, there is an approximate 40% increase in preference for "community" (see Table 2).

*Table 2.***Course Experiences**

	B	S.E.	Significance
Course Experiences	.220	.044	>.0001
Constant	-1.037	.165	>.0001
Cox & Snell R Squared=.024 Nagelkerke R Squared=.033			

Dependent variable is preference for school or community

9. As learners gain experience, which cannot be attributed solely to course-based experience, they are more likely than less experienced learners to report that peer assessment was a viable assessment technique.

10. The findings are consistent over time whether examined from age or course experiences, though the findings are slightly less pronounced in the latter.

The figures below illustrate the frequency distributions by term and experiences—fall, spring—and combined by experience associated with age in figures 1–3. Figures 4–6 are frequency distributions by term and experiences associated with courses completed over the same period.

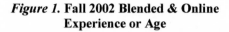

Figure 1. **Fall 2002 Blended & Online Experience or Age**

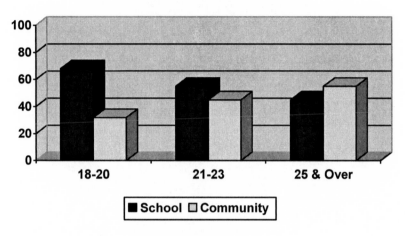

Figure 2. **Fall 2003 Blended & Online Experience or Age**

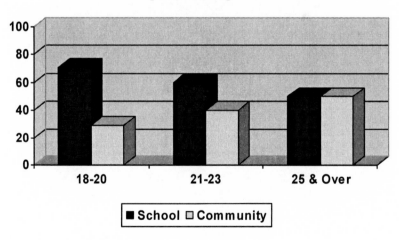

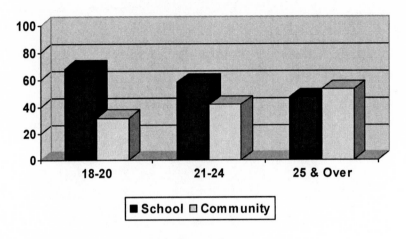

Figure 3. Combined 2002 & 2003
Experience or Age

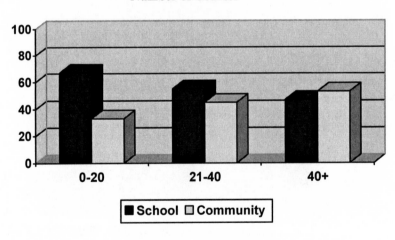

Figure 4. Fall 2002
Number of Courses

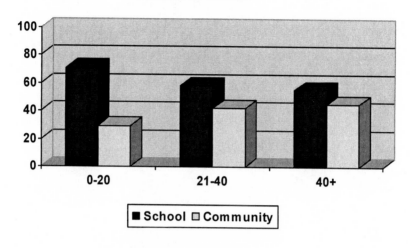

Figure 5. **Fall 2003**
Number of Courses

Figure 6. **Combined 2002 & 2003**
Number of Courses

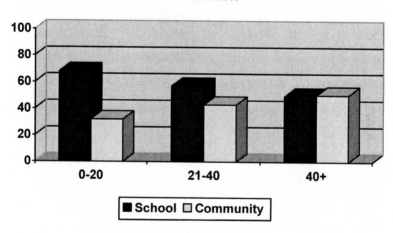

Discussion

Though the aggregation of blended and fully online populations and the various technology functions in the analysis might be perceived of as a limitation, the intention of this study was not to compare technologies or implementation variables (chats, online tests, threaded discussions, document sharing, etc.) but to isolate and examine underlying *learning constructs* necessary for the effective implementation of efficacious learning experiences. In this case the learning constructs were the different grading strategies used and students' corresponding perceptions of the value of those strategies. Certainly future research will continue to focus on the effects of

155

different technologies on different populations and how those technologies alter students' perceptions, but those variables were not the focus here and, further, often needlessly confound the implementation of principles of best practice.

With that in mind, and given the expected limitations related to population samples and response rates associated with survey research conducted across multiple courses of various technology use, the results are remarkably stable and support the assertion that students' perceptions of assessment strategies obtund the effect of the particular technologies used to implement those strategies. The picture emerges clearly and confirms the hypothesis: The perception of the efficacy of "school," defined as those activities that isolate interaction to the exclusive dyad of teacher and student, diminishes as students' perceptions of learning matures, regardless of whether that maturation reflects age, life experience, or course experiences. Conversely, the perception of the efficacy of "community" assessment activities or tasks increases as students' perceptions of learning matures. If the pattern is clear and consistent, however, the implications for practice are more complex.

First, it is important to note that though the perception of the value of "school" assessment strategies diminishes after students begin college, "school" is not synonymous with learning. As one student in this study lamented, "I am very upset that my time was so taken up trying to pass the quizzes rather than enjoying the learning that could have taken place."

Multiple choice tests, term papers, and even essay writing to the extent that writing assignments are often one-way student-to-teacher dyads in the traditional context of "school" is often viewed, as Johns and Swales (2002) observed, as *pseudocommunicative*. But in fact it appears that learning as described by Bruffee (1984) as "that which distinguishes human beings from other animals" by engaging participants in the larger "conversation" (p. 86) increases significantly as learners mature and gain experience. A student clarifies the distinction, "I think essay based exams where a case study could be evaluated would be the best method of 'graded' assessment—but comments to threaded discussions are by far the best way to see if we have grasped the course work's objective."

Mature learners recognize a difference between *grading* and *learning*. The distinction is a good indicator of the progression of the novice to the mature learner. A novice learner, for instance, expresses concern for the lack of "objectivity" associated with discussions and peer critiques, "It would be nice to have some more objective evaluation like a multiple choice test or something." Alternately, the more experienced learner observes, "I have also found that every professor has their own style to a multiple choice test."

The novice learner tends to hold the more simplistic view of learning, more likely to be constrained by the principles and habits that have defined a more limited experience associated with "school." Students who hold the view that grades are objective measures of their performance are less likely to value peer critiques or peer evaluations and are less likely to value the multiple perspectives one encounters in a broader conversation, "I find the peer evaluations to be somewhat unfair as different students place emphasis on different things, or may not grade other students fairly depending on how much they actually scrutinized their classmates' work."

One might argue that such findings are consistent with developmental theories and that the phenomenon reflects student maturation independent from teaching strategies. Yet concluding that maturation as synonymous with aging fully explains the findings ignores the fact that the evidence here also implies that younger students generally appear to have had less exposure to more sophisticated learning opportunities. Age and course experiences yield essentially the same pattern. Maturation is experience as well as biological aging, and there is scant evidence to suggest that "school" has done all that it might to provide "community" and richer experiences that foster more sophisticated learners.

In fact, it is important to consider that there is ample evidence from other quarters to suggest that younger learners are predisposed to have greater appreciation of "community learning" opportunities than the results of this study suggest. Citing neuroscience, Caine and Caine (1997) report that humans and human brains are innately social. Even for children, interpersonal relationships are essential for healthy development of the brain and mind.

> It is now clear that throughout our lives, our brain/minds change in response to their engagement with others—so much so that individuals must always be seen to be integral parts of larger social systems. Indeed, part of our identity depends on establishing community and finding ways to belong. Learning, therefore, is profoundly influenced by the nature of the social relationships within which people find themselves (Caine & Caine, http://www.newhorizons.org /neuro/caine.htm).

In this context, the implications of the findings in this study suggest that students have been habituated in ways that have delayed their maturity as learners. The novice students who say things like, "I like to get feedback from the teacher, and I don't like having to critique another student's work..." demonstrate a sensibility that has not been provided with what Wiggens (1993) means when he calls for opportunities to recognize and develop sophisticated habits of mind.

Citing Holt's 1971 ironically Internet prescient work, *The School without Walls*, Bruffee (1984) points out that it has been "traditional classroom learning that [leaves] students unprepared in the first place." What students need, Bruffee argues, are learning opportunities that are "not an extension of but an alternative to traditional classroom teaching" (Wily, Gleason, & Wetherbee Phelps, 1996, p. 86). In other words, it is reasonable to conclude that if we believe, as we should, that helping learners mature requires opportunities to establish community, then the evidence from this study suggests that capitalizing on technologies creates a potent path for doing so, for engaging even novice learners into the larger conversation.

Of course the caveats from skeptical colleagues are also echoed by students even as they make the argument more salient. For instance, a student from this study also observes, "Although peer reviews are sometimes helpful, I sometimes feel that we are the blind leading the blind. I really rely on the instructor's guidance when a post misses the mark. In some of the other web classes, we never get one comment from the instructor, only a grade. How would we know what we do not know? Most of the peer reviews are kind. While I am thankful for that, I notice that they seldom do the job they are intended to do."

Certainly this concern echoes discussions about student collaboration heard on campuses for years even as they make the opposite point ("We never get one comment from the instructor, only a grade) that recalls Wiggens' exhortation that people "cannot always be dependent upon another person for assessment" (1993, p. 54). In the larger increasingly global context, the conversation that educators must both shape and reflect requires an understanding that community is both an end and a critical means. Recall, finally, that designing and facilitating effective collaborative or communities of practice is itself an area that merits attention. As Bruffee observed more than twenty years ago:

> Organizing collaborative learning effectively requires doing more than throwing students together with their peers with little or no guidance or preparation. To do that is merely to perpetuate, perhaps even aggravate, the many possible negative efforts of peer group influence: conformity, anti-intellectualism, intimidation and leveling down of quality. To avoid these pitfalls and to marshal the powerful educational resource of peer group influence requires us to create and maintain a demanding academic environment that makes collaboration—social engagement in intellectual pursuits—a genuine part of students' educational development. (Wiley et al., 1984, p. 96)

The emergence of a new global knowledge society (Drucker, 2001) affirms that changing demographics will be increasingly apparent in higher education, and that higher education will increasingly be happening online. As more sophisticated and subsequently more demanding students enroll in courses that are increasingly blended, there is the obligation and opportunity to integrate and foster more sophisticated learners to meet more sophisticated learning requirements or, finally, to extend and thereby deepen the conversation.

References

Angelo, T. & Cross, K. P. (1993). *Classroom assessment techniques – A handbook for college teachers* (2nd ed.). Hoboken, NJ: Jossey-Bass.

Bereiter, C., & Scardamalia, M. (1993). *Surpassing ourselves : An inquiry into the nature and implications of expertise.* Chicago: Open Court.

Bloom, B. S., Mesia, B. B., & Krathwohl, D. R. (1964). *Taxonomy of educational objectives: The affective domain and the cognitive domain.* New York. David McKay.

Bruffee, K. (1984). Collaborative learning and the "conversation of mankind." *College English, 46,* 635–652.

Caine, R. N. & Caine, G. (1997). Mind/brain learning principles. New Horizons for Learning. Retrieved January 31, 2005, from http://www.newhorizons.org /neuro/caine.htm.

Chickering, A. & Gamson, Z. (1987). Applying the seven principles for good practice in undergraduate education. In A. W. Chickering & Z. F. Gamson (Eds.), *New directions for teaching and learning, No. 47* (pp. 63–69). Hoboken, NJ: Jossey-Bass.

Carnevale, D. (2002, November 8). Distance education attracts older women who have families and jobs, study finds. *The Chronicle of Higher Education,* p. A33.

Donald, J. (2002). *Learning to think: Disciplinary perspectives.* San Francisco, CA: Jossey-Bass.

Drucker, P. (2001, November 1). *The next society.* Retrieved January 28, 2003, from http://www.economist.com/surveys/PrinterFriendly.cfm?Story_ID= 770819.

Elder, L., & Paul, R. (1996). *Critical thinking development: A stage theory.* Retrieved January 11, 2005, from http://www.criticalthinking.org/resources /articles/ct-development-a-stage-theory.shtml.

Johns, A. M., & Swales, J. M. (2002). Literacy and disciplinary practices: Opening and closing perspectives. *Journal of English for Academic Purposes, 1*(1), 13–28.

LeBaron, J., & Santos, I. (2005). Authentic engagement of adult learners in online learning. *MountainRise,* 2(1). Retrieved April 9, 2006 from http://facctr.wcu.edu/mountainrise/archive/vol2no1/html/authentic _engagement.html.

Meyer, K.A., (2003). Face to face versus threaded discussions: The role of time and higher-order thinking. *Journal of Asynchronous Learning Networks,* 7(3), 55–65. Retrieved January 30, 2005, from http://www.sloan-c.org /publications/jaln/v7n3/v7n3_meyer.asp.

National Center for Educational Statistics (1999–2000). *A profile of participation in distance education: 1999–2000.*

Picciano, A. G. (2002). *Beyond student perceptions: Issues of interaction, presence, and performance in an online course.* Retrieved December 12, 2005, from http://www.sloan-c.org/publications/jaln/v6n1/index.asp.

Paul, R. (1993). *Critical thinking: What every student needs to survive in a rapidly changing world.* Dillon Beach, CA: Foundation for Critical Thinking.

Paxson, M. C. & Tarnai, J. (2005). *A decade of results using the ETS major field test in business.* Assessment and Evaluation in Higher Education.

Perry, W. G., Jr. (1981). Cognitive and ethical growth: The making of meaning. In A. W. Chickering (Ed.), *The Modern American College* (pp. 76–116). San Francisco: Jossey-Bass.

Russell, T. (2005). *The "No Significant Difference" phenomenon as reported in 248 research reports, summaries, and papers.* Retrieved January 30, 2005, from http://www.nosignificantdifference.org/nosignificantdifference/.

Swan, K. (2002). Building learning communities in online courses: The importance of interaction. Education, Communication and Information, 2(1), 23–49.

Underwood, D., Kim, H., & Matier, M. (2000). *To mail or to web: Comparisons of survey response rates and characteristics.* Paper presented at the Annual Forum of the Association for International Research. Cincinnati, OH. ED446513.

Wiggens, G. P. (1993). *Assessing student performance: Exploring the purpose and limits of testing.* San Francisco: Jossey-Bass.

Wildman, T. M. (2005). From the outside in: Lessons in learning beyond the school walls. *About Campus, 10*(1), 16–22.

Wilgoren, J. (1999, December 22). Golden years now bring new emphasis on learning. *The New York Times.* Section 1, Page 14, Column 1.

Wily, M., Gleason, B., & Wetherbee Phelps, L. (1996). *Composition in four keys: Inquiring into the field.* Mountain View, CA: Mayfield.

Wright, J. C., Millar, S. B., Kosciuk, S. A. & Penberthy, D. L. (1998). A novel strategy for assessing the effects of curriculum reform on student competence. *Journal of Chemical Education, 75*(8), 986–992.

Zernike, K. (2002, August 4). Tests are not just for kids. *The New York Times, Education Life Supplement.* Section 4A, Page 27, Column 1.

The authors of this chapter gratefully acknowledge the help and assistance of Carrie Meyers, Filip Wieko, and Harish Mohan.

Enhancing Student Interaction and Sustaining Faculty Instructional Innovations through Blended Learning

Michael Starenko
Rochester Institute of Technology
Karen Vignare
Michigan State University
Joeann Humbert
Rochester Institute of Technology

Rochester Institute of Technology (RIT) is a large, privately endowed, career-focused technology institute in western New York State. Like many of its peer institutions (e.g., Drexel University, New Jersey Institute of Technology, Rensselaer Polytechnic Institute), RIT has had a sustained involvement with asynchronous learning networks (ALNs) that stretches back to 1991, when RIT offered its first set of fully online distance courses. With faculty and student support provided by its Online Learning Department, RIT currently offers over 38 fully online distance programs and degrees, has 450 courses offered annually, and over 350 faculty teach online annually. There have been over 3000 graduates from the online distance learning programs since 1991. These programs are successful as measured by student graduation, retention, and course withdrawal rates (Vignare, 2002).

Unlike any of its peer institutions—or most colleges and universities for that matter—RIT has a very large population of deaf or hard-of-hearing students and faculty. One of RIT's eight colleges is the National Technical Institute for the Deaf (NTID), the world's first and largest technological college for students who are deaf or hard-of-hearing. More than 1,100 deaf and hard-of-hearing students study, share residence halls, and enjoy social life together with approximately 14,000 hearing students at RIT. The presence of so many deaf and hard-of-hearing individuals has a positive and distinctive impact upon every aspect of RIT, including the design of online courses.

In 2002, under a directive from the Provost of RIT, the Online Learning Department commenced offering new technologies and services to encourage campus-based faculty to use a greater number and a wider range of instructional strategies, including introducing blended learning. It was only natural for Online Learning to assume this broader role, as the department has a long and successful history of working with faculty to design, develop, and teach distance courses. The introduction of blended learning by the department extends these proven pedagogical strategies and services to faculty teaching campus courses. As an added benefit, blended learning leverages the full capacity of and investment in myCourses, the courseware management system that is currently associated with every RIT course.

Because it houses NTID, RIT has an explicit commitment to deaf and hard-of-hearing students, one that requires having equal access to all forms of learning. This commitment to equal access is shared by the Online Learning Department. Consequently, all audio content used in distance learning courses at RIT must be transcribed and made available to all students. To minimize costs for the Blended Learning Pilot Project, which extended from the Fall 2003 to Spring 2005, no audio components were put online. The introduction of blended learning meant not only measuring the impact of combining classroom and online learning technologies, but also meant that any data collected would also need to measure whether this learning format is beneficial for deaf and hard-of-hearing students. The purpose of this study was to investigate the impact of the Blended Learning Pilot Project on the teaching and learning environment at RIT.

Review of the Literature

RIT's Blended Pilot was based largely on the expectation that asynchronous, Internet-based communication technologies and pedagogical strategies—the same technologies and strategies that were developed in RIT's successful distance leaning programs—could be adapted for blended learning courses. Several theoretical frameworks exist for distance learning (Amundsen, 1993; Garrison, 1989; Keegan, 1993; Bransford, Brown & Cocking, 2000). Bransford et al. provides the most fluid model for blended learning, since their work is broader than a distance education model. In the Bransford model, the learning environment is surrounded by the community and formed from three overlapping circles that are knowledge centered, learner centered, and assessment centered. Bransford recognizes several purposes for technology, but does not fully explore the communication and interaction of community to promote enhanced learning. Garrison, Anderson and Archer (2000) used the same visual pattern, but termed the elements cognitive, teaching and social presence, all inside a community of inquiry. According to this model, blended learning requires the deliberate and thoughtful integration of both classroom and online learning environments (Garrison & Kanuka, 2004). One of the challenges, then, in adapting distance learning models to blended learning is that none of these models consider all the variables of a more complex blended learning environment, one in which both online and traditional classroom environments must be individually well designed, but also integrated to gain the greatest impact.

Statistically significant improvement in cognitive presence, such as that in online learning environments, has not yet been reported for blended learning environments (Vaughan & Garrison, 2005; Shea, Swan, Fredericksen, & Pickett, 2001). For blended learning, the struggle seems to be how to make the shift toward cognitive presence. In the fully online environment, in which the instructor is never physically present, it may be easier to get the students to participate in a valuable online discussion. Still, even with sparse evidence, the value of increasing cognitive presence supports using a research framework that relies on better mix of teaching, cognitive, and social presence in a community of inquiry.

While an improved learning environment remains a laudable goal, academic technology support departments like Online Learning at RIT are also needed to guide and support the effective use of technology in all academic settings (Hitt & Hartman, 2002). The investment in technology is only a part of the systematic changes that need to occur for a campus to support improved teaching and learning through the effective use of technology. At RIT, additional consideration must be given to technology use, insofar as technology cannot impede equal access for deaf and hard-of-hearing students. Deaf and hard-of-hearing students enrolled in college face a multitude of barriers to inclusion in the classroom (Stinson & Liu, 1999). In the online classroom though, the barriers tend to be lower and mostly depend upon the students' intellectual capability to participate (Mallory & Long, 2003). One of the pedagogical strengths of text-based asynchronous communication technologies is their ability to provide a barrier-free or level playing field for all students in the classroom (Harasim, 1995). An environment in which communications are open and accessible is very conducive to deaf or hard-of hearing students. In the traditional classroom all communication is triangulated through the interpreter or others (Lang, 2002). Deaf students often feels they are behind the classroom dialogue and often do not wish to ask questions or interject thoughts (Long & Beil, 2005). In a text-based asynchronous online learning environment, by contrast, there are no longer these communication barriers (Richardson, Long, & Woodley, 2003).

RIT'S Instructional Design Model for the Pilot

During Spring and Summer of 2003, Online Learning developed an instructional design model for a Blended Learning Pilot Project that drew upon: (1) the department's long experience with and commitment to asynchronous Internet communication technology for distance education, and (2) interest in the relative opportunities and constraints of different educational media or environments.

For the purposes of the pilot, a blended course was defined as any course in which approximately 25% to 50% of classroom lectures and other seat time is replaced by instructor-guided online learning activities or experiences—primarily asynchronous discussion (whole and/or small group)—but also synchronous chat sessions, as well as online quizzes, games, discovery labs, and simulations. Because it recognizes the relative opportunities and constraints of each media environment, the model encourages, for example, online interaction that extends discussion beyond

163

the four walls of the classroom. Since the on-site classroom is readily available for laboratory—or studio-style demonstrations, the model likewise discourages elaborate and expensively captioned audio-visual productions of the kind found in many online distance courses.

As Garrison and Kanuka (2004) have noted about the affordances and constraints of blended learning, the classroom experience affords a rich dynamic of fast-paced, spontaneous verbal communication, whereas the largely text-based online experience affords reflection and precision of expression. In small-group work, for instance, it may be advantageous for groups to initially meet face-to-face, or when reaching a consensus. In contrast, discussing a complex case study that requires reflection and negotiation may be better accomplished through an online discussion board. When the two environments are thoughtfully integrated, the educational possibilities are logically multiplied.

An example of this approach is RIT faculty member Roberta Klein's blended Basic Taxation course, first offered in Winter Quarter 2003–2004, which illustrates the multitude of education possibilities that appear in the blended format. Like many accounting and finance faculty, Klein faced the challenge of engaging students in a subject that many consider to be both dry and intimidating. Like many instructors in MBA programs that serve working adults, Klein was searching for a way to make better use of the classroom sessions, and, at the same time, to re-distribute more of the learning activities outside of class. Here is the blended solution that Klein created to address these challenges:

1. Replace 50% of classroom seat time (mostly lectures and homework review) each week with online discussion groups and team projects that extend across the entire week.

2. To encourage learning by discovery, develop online discussion assignments in which students find, summarize, and evaluate a recent article on a taxation issue.

3. Students work in online discussion groups to solve collaboratively the homework problem sets. This strategy makes better use of classroom time because Klein knows before class those problems that are most difficult for students and therefore need to be reviewed in class. For example, Klein organizes the students into four online teams to analyze and present the pros and cons of President Bush's and Mr. Kerry's respective tax policies.

Method

At the onset, the Blended Learning Pilot Project at RIT was intended to be an action research project that focused its efforts on using data collection to improve instructional processes. A hybrid research design using multiple data sources was employed in the pilot. Data sources included qualitative input from faculty regarding initial course design for their blended courses, faculty narratives reflecting upon their experiences teaching a blended course, and interviews with the faculty participants. Faculty members were also invited to quarterly luncheons to share and reflect on blended teaching practices with other pilot participants. Student data collected included a week three survey in the first year and end-of-course surveys in both years of the pilot. First- and second-year surveys included 10 of the same questions. The second year survey was enhanced to include more questions on how blended learning impacted communication for different groups of students: namely, deaf students, hard-of-hearing students, English as a Second Language (ESL) students, and hearing students. Course statistics were collected on completion rates and grade distribution as well.

There were a total of 69 faculty members, 80 unique blended courses, and 115 blended sections upon the conclusion of the pilot in Spring 2005. Participating faculty received a one-time $500 stipend and comprehensive instructional design support from Online Learning instructional designers. Faculty members from all eight RIT Colleges including five from NTID participated in the pilot. Two of the participating faculty members are deaf. Participating faculty varied in teaching and technology experience, ranging from full professors to assistant professors, tenured to adjuncts, technologically savvy to simply computer literate. While participating faculty were motivated by a variety of factors, most said they wanted to solve an instructional problem.

Twenty-five RIT faculty members participated in the Blended Pilot in the 2003–2004 academic year; forty-four participated in the 2004–2005 year. Participants were recruited in three different ways: blended workshops, invitations to faculty who were heavy users of the courseware management system, and distance learning faculty. The blended learning workshops were sponsored by Online Learning and began in late Spring 2003. Often faculty who had experience with online teaching coached and facilitated these workshops as well. Direct email invitations to heavy users of the courseware management system attracted many prospective faculty participants. The other method of soliciting faculty participants was to ask distance learning faculty. Nearly half or 13 faculty in on the first year had taught distance learning courses, and another seven faculty with distance learning experience taught blended courses in the second year.

Once accepted into the pilot, participating faculty were expected to:
1. Complete and submit online a "Blended Application" form.
2. Work with an Online Learning instructional designer to develop their blended course.
3. Learn the myCourses course management system.
4. Inform their department chair and scheduling officer that they will be offering a blended course.

5. Attend a Blended Luncheon in the quarter in which they are teaching their blended course.
6. Allow Online Learning to survey their students at the end of the course.
7. Write a 750–1500 word narrative of their experience with blended learning (second year only).

Results

Faculty Satisfaction

Online learning supported and solicited faculty feedback in three ways: informal luncheons, narratives or reflective writing, and structured interviews. While the luncheons provided social cohesion and ideas to share within the pilot, the narratives and structured interviews offered the richest data about faculty perceptions of and experience with blended learning.

Reflective writing in the form of personal narratives about experience with the blended format was a major form of faculty feedback. Three of the 25 first year pilot faculty wrote narrative accounts of their experience with the blended format; 32 of the 44 second year faculty wrote such narratives. Although no writing style was mandated and no template was provided, most faculty used the familiar academic triad of objectives-methods-results to organize their narratives.

The major identified theme of the 35 submitted narratives was that pilot faculty were attracted to blended learning by the prospect of increased student-to-student interaction. Though not always expressed in negative terms (i.e., as an instructional problem in search of a solution), faculty clearly desired more and better interaction, discussion, dialogue, participation, engagement, and so forth in their courses, and they clearly thought that blended learning promotes such interaction. In particular, faculty teaching primarily lecture-based courses said that their new blended course(s) produced more interaction; and faculty teaching primarily discussion-based or seminar-style courses said that their new blended course(s) deepened or intensified the discussions.

Four additional themes—all sub-themes on the major theme that blended learning promoted more and better interaction—could be discerned within the faculty narratives. These included:

1. Blended learning offered multiple modes of communication. As one NTID instructor remarked, "This class is typically attended by both deaf and hearing students who have various levels of proficiency in sign language and in spoken and written communication. Both face-to-face and online interactions present some communication barriers for different students. Therefore, it is important to have options for communication with peers that include efficient sharing of text as well as more

traditional face-to-face interaction during class using signing and speech."

2. Blended learning leveled the playing field or otherwise promoted widespread and even participation. As one social work instructor explained, "Often students are fearful of introducing in the classroom format a perceived 'different' way of viewing the world. Moreover, deaf students may not always interact with those students who do not use ASL. The online interactive discussions offered the opportunity for all persons to be heard and for peer learning to unfold."

3. Blended learning encouraged peer-to-peer teaching and learning. As one art history instructor put it, "The students within the (online) groups were 'talking' to each other, not at me or at the authors of the readings. In responding to other postings within their groups, they would write things like, 'I never thought of that before...' or 'What the author really meant was...'"

4. Related to the above sub-theme, blended learning shifted the faculty role from imparting knowledge to facilitating learning. As one foreign language instructor acknowledged, "While in the past I often felt the weight of encouraging the students to do their studies, the students took this responsibility on themselves in the blended course, and I felt more like the facilitator of their language study."

A former associate dean and professor at RIT interviewed 29 pilot faculty participants via in-person, telephone, and email sessions on an extensive range of issues. Her major finding, which also supports the findings of the faculty narratives, was that the "great majority of faculty members decided to try a blended learning format in order to address some 'problem.' In a few cases the problem involved a classroom scheduling issue, but more generally the issues involved communication among and with students."

When asked what had worked best in their blended learning courses, faculty members reported the following to the interviewer:

- Improvement in the quantity and/or quality of the communications among the students in online discussion boards
- Good group or team activities
- Improved contacts between faculty member and students
- The immediate feedback that could be given to students
- Student appreciation of opportunities to review subject matter online and determine how well they were doing
- Students maintaining contact with the course throughout the week in a course that was scheduled to meet only once a week
- An enhancement of the time actually spent face-to-face in class

When asked what was the most disappointing or troublesome aspect, faculty members identified:

- Their own lack of preparation and planning time, organization, or skills
- The failure of online PowerPoint presentation of lecture material to meet student expectations
- Student lack of enthusiasm or actual resentment at being in a blended course
- Students not working well together in groups
- The difficulty in developing non-redundant, interesting, and meaningful online activities for the students

Student Satisfaction

During the first year of the pilot, Online Learning surveyed students in blended courses twice during the quarter—once during week three and again at the very end of the quarter. Most of these surveys were handed out in the classroom and entered manually into an online survey system. In the second year of the pilot, Online Learning surveyed students only at the end of the quarter, and only in an online form. In the last weeks of the course, Online Learning emailed students the hyperlink to the end-of-course survey form for their respective blended courses. As expected, the response rate was lower than the in-class surveys, though still large enough to provide a reliable sample. Both surveys and the respondents' answers can be found in the appendix.

The purpose of the end-of-course survey was to investigate how students felt about their blended learning experience. It was also designed to gauge student opinions on interaction and community. The questions developed for the survey were generally questions used before by Online Learning and/or adapted from the Flashlight Online survey bank with Technology survey instruments. The questions on whether faculty-to-student or student-to-student communication increased quantitatively or qualitatively in the survey were the ones used by the University of Central Florida (UCF), which has used these questions for more than seven years and has received well over 150,000 responses (Dziuban, Hartman, Moskal, Sorg, & Truman, 2004). Several open-ended questions were also added and modeled on the UCF surveys.

The survey and demographic results strongly support offering blended learning as regular mode for teaching and taking courses at RIT. Course completion remained consistent with last year's statistics. Ninety-five percent of students successfully completed their blended courses. Students continued to like blended learning. Students agreed that faculty used different strategies in blended learning courses. They also agreed that the online learning activities allow them to learn in different ways than classroom activities. Students also agreed that instructors use more and different teaching resources in blended learning courses.

While all these findings are supportive, there are two important general points to note about the second year data: the percentage of students who agreed or strongly agreed on the above categories is down from last year, but students in all of the above categories are overwhelmingly more positive than they are negative.

The survey also uncovered some very valuable information about how students who belong to subpopulations of deaf and hard-of-hearing and those who speak English as a Second Language (ESL) view blended learning. As we have seen, RIT's commitment to deaf and hard-of-hearing students having equal access to all forms of learning is a constant goal for the Online Learning Department. For the Blended Learning Pilot, for example, no audio components were added. Moreover, the pilot instructional design model encourages classroom interaction to be moved online, where, due to the writing-intensive nature of online discussion boards, it was expected that classes with higher percentages of deaf and hard-of-hearing students would be positively impacted.

For the 2004–2005 academic year, the survey asked students to complete additional demographic questions. One question asked students to indicate whether they were hearing, deaf, or hard-of-hearing. Another question asked whether English was their first language. In this second year of the pilot, 4% of the respondents were deaf, three percent were hard-of-hearing, and 93% were hearing. Within the hearing group, 10% of the respondents indicated that English was a second language. The results, while considerably more positive for deaf and hard-of-hearing students than ESL students, show that deaf and hard-of-hearing students feel like their interaction with other students increased much more so than hearing students. ESL students are more positive about their interactions than hearing students but not nearly at the rate of the deaf and hard-of-hearing students. Given that both these populations expressed stronger positive feelings to blended learning, further investigation of these trends is certainly called for. Blended learning appears to offer a compelling way to offer integrated classrooms for the deaf and hard-of-hearing with hearing students.

Tables 1 and 2 in the appendix summarize the survey findings for the two years of the Blended Learning Pilot Project. The first table shows the results from the 2004–2005 student survey. Students' agreement ratings have declined while neutral and disagreement have risen. These data seem somewhat disappointing—but are to be expected. There is a much larger group of students involved in the second year pilot. Some of the positives from the first year may have been induced by the excitement of faculty trying something for the first time. In addition, there were several faculty members who had difficulty adopting the blended learning strategies they had expected to initiate in their course.

Table 2 shows the differences in questions on the survey that were the same in both years. Only nine of the 16 total questions remained the same on the first- and second-year surveys. The change in the survey was due in part to the inclusion of student subpopulations and an attempt to determine if the deaf and hard-of-hearing students were viewing blended learning as different from the conventional classroom experience. While the data show some decreases, the trends remain positive, and, given that deaf and hard-of-hearing students feel more than twice the interaction with other students, there seems to be more than ample reasons to believe that introducing online learning, via blended learning, to the traditional classroom is well worth the effort.

Faculty Perceptions of Student Engagement

In the structured interviews with pilot faculty (discussed in the previous section), most responses to a question on student satisfaction with the blended course suggested a range of student reactions. Some students were identified as liking the increased flexibility with their time and a reduction of actual classroom time that came with the blended format. Some students would have liked better linkage between the online and face-to-face portions of their courses. Some faculty reported that students recognized the enhancements to their learning experience, but in some cases the students tired of online responses.

Some faculty members identified student lack of prior knowledge that their course would be a blended course as a major factor in their degree of satisfaction with the blended course in which they found themselves. Faculty members also suggested that some students simply prefer face-to-face instruction or sitting in class. Another variable in student response to the blended format was whether the student elected to take the course that was offered in blended format or whether it was an institutional requirement to take the course.

Faculty generally perceived that some students benefit more from the blended format than others. Students who prefer direct person-to-person contact do not do as well online, whereas quiet, shy people tend to do better online. Some students are more open to alternative teaching techniques and are more self-motivated and independent than others, and therefore flourish more with a blended format than the less flexible, more dependent student. Several faculty members identified international and older students as particularly benefiting from the blended course format, while other faculty members noted that international students preferred face-to-face course time. Twenty-three instructors detected improvements in communication among their students and 19 instructors felt that communications between themselves and their students were improved in their blended format courses.

The faculty members described increases both in the quantity as well as quality of communications among their students. They described the student communications as more open, more sharing, and more analytical with better critical thinking. They noted improvements in the areas of: students accepting challenges to their points of view as well as more willing to challenge, in-class discussions after online discussions, the level of intellectual curiosity, and the quality of ideas. Some faculty observed increased openness in online discussions of sensitive topics. In some cases the quality of group interactions was also seen as improved.

Most instructors described increased communication between themselves and their students. Among the differences noted were more contact with students and getting to know them better, greater insight into some students, finding a more friendly and helpful role with students with less conflict, and the ability to respond more thoughtfully and in a more timely fashion to students.

Faculty Perceptions of Special Student Populations

Of the 29 faculty members interviewed, 18 had at least one deaf or hard-of-hearing student in their blended learning courses. Ten of these observed no differences in performance of the students in a blended setting. Deaf or hard-of-hearing students were the majority in one class so observation of performance differences was not possible. Eight instructors noted some differences in performance in the blended format versus other classroom formats:

- An opportunity for the deaf and hard-of-hearing to be more deliberative both in class and online
- One deaf student who would have typically been on the sideline took on more of a leadership role online
- Hearing students with limited signing skills were on a more equal footing online
- Hearing students were more likely to engage in a conversation with the deaf and hard-of-hearing
- Instructor communication was improved with the deaf and hard-of-hearing, even in face-to-face situations
- Deaf students were more likely to be included in mixed hearing groups in online situations, and
- Greater and more enthusiastic online participation of the deaf students in discussions than in the face-to-face environment.

Course Completion and Grades in Pilot Courses

According to a review of all individual course grades in the first year of the pilot, the overwhelming majority of the students did well in blended courses. If the measure of course success is defined as completion for those receiving "Cs or above" grades, then 95% of the students in the pilot succeeded. A total of 87% of all students received "As" and "Bs." During the second year, nearly 85% of the courses were reviewed. Grade distributions and overall completion rates remained the same. The data was comparable to the information available from reviews of distance learning courses. No attempt was made to compare the data to entirely face-to-face courses.

Discussion

Solving Instructional Problems for Faculty

Findings support the conclusion that pilot faculty were highly satisfied with blended learning in general, and with their participation in the pilot in particular. All of the 29 interviewed faculty, and all 35 of the faculty who contributed reflective narratives, said they were satisfied with blended learning and that they were either planning to offer, or would consider offering, blended courses in the future. In fact, thirteen of the 69 pilot faculty repeated or offered new blended courses during the two years of the pilot. As this chapter went to press in early 2006, just 14 of the 53 pilot faculty participants who are still at RIT or teaching this academic year have yet to offer a repeat or new blended course.

Another major finding from the faculty data is that blended learning appears to provide a solution to the implied or explicit problem of student participation and engagement. When specifically asked in the structured interviews about their motivation for joining the pilot, the majority of the faculty said they expected blended learning to provide a solution to an instructional problem. Further analysis of the interview sessions and reflective writing reveal that the dominant instructional problem perceived by pilot faculty is a lack of student participation and engagement. Stated in positive terms, pilot faculty clearly expected that a blended course design would result in more and better student participation, engagement, communication, and discussion—in short, more and better student-to-student interaction—in their courses.

Did blended learning live up to these expectations? Again, the faculty data supports the conclusion that faculty perceived an increase in both the quality and quantity of student-to-student interactions. Faculty participants were not only satisfied with these results, but were often pleasantly surprised by them. In the reflected narratives especially, faculty remarked that blended learning levels the playing field or enabled everyone in the course to be heard or become visible. Many expressed surprise by the great quantity and quality of peer-to-peer teaching and learning that occurred in their blended courses. Similarly, many faculty members were pleased to see their own role shift from that of imparting knowledge to facilitating learning.

172

Improving Course Communications for All Students

On the whole, students were positive about courses that used a blended learning format. When subgroups of students were examined, deaf and hard-of-hearing students were the most positive. In traditional classes, these students are faced with the challenge of peer and teacher interactions being filtered through a third party, the interpreter.

The results of the present study indicated that the blended learning instructional format offers some appealing advantages for students with hearing loss. The addition of discussion boards and other online tools that facilitate written communication provide ways for deaf and hard of hearing students to interact directly with hearing instructors and peers. Often questions are posted and students are asked to share their answers or opinions based on their reading of course materials and personal experience. Because of the online format, students with hearing loss do not need to go through a third party to respond. They also have more time to compose their responses than they do in a traditional lecture class. Blending allows for a free sharing of opinions and ideas by students who are challenged to do so in a traditional class. They also are able to process and learn from the ideas and opinions of their classmates and instructors without the information going through a third party. In some ways, providing an option for online communication helped level the playing field and allowed these students greater ease of communication with peers and instructors. This may be why over 75% of the students with hearing loss said that other students should have the opportunity to take a class like this in the future.

Conclusion

The purpose of the pilot was to investigate the potential impact that blended learning would have on the teaching and learning environment. Two main reasons explain the decision to base the pilot on asynchronous Internet-based discussion: the successful model that had been established in distance courses using online discussion as a core design element, and the need to use academic technologies effectively. The pilot supported the research evidence that online learning strategies did indeed improve cognitive presence (Garrison et al., 2000; Shea et al., 2001; Garrison & Kanuka, 2004). The Hitt & Hartman (2002) research provided the strategic view of integrating technologies to use them more effectively for all types of learning. The pilot, as measured on these two parameters, was clearly successful. The additional and related findings that students perceived blended learning to improve the quantity and quality of their interaction with other students is important; but, for RIT, what may be more important is that deaf and hard of hearing students found the improvement in communication with other students to be significantly better than even the (hearing) students. What this implies for RIT is that blended learning can provide a cost effective way of significantly improving the teaching and learning environment when deaf and hard of hearing students participate in courses with hearing students and professors. Blended learning clearly helped faculty solve instructional problems; while this finding may not be generalizable, it does seem worthy of further investigation.

Future Research

The opportunities for future research can be grouped in two basic categories: those research opportunities that might apply to all colleges commencing blended learning, and those that remain much more specific to RIT and its unique characteristics. General research questions relating to issues of faculty satisfaction, learning effectiveness, access, and student satisfaction should be investigated. In the faculty satisfaction arena, questions include whether the ability to use technology coupled with academic support lead to a sustainable course redesign. Are traditional, on-campus faculty members more satisfied or effective when introduced to online learning through blended learning, rather than through fully online courses? Does the faculty data or other statistics show that learning outcomes are actually improved in blended learning? Traditional methods of comparing grades and successrates is likely to point to no significant difference as it did at RIT. However, is it important to recognize that blended learning, which offers students a more complicated and integrated set of learning strategies, may require new methodologies for measuring learning effectiveness? Does blended learning better address the communication needs of all learners? Finally, is it important to learn whether student satisfaction is critical to successful blended learning courses?

For RIT, other questions persist. Because an asynchronous discussion model was supported, did we mostly attract faculty who were already interested in and committed to the project of increasing student interaction? If we had promoted or encouraged other options, such learning outside of communities of inquiry or in sophisticated multimedia environments, for example, would we have seen different results in the satisfaction levels and experiences reported by both faculty and students? Does the blended model assist faculty in addressing the many learning styles and needs of students? If students had the information whether a course would be in a blended format before they registered, and an option to choose either a blended or completely face-to-face format, would we have seen different results in our satisfaction levels? Further investigation of the deaf, hard-of- hearing, and ESL students should be conducted to determine whether the blended format, or asynchronous discussion, should be a standard strategy for faculty wishing to establish a healthy learning community within the classroom environment. Is it important to have blended learning as an institutionally supported initiative, or can blended learning flourish with faculty support alone?

References

Amundsen, C. (1993). The evolution of theory in distance education. In D. Keegan (Ed.), *Theoretical principles of distance education* (pp. 61-79). New York: Routledge.

Bransford, J.D., Brown, A.L., & Cocking, R.R. (2000). *How people learn: Brain, mind, experience and school.* National Research Council. Washington, D.C.: National Academy Press.

Dziuban, C., Hartman, J., Moskal, P., Sorg, S., & Truman, B. (2004). Three ALN modalities: An institutional perspective. In J. Bourne & J. C. Moore (Eds.), *Elements of quality online education: Into the mainstream* (pp. 127–148). Needham, MA: Sloan-C.

Garrison, D. R., & Kanuka, H. (2004). Blended learning: Uncovering its transformative potential in higher education. *The Internet and Higher Education, 7*(2), 95–105.

Garrison, D. R, Anderson, T. & Archer, W. (2000). Critical inquiry in a text based environment: Computer conferencing in higher education. *The Internet and Higher Education, 2*(2–3), 1–19.

Garrison, D.R. (1989). *Understanding distance education: A framework for the future.* New York: Routledge.

Harasim, L., Hiltz, S.R., Teles, L. & Turroff, M. (1995). *Learning networks: A field guide to teaching and learning online.* Cambridge: MIT Press.

Hitt, J. C. & Hartman, J.L. (2002). *Distributed learning: New challenges and opportunities for institutional leadership.* Washington, D.C.: American Council on Education, Center for Policy Analysis.

Humbert, J., & Vignare, K. (2004). RIT introduces blended learning—successfully! In J. C. Moore (Ed.), *Elements of quality online education: Engaging communities, wisdom from the Sloan Consortium, Volume 2 in the Wisdom Series.* Needham, MA: Sloan-C.

Keegan, D. (1993). *Theoretical principles of distance education.* New York: Routledge.

Lang, H. (2002). Higher education for deaf students: Research priorities for the new millennium. *Journal of Deaf Education and Deaf Studies, 7*(4), 267–280.

Long, G. & Beil, D. (2005). The importance of direct communication during continuing education workshops for deaf and hard-of-hearing professionals. *Journal of Postsecondary Education and Disability, 1*(8), 5–11.

Mallory, J.R. & Long, G.L., (2003). Learning preferences for deaf and hard of hearing remote, online learners. *Instructional Technology and Education of the Deaf Supporting Learners.* Rochester, NY. Retrieved from http://www.rit.edu/~techsym/2003/detail.html#T3B.

Richardson, J., Long, G., & Woodley, A. (2003). Academic engagement and perceptions of quality in distance education. *Open Learning, 18*(3), 223–244.

Shea, P. J., Swan, K., Fredericksen, E. E., & Pickett, A. (2001). Student satisfaction and reported learning in the SUNY Learning Network. In F. Mayadas, J. Bourne & J.C. Moore (Eds.), *Elements of quality online education, Vol. 3* (pp. 145–156). Needham, MA: Sloan-C.

Stinson, M. & Liu, Y. (1999). Participation of deaf and hard-of-hearing students in classes with hearing students. *Journal of Deaf Studies and Deaf Education, 4*(3), 190–202.

Teaching, Learning, and Technology Group. *Flashlight online data bank.* Retrieved January 16, 2006, from http://www.tltgroup.org/subscription /Matais-II.htm.

Vaughan, N. & Garrison, D.R (2005). Creating cognitive presence in a blended faculty development community. *Internet and Higher Education, 8*(1), 1–12.

Vignare, K. (2002). Longitudinal success measures for online learning students at the Rochester Institute of Technology. In J. Bourne & J. Moore (Eds.), *Elements of quality online education: Practice and direction, Vol. 4* (pp. 261–278). Needham, MA: Sloan-C.

Appendix

*Table 1.*Blended Learning Survey Data Second Year

Question	Disagree	Neutral	Agree
I liked having part of the course online and part of it in the classroom.	21%	15%	61%
I liked learning from online activities.	24%	22%	51%
I learned more about my fellow students because part of this class was online.	42%	23%	32%
I interacted more with other students because part of this course was online.	40%	27%	31%
I had to work harder in this course than I would have if the course had been held only in the classroom.	31%	33%	32%
The professor used a greater variety of teaching resources (e.g. web, print, video) because part of this course was online.	21%	26%	49%
The professor used a greater variety of teaching strategies (e.g. group work, discussion, projects, and testing) because part of this course was online.	17%	21%	57%
The online activities gave me the opportunity to learn in different ways than I do in the classroom.	22%	19%	57%
The technology used for the online portions of this course was reliable.	19%	17%	61%
The time I spent online would have been better spent in the classroom.	41%	23%	32%
The time I spent in the classroom would have been better spent online.	54%	29%	14%
Other students should have the opportunity to take a class like this in the future.	16%	25%	56%
The amount of your interaction with other students (agree or disagree).	22%	35%	39%
The quality of your interaction with other students (agree or disagree).	19%	42%	35%
The amount of your interaction with the professor (agree or disagree).	24%	41%	31%
The quality of your interaction with the professor (agree or disagree).	20%	46%	32%

Table 2. Two Year Comparative Data

Question		Disagree	Neutral	Agree
I liked having part of the course online and part of it in the classroom.	Year 2	21%	15%	61%
	Year 1	17%	11%	72%
The time I spent online would have been better spent in the classroom.	Year 2	41%	23%	32%
	Year 1	50%	23%	27%
The professor used a greater variety of teaching resources (e.g. web, print, video) because part of this course was online.	Year 2	21%	26%	49%
	Year 1	23%	24%	53%
The professor used a greater variety of teaching strategies (e.g. group work, discussion, projects, and testing) because part of this course was online.	Year 2	17%	21%	57%
	Year 1	16%	16%	68%
Other students should have the opportunity to take a class like this in the future.	Year 2	16%	25%	56%
	Year 1	8%	21%	71%
The amount of your interaction with other students (agree or disagree).	Year 2	22%	35%	39%
	Year 1	19%	30%	51%
The quality of your interaction with other students (agree or disagree).	Year 2	19%	42%	35%
	Year 1	15%	37%	49%
The amount of your interaction with the professor (agree or disagree).	Year 2	24%	41%	31%
	Year 1	23%	45%	32%
The quality of your interaction with the professor (agree or disagree).	Year 2	20%	46%	32%
	Year 1	17%	49%	34%

Reactive Behavior, Ambivalence, and the Generations: Emerging Patterns in Student Evaluation of Blended Learning

Charles Dziuban
Patsy Moskal
Linda Futch
University of Central Florida

Introduction

As higher education responds to technological advances, blended learning is becoming a preferred model for using the Internet to maximize instructional effectiveness. Growing interest in this instructional mode is evident by the number of books, articles, and presentations that describe its application to higher education and industry (Bonk & Graham, 2006; Dziuban, Hartman & Moskal, 2005; Dziuban, Hartman & Moskal, 2004; Dziuban, Hartman, Juge, Moskal, & Sorg, 2006). With a prevailing use of technology among younger students, one is not surprised at the proliferation of blended approaches in higher education. Vail (2005) found that 90% of students between ages 5 and 17 use computers, while 94% of teens use the Internet for schoolwork. Similarly, McHugh (2005) found that 86% of students between ages 8–18 owned computers and 74% had Internet access. Blending allows faculty to enhance and improve course instruction, accommodate broader strategic institutional initiatives, experience professional growth, and discern better interaction with their students. At the same time, students express satisfaction with their blended courses, preferring a combination of face-to-face and online learning. In economic terms, blended learning reduces opportunity costs for students, thus making college more attractive and accessible to them.

No universal definition for blended learning currently prevails. With definitions predominantly based on the proportion of face-to-face and online learning (50%–50%, 60%–40%, etc.), determinations vary by institution, discipline, and even instructor. This phenomenon requires what Lakoff (1990) calls a prototype: the best example of the category "blended learning." To better understand this definition challenge, consider an example of Diamond's (1999) *blueprint copying* versus *idea transmission*. If someone visited the University of Central Florida (UCF), observed our blended learning components, and decided to replicate them at his or her university, that is *blueprint copying*. If that visitor, however, arrived on campus and became aware of our blended learning program, but had no details, and decided blending had potential, then designed a program with no

UCF elements, that is *idea transmission*. Because varying circumstances and differing contexts exist on college campuses, *idea transmission* is the approach by which blended learning develops in higher education. The possibilities of *blueprint copying* are remote because blended learning is by nature flexible and adaptable. We hope our research fosters *idea transmission*.

Study Concept

We examine three separate theories that have meaning for blended learning—sociological through generational cohorts, psychological through reactive behavior, and metaphoric through ambivalence. The statistical methods that we employ to examine these theories include principal components, Monte Carlo analysis, and decision trees. Figure 1 illustrates our model.

We examine generational cohorts (Oblinger, 2003; Wendover, 2002) to determine students' satisfaction with their blended learning experiences mediated by the political, economic, technological, and social influences of the time period in which they matured. Employing the theory of reactive behavior (Long, 1975), we examine students' satisfaction through the template that they use to communicate and react to blending learning courses—a notion analogous to learning styles, but grounded in energy levels and need for approval. We then examine the interaction between students' reactive behavior and their generational cohorts mediated by metaphors of ambivalence.

Figure 1. **Study Design**

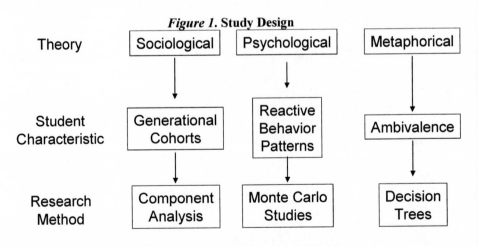

The survey in this study involves relatively standard construction, sampling, and data collection techniques, however, the scaling and analysis deviate from methods in similar research studies. We address specific difficulties with rating scale investigation by rescaling data to accommodate student ambivalence toward blended learning.

The Theories

Generations

Student generational research focuses on the environmental forces that shape students' interactions in their academic and personal lives. It also provides understanding about how these forces impact learners' reactions and communication with professors and each other, and how they obtain and evaluate information. There are four generational cohorts on campuses today, but the *Mature* generation, born prior to 1946, is barely represented in our blended classes or on campus at all. Because of this, we exclude them from our analyses.

Baby Boomers, born from 1946–1964, have had a tremendous impact on American society, changing our economy in profound ways (Howe & Strauss, 2000; Lancaster & Stillman, 2002; Wendover, 2002). This generation of 80 million grew up in a period of rapid and sustained economic growth. This economic sense of security allowed Boomers to enjoy a comfortable lifestyle. They moved to the suburbs, discovered credit spending, and had no problem with debt service. Boomers live by the mantra "optimism." They think anything is within their grasp. Even as they experienced increased divorce rates, the brink of nuclear war, the Cuban missile crisis, and the Vietnam War, Boomers remained optimistic. They are nostalgic about their youth, exemplified by the number of "golden oldies" radio stations now available. The single most important technological development in this period was the television; it permitted Boomers to experience real time world events. For them, technologies such as microcomputers and programming languages were just evolving. Today, many Boomers occupy high positions in government, education, and industry.

Generation X, born from 1965–1980, experienced the overwhelming impact of technology and the media in their lives (Coupland, 1991; Oblinger, 2003; Wendover, 2002). Born in the chaotic time of Watergate, the Jonestown massacre, corporate downsizing, AIDS, the Challenger explosion, and the Exxon Valdez oil spill, Gen Xers are skeptics: about education, government, and industry. They were the first "latch-key kids," who spent part of their day at home unsupervised because both parents worked, an experience that taught them resourcefulness. Gen Xers never experienced a world without TV, MTV, CNN, and cable channels, and they expect to be entertained. They experienced an historic proliferation of information technology. Gen Xers live in the present and focus on their personal well-being. Frequent job changes are commonplace and money is only a part of their larger perspective about life—this generation works to live instead of living to work. Older generations might view them as disrespectful because they are outspoken.

Millennials, born from 1981–1994, come to campus with a complement of skills and attitudes that have changed the academy (Howe & Strauss, 2000; Oblinger & Oblinger, 2005; Prensky, 2001). They have more technology experience than any other generation—including the majority of their professors. Millennials, also, live in the present and expect immediacy of technology. They respond well to group activity, relate to their parents' values, showcase their abilities, and participate in service activities. Millennials have well developed visual-spatial skills acquired by electronic game use. Allegedly, Millennials multitask and change contexts seamlessly and expect this from others. Today's media bombards them with messages that tell them what to think, buy, wear, and eat. These students readily acknowledge that the Internet is their first source of information. Howe and Strauss (2000) assert that Millennials are the most diverse generation in history and are much more capable intellectually than those cohorts that preceded. Generally, Millennials feel that they are at the frontier of progress.

Reactive Behavior

Long (1975, 1985, 1989), in training practitioners in adolescent medicine, developed his theory of reactive behavior that has proved to be a useful alternative for assessing learning styles in blended learning. The model builds a typology of how students react and communicate in various educational situations predicated on energy levels and the need for approval. Long and Dziuban (Dziuban, Moskal, & Dziuban, 2000) developed and validated an assessment protocol that allows students to accurately classify themselves in the typology so that instructors can determine their learning preferences. The instrument identifies four Long types and four ancillary traits that modify the basic types. The distributed learning program at the University of Central Florida is using reactive behavior pattern theory to improve online and blended learning by working with groups of instructors and students in a collaborative effort to develop communication methods with students and to increase their engagement in the learning process.

Students classify themselves into one of four categories: Aggressive Independent, Passive Independent, Aggressive Dependent, or Passive Dependent.

Aggressive Independents (AIs) are energetic and outspoken. Because they are independent, they do not need approval from their peers or instructors. AIs bring energy to class and create a lively atmosphere in both face-to-face and online situations. Their preferred method for resolving disagreement, stress, or ambiguity, is confrontation that can sometimes make them appear argumentative. They have no problem challenging the instructor and prefer direct and succinct treatment. Occasionally, they can act or speak out before thinking which can get them into trouble. Aggressive Independents have innate leadership ability and are often in positions of authority and responsibility in their peer groups, and subsequently in life.

Passive Independents (PIs) exhibit lower energy levels and are unmotivated by approval. Because they are non-communicative, instructors regard them as students who prefer to work alone. PIs interpret directions or constructive criticism as nagging and they passively resist expectations. Their independent nature makes them appear stubborn, especially when they fail to meet deadlines. Eventually, instructors become frustrated with these students' non-engagement in courses. In the online environment, professors must verify that the Passive Independents are keeping up with postings and other day-to-day aspects of the class. Without the need for approval, these students are not persuaded by outside influences when making decisions. As they mature, they become strong, self-sufficient individuals who can be relied on in almost any situation.

Aggressive Dependents (ADs) have the same high energy levels as their Aggressive Independent counterparts, but derive pleasure and motivation from the approval of their peers and teachers. ADs are the achievers of the world. In class, they are the first to speak up, volunteer and complete their assignments on time. These students thrive on harmony and they accommodate and facilitate interactions with their peers and instructors. Disapproval or criticism is distasteful to these students. Often, they achieve leadership positions in athletics, co-curricular activities, service organizations, and honor societies. Interestingly, the leadership role can make them uncomfortable and ineffective because leaders can be challenged and criticized. ADs pressure themselves to excel and please, behavior that causes more anxiety. Aggressive Dependents, however, accomplish most tasks they undertake and derive great pleasure from a job well done.

Passive Dependents (PDs) are caring, sensitive, and affectionate students, who accommodate their instructors and peers. They follow directions exactly and derive satisfaction from another's approval. PDs prefer a supportive role, in which expectations are clear. They can be perceived, however, as overly compliant and interpret criticism as personal rejection. Instructors need to help these students take initiative and realize that we all make mistakes. These students are consistent and cooperative and are often employed in care-giving positions, social work, and community service.

The Long Traits

The Long types are moderated by four traits. Students can possess any combination of these traits, from none to all.

Phobic students are thoughtful and careful about their work. They are reluctant to rush to conclusions, a positive when facing multiple possibilities and alternatives, but a hindrance when responding to assessment devices such as multiple choice tests. If a problem contains multiple possible solutions, however, the phobic student will meticulously sift through the alternatives. Their preferred assessment modes include simulations, scenarios, games, and actual workplace case studies.

Compulsive students in the learning environment are organized, efficient, methodical and possess self discipline. These students are inherently tenacious when completing work and solving problems, a trait that, if taken to extremes, can become ritualistic and impede progress. Lack of spontaneity, in certain academic situations, can frustrate and exhaust these students, especially without methodical preparation.

Impulsive students in the classroom situation are energetic, never dull, and they can use this energy to motivate other students. Sometimes, however, they are capricious, as when answering a question before the instructor has finished asking it. Their motto is "damn the torpedoes." They will push buttons until something happens: either solving the problem or crashing the machine. If the latter occurs, they will likely abandon the assignment and move on to another.

Hysteric students are interesting, colorful, dramatic, compassionate, and entertaining. Their behavior creates a positive environment filled with contagious energy. Hysterics, however, are also attracted to crises, bringing disorganization, chaos, and histrionics to the classroom situation and their personal lives. Triggers include a failed examination, a poor grade for an assignment, or computer connection problems. Online instructors can be flooded with e-mail messages from just one hysteric when a problem arises, real or imaginary. When planning group presentations, we include some hysterics in the first group with some compulsive Aggressive Dependents. The compulsive, overachieving Aggressive Dependents get the work done and the hysterics make the presentation interesting and entertaining.

Ambivalence

Underpinning Long's reactive behavior theory is ambivalence—the simultaneously counterpoised feelings toward a given set of stimuli. The confusion an adolescent feels when striving to become independent, yet still wanting to be dependent, is ambivalence. Long considers adolescence as a behavioral stage rather than a chronological or developmental period, noting that many adults exhibit adolescent behavior. Students, therefore, react ambivalently to stimuli that they encounter at these stages in their lives: leaving home for college, changing their relationships with their parents and instructors, serving in the military, responding to the pressures of social life, choosing an academic major, or taking blended courses.

Lakoff and Johnson (2003) provide insight into the nature of ambivalence by their research on metaphors. They contend that most of our conceptual functioning is metaphorical and that without realizing, we use metaphors in our day-to-day living. Metaphors structure our perceptions and understanding, how we relate to others, and how we act. They reflect our ideas and shape how we think.

Consider *argument* as a prevailing metaphor for *war*:

That criticism was right on *target*.

Okay, *shoot*

If you use that *strategy* he will *wipe you out* (p. 4).

Another example is that *time is money*: that flat tire *cost* me an hour (p. 8). We also use metaphors related to our physical orientation: things are looking *up* or things are at an all time *low* (p. 16). Meyer (2005) emphasizes that computer and technology language is replete with metaphors. The Web is a metaphor for the Internet that led to the term "browser," a term borrowed from browsing the stacks in the library. Metaphorically, at times, we become one with the computer as in "I was surfing the Web last night" (p. 1604).

Literature also provides many examples of ambivalence that enrich our understanding: Edna Pontellier in *The Awakening* (Chopin, 1899), Nel in *Sula* (Morrison, 1973) and Stephen Dedalus in *A Portrait of the Artist as a Young Man* (Joyce, 1916) are just three examples of protagonists whose major motivating force was ambivalence. The archetype for ambivalence is in Shakespeare's (1604) *Hamlet*. We recognize common metaphors of ambivalence in our everyday speech:

Metaphor	Ambivalent Language
Weapon	It's a double-edged sword *and* It's a corollary that cuts both ways
Body part	On the other hand
Performance	That's a balancing act
Boundary	Both sides of the fence
Color	It's a gray area
Position	The ins and outs of a situation
Distance	Neither here nor there

The Study

The investigators distributed the student satisfaction instrument to 14,794 students that enrolled in a blended course section from Summer 2004 through Fall 2005. They electronically invited students to participate and provided a link to the survey webpage. Students returned 980 questionnaires that investigators coded for analysis. With no accurate way to determine how many students actually received and opened the e-mail, it is impossible to know the exact number of instruments that reached the intended audience. A reminder e-mail was sent approximately one week after the initial e-mail.

The 22-item questionnaire asked students to provide a demographic profile and to answer several questions related to their satisfaction with blended learning. Questions addressed overall satisfaction, amount and quality of interaction with other students, amount and quality of interaction with the instructor, course organization, and the degree to which class activities encompassed online assignments. These evaluative questions appeared in the five-point Likert format ranging from strongly positive to strongly negative with a neutral point. Students also provided a number of written comments about their blended experiences and indicated their preferred Long-Dziuban types and traits. Demographic questions indexed age, ethnicity, and academic level.

The Analysis

The Rating Scales

As is characteristic with five-point Likert scales, the distribution of responses was not even for each of the categories. Although it appears that the distances among the points on the scale are equal, they are not equidistant. Likert built the scales on the cumulative frequencies in the unit normal distribution so that the scale point distances determine themselves by the proportion of responses in each category. For example, the distance between two adjacent categories (e.g., agree and strongly agree) in which one category has very few responses and the other has a large number of responses is much further than one unit because the scale points move a long way in the cumulative distribution. The only way the point distances will become equal is when 20% of the responses fall into each of the five categories. A common strategy with these data, therefore, is to combine them (e.g. agree and strongly agree) into one response set. The problem with this procedure, however, is that it "washes out" the responses when making comparisons with demographic and other variables. When Likert (1932) designed his scale, he knew of this consequence and item response theorists have attempted to accommodate it in recent years.

A typical rating scale item might take the form:

1	2	3	4	5
Very Unsatisfied	Unsatisfied	Neutral	Satisfied	Very Satisfied

In theory, it seems reasonable that students responding at the extreme points of the scale should express less ambivalence toward blended learning than those in a more central position. Examining some typical responses for the very satisfied category we find:

- *"With partially online classes, it is nice not to waste time in class taking tests or tests that we can do at home. In partially online classes, instructors usually organize course[s] better and make better use of time."*
- *"They are very well organized and instructors are very clear and concise on what is to be done since you may not be able to ask questions as in a face-to-face class."*
- *"I used new technology with excellent feedback for instructor and GTA, like instant results on graded work."*

These responses are typical of highly satisfied students and show very little ambivalence toward blended learning.

Examining a similar set of response for students in the very unsatisfied category we find:

- *"The group projects are difficult. We spend so little time with each other. We have to get together at inconvenient times and locations. Also, we can't build a relationship on one and a half hours per week. It is awkward."*
- *"The face-to-face portion was inconvenient and totally unnecessary."*
- *"The whole course was a challenge for me. For my personal learning style, I cannot do online or mixed mode classes. I need a physical person lecturing and me physically taking notes."*

There is very little ambivalence in the comments of these students. They are unequivocal in their dissatisfaction.

Finally we submit some responses from the neutral category.

- *"I like submitting assignments online but I worry about my computer skills. Sometimes I just don't know what to do."*
- *"The subject matter in the partially online course was extremely complex, and despite passing the class I don't understand the majority of it."*
- *"Online learning gives the same attention to every student. Although I learn well by myself, others may not, and others may require face-to-face interaction."*

These statements are typical of students that respond nearer the midpoint of the scale. Each one demonstrates mixed feelings toward the blended learning experience. Almost all responses from students in the middle have some form of "on the other hand" a "double edged sword" or a "shade of gray." We suggest that the ambivalence model for these rating scales conforms to Figure 2 where the strongly positive and strongly negative points convey very little ambivalence. The middle three categories, however, all confound with some degree of uncertainty that produces a strong noise to signal ratio.

Figure 2. **Levels of Ambivalence in Likert Scale Choices**

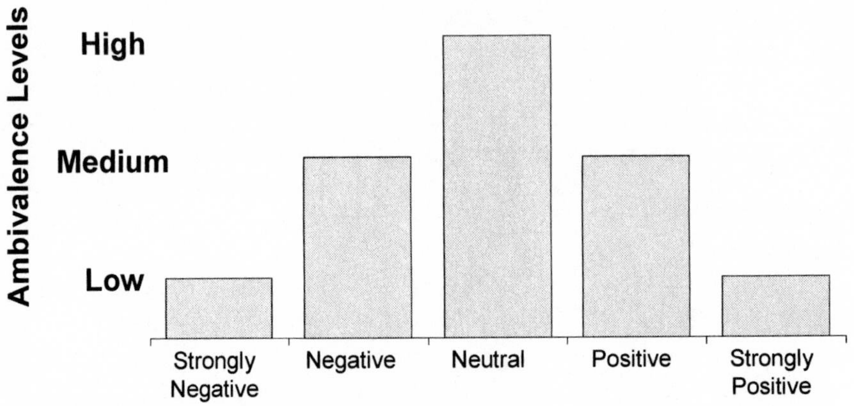

We, therefore, rescaled the measures according to the following protocol:
- Strongly positive or not as a 1 or 0, respectively
- Strongly negative or not as a 1 or 0, respectively
- In one of the three middle categories or not (ambivalent) as a 1 or 0, respectively.

These binary responses were outcome measures for student satisfaction, dissatisfaction, and ambivalence with blended learning.

A Demonstration of Ambivalence at Work

To assess the impact of ambivalent responses on the analysis of student satisfaction responses, we conducted principal component analyses (Hotelling, 1933) of student responses under four scoring protocols: the scales in their original formats (1 through 5), positive but not ambivalent, negative but not ambivalent, and ambivalent. Components were retained according to the eigenvalues of the correlation matrices greater than one and transformed according to the promax criterion (Henderickson & White, 1964). We used these procedures to determine if what Thurstone (1935) called *simple structure*, applies to the data. If so, then each variable in the solution "loads" with only one component, and indicates an underlying clarity in structure. When this is not the case, students' responses to a single question "load" on multiple components so that it becomes impossible to determine to which dimensions a student is responding. These complex variable solutions are undesirable in component analysis because they usually negate any meaningful interpretation. The transformed pattern matrices for the four scoring protocols are presented in Table 1.

Table 1. **Promax Transformed Component Solutions for Student Responses to Blended Learning Under Four Scoring Protocols**

Solution	1		2		3		4	
	1–5 Scoring		Positive Non-Ambivalent		Negative Non-Ambivalent		Ambivalent	
	1	2	1	2	1	2	1	2
Overall satisfaction	33	76		70		52		72
Amount of interaction with other students	87		82		87		77	
Quality of interaction with other students	87		82		89		80	
Amount of interaction with the instructor	77	33	42		76		81	
Quality of interaction with the instructor	75	45	81		76		82	
Course was well organized		87		89		72		86
Online assignments fit the course		84		87		71		85

*Decimals omitted—pattern coefficients >30

Solution one, for the scales in their original form (1 to 5 ratings containing ambivalent responses), produced a complex component matrix with several variables loading (>.3) on more than one component: overall satisfaction, amount of interaction with the instructor, and quality of interaction with the instructor. These confounds hinge on students' evaluations of their interaction with the instructor and their overall satisfaction. The other three solutions (2, 3 and 4) that accounted for ambivalence by either eliminating it (extreme positive or negative satisfaction) or by using ambivalence as an outcome measure all produced much clearer patterns showing easily identifiable "interaction" and "effectiveness" components.

Interaction between the Generations and Reactive Behavior

Table 2 presents the percentage of Long reactive behavior types that participated in blended learning courses by generational cohort. The Monte Carlo probability of .006 indicates that the two theories are not independent. The most noteworthy differences in types by the generations occur for Aggressive Independents and Passive Dependents. Approximately twice the proportion of Baby Boomers designated themselves as Aggressive

Independents than did Generation X or Millennial students. This seems consistent with both theories. The optimistic and free-spirited Baby Boomers, who rebelled against the establishment in their early years and assumed leadership positions later in life, seem compatible with the energized lifestyle of Aggressive Independents. Generation X's philosophy—"every personal relationship is a negotiated contract"—is much less compatible with Aggressive Independent behavior. Millennial students, who accept parental values and tendencies and tend to conform, also seem less compatible with this behavior. Millennials described themselves as Passive Dependents three times more than Baby Boomers, again validating the assumption that they adopt the values of their parents and society. Table 2 yields one additional conclusion: the largest single proportion of students in college tend to be Aggressive Dependent, a type that thrives on achievement.

***Table 2.* Percentage of Long Types in the Generations Registering for Blended Learning Courses**

	Aggressive Independent	Passive Independent	Aggressive Dependent	Passive Dependent	n
Boomers	31	19	47	4	130
Gen X	15	23	50	11	123
Millennials	18	19	48	14	684
n	199	166	452	120	

*Decimals omitted, percentages rounded   Monte Carlo p=.006

Table 3 presents the intersection of the Long traits with the generations. The table represents a summary of four separate analyses because the traits may attach themselves to any one type individually. Therefore, the columns should be read separately with each having a significance test of proportional differences. The results show substantial changes in Long traits across the generations. Millennials claim to be phobic learners at higher rates than the other generations, indicating a tendency to work cautiously and carefully in their blended learning classes. This finding runs counter to most theorists, who speculate that this generation parallel processes with tasks and operates at quick speed. Millennials and Generation Xs are less compulsive than Baby Boomers, another finding that is also inconsistent with theory. Most researchers believe that the Millennial generation are the most driven in history—even more so than the Baby Boomers, who strive for perfection. In Table 3, Millennial students are, however, significantly more impulsive than the other two generations—a finding much more consistent with current beliefs. They never read the directions and they learn by doing, pressing buttons until they learn how it works. Millennials also show more hysteric tendencies than Baby Boomers or Generation X students. Once again, this finding validates this generation's propensity to show compassion and perform community service, a prevailing characteristic of hysterics. These major changes in traits across generations deserve further study because they have potential for impacting pedagogy and instructional design in technology-mediated learning, especially since some of these findings contradict current theory and practice.

Table 3. **Percentage of Generational Cohorts Displaying Each of the Long Traits**

	Phobic	Compulsive	Impulsive	Hysteric	n
Boomers	38	82	15	20	131
Gen X	44	67	21	25	124
Millennials	56	68	27	32	695
p (Monte Carlo)	.000	.015	.009	.031	
n	494	663	234	280	

*Decimals omitted, percentages rounded

Student Satisfaction by Demographics

Examining the correlation matrix among the seven rating scales mentioned in Table 1, the largest positive vector related overall student satisfaction with the remaining six variables. All were moderately positive and statistically significant. This finding led the researchers to focus on overall satisfaction as the outcome measure. Replication of these methods with the other six scales, however, produced identical results to the findings reported here. Correlation analysis of three binary measures (satisfied, dissatisfied, and ambivalent) showed them to be virtually independent, accounting for less than 1% of pairwise variance.

Table 4 presents the percentages of satisfied, dissatisfied, and ambivalent students in blending learning by gender, work status, and academic level. A typical pattern emerges in the data for student satisfaction. The highest percentage of students in all cases is ambivalent. This finding is a function of two considerations, one an artifact, another possibly a noteworthy outcome. Our first consideration is an artifact because the researchers used three original scale points to place students in the ambivalent category: satisfied, neutral, and dissatisfied. The authors considered using "satisfied" and "unsatisfied" as threshold points, but decided that the middle three scale positions each contained some degree of ambivalence, and therefore combined the three categories into "ambivalent." This point is arguable and thresholds should be investigated in further research. Our second consideration may be important, suggesting a genuinely large percentage of students hold some ambivalence toward blended learning.

Table 4. **Percentage of Satisfied, Dissatisfied, and Ambivalent Student Responses to Blended Learning by Gender, Work Status, and Academic Level**

	Satisfied	Dissatisfied	Ambivalent	n
Gender				
Male	26	5	69	704
Female	35	4	61	239
p	.005	.338	.041	
Work Status				
Full-time	38	4	58	356
Part-time	31	4	65	354
None	28	6	66	236
p	.031	.539	.072	
Academic Level				
Lower Undergraduate	25	6	69	208
Upper Undergraduate	34	5	66	434
Graduate	36	2	62	289
p	.014	.146	.073	
n	305	40	587	

*Decimals omitted, percentages rounded

Table 4 shows that females are significantly more satisfied and less ambivalent toward blended learning than males, full-time workers are more satisfied than part-time workers or the unemployed, and graduate students are more satisfied than undergraduates. Each of these findings is consistent with several years of research on blended and online learning at the University of Central Florida (http://rite.ucf.edu). Overall, a small percentage of the students express dissatisfaction with blended learning and the differences are not significant across demographic categories. The ambivalence measures, although large, show no significant differences in examining employment or academic level in the blended environment.

Student Satisfaction by Generation and Reactive Behavior

Table 5 depicts the satisfaction, dissatisfaction, and ambivalence status of the generational cohorts and Long reactive behavior pattern types. Millennials are significantly less satisfied and more ambivalent toward their blended experience than the Boomer or Gen X cohorts. Speculation indicates that when institutional technologies are not consistent with Millennials' personal technologies, they are less satisfied (AASCU, 2004).

The response patterns for the Long behavior categories show that Passive Dependent students tend to exhibit a somewhat lower satisfaction rate (p=.084) with their blended learning experiences when compared to the other types. They are also significantly (p=.010) more ambivalent. These findings concur with earlier results indicating that Passive Dependents do not respond as favorably to fully online environments as other types (Dziuban, Moskal, & Dziuban, 2000). The dissatisfaction responses, like previous trends, show only minimal differences in the generations or Long types.

Table 5. **Percentage of Satisfied, Dissatisfied, and Ambivalent Student Responses to Blended Learning by Generations and Long Type**

	Satisfied	Dissatisfied	Ambivalent	n
Generations				
Boomer	41	3	56	131
Gen X	43	5	52	124
Millennial	29	5	66	695
p	.002	.717	.002	
Long Type				
Aggressive Independent	38	7	55	206
Passive Independent	31	3	66	169
Aggressive Dependent	33	4	63	461
Passive Dependent	24	4	72	122
p	.084	.139	.010	
n	311	42	594	

*Decimals omitted, percentages rounded

Table 6 shows perplexing results for the satisfaction, dissatisfaction, and ambivalence levels for the Long ancillary traits. Table 3 contained rather dramatic changes in the trait affiliations across generation, however, the student ratings of blended learning by their traits produced only trivial differences. Once again, this raises the question of what satisfaction interactions exist in the generation and reactive behavior pattern systems.

Table 6. **Percentage of Satisfied, Dissatisfied, and Ambivalent Responses to Blended Learning by Long Traits**

	Satisfied	Dissatisfied	Ambivalent	n
Phobic	35	2	63	492
Compulsive	33	4	63	660
Impulsive	31	4	65	234
Hysteric	32	5	63	279
p	.693	.834	.899	
n	311	42	592	

*Decimals omitted, percentages rounded

Interactions and Decision Trees

To predict student satisfaction interaction by generations and reactive behavior in blended learning, the investigators used classification and regression trees (CART) (Breiman et al., 1984). Tree methods are recursive and bisect data into disjoint subgroups called terminate nodes or leaves. CART analysis involves three stages of analysis: data spitting, pruning, and homogenous assessment. In our study, the dependent measures were student satisfaction, dissatisfaction, and ambivalence, and the predictor variables were demographic status, generation, and the Long membership categories. Through a series of decision rules, CART assesses which of the variables that best predicts, after examining each of the candidates. Then the procedure begins building a tree-like structure by splitting the first predictor in two homogenous nodes or leaves. The process begins again by finding the second best predictor of student satisfaction and splits those into subcategories under the first two nodes. The tree continues to split until the numbers in the nodes become extremely small or all observations in a subset belong to one category. Typically, this growing procedure results in far too many nodes for the model to be useful, therefore, researchers solve this problem by a pruning procedure that reduces the dimensionality of the system. The final step of decision tree analysis validates the original model on a data set that has been kept out of the development phase. There are several advantages to the decision tree procedure. The procedure accommodates all possible interactions among the variables, efficiently handles missing data by building surrogates from the remaining predictor variables, and produces rules that have an if-then structure that is intuitive, easily understood, and practically applicable.

Table 7 presents the important decision rules for satisfaction, dissatisfaction, and ambivalence across demographic characteristics of blended learning students. The most effective rule for satisfaction shows that full-time employed, upper undergraduate females are approximately 1.4 times more likely to be satisfied than an individual selected at random from the population. Full-time or unemployed undergraduate males were approximately 2 times more likely to be dissatisfied with their blended learning course. The rule for ambivalence shows that males, who are working part-time or are unemployed, are, on average, slightly more ambivalent about blended learning.

Table 7. Decision Rules for the CART Analysis for Predicting Student Satisfaction, Dissatisfaction, and Ambivalence toward Blended Learning Using Gender, Employment, and Academic Class

Satisfied
p=.328

	Male	Female	Work Full-time	Work Part-time	Not Employed	Lower Under-graduate	Upper Under-graduate	Graduate Student	Probability
Rule1		•	•					•	.467

Dissatisfied
p=.043

	Male	Female	Work Full-time	Work Part-time	Not Employed	Lower Under-graduate	Upper Under-graduate	Graduate Student	Probability
Rule 2	•		•		•	•	•		.095

Ambivalent
p=.623

	Male	Female	Work Full-time	Work Part-time	Not Employed	Lower Under-graduate	Upper Under-graduate	Graduate Student	Probability
Rule 3	•			•	•				.706

Table 8 shows the predictive interactions among the generations, Long types, and traits. Rule 1 for satisfaction indicates that Passive Dependent, Millennial students are about half as likely as the average for the population to express satisfaction with their blended courses. Rule 2 shows that if a student is a member of the Generation X or the Baby Boomers, then he or she is about 1.4 times more likely to be satisfied.

Rule 1 for dissatisfaction depicts students who are Passive Independent or Aggressive Dependent and hysteric are 1.7 times more likely to be dissatisfied than the average blended learning student. Rule 2 shows that students, who are either Aggressive Independent or Passive Dependent, have 2.4 times the chance of being dissatisfied. When examining ambivalence, generational and Long theories produce two important decision rules. Students that belong to Generation X or Baby Boomers are less likely to be ambivalent than the average for the population. Millennial students who are Passive Dependent, however, are somewhat more likely to express ambivalence toward the blended learning environment.

Table 8. Decision Rules for the CART Analysis for Predicting Student Satisfaction, Dissatisfaction, and Ambivalence toward Blended Learning Using Generation, Long Type, and Long Traits

Satisfied
p=.327

	Boomer	Gen X	Millennial	AI	PI	AD	PD	Phobic	Compulsive	Impulsive	Hysteric	Probability
Rule 1			•			•						.188
Rule 2	•	•										.460

Dissatisfied
p=.044

	Boomer	Gen X	Millennial	AI	PI	AD	PD	Phobic	Compulsive	Impulsive	Hysteric	Probability
Rule 1				•		•					•	.074
Rule 2			•			•						.109

Ambivalent
p=.623

	Boomer	Gen X	Millennial	AI	PD	AD	PD	Phobic	Compulsive	Impulsive	Hysteric	Probability
Rule 1	•	•										.473
Rule 2			•			•						.772

Demographically, upper division, full-time employed females have the higher probability of being satisfied, while undergraduate, unemployed or full-time employed males are most likely to be dissatisfied. Ambivalent students tend to be male and are either unemployed or working part-time. Baby Boomers and Generation X students are most apt to show satisfaction with blended learning. Millennials are less likely to be satisfied. Dissatisfied students tend to be Aggressive Independent or Passive Dependent. Ambivalence tends to show up most often in Millennials who are Passive Dependent.

Conclusion

We have attempted to build some predictive models for student satisfaction, dissatisfaction, and ambivalence in blended learning environments. The concept of blended learning varies widely in universities depending on many considerations. We contend, therefore, that blending learning is a mental model that is evolving, rather than a well-defined pedagogical entity.

Figure 1 depicts the interactive design that guided the study. We emphasize interaction in this study to argue that interactions among various student components, such as generation and reactive behavior, affect student satisfaction and predict more effectively than separate elements. Blended learning is not a main effect that can be summarized with one hypothesis test or summary statement. An investigator enters difficult territory when attempting to answer the question: "Is blended learning more or less effective than face-to-face instruction?" They face a conundrum: a simple questioned answered incorrectly (Is blended learning effective?) or a complex question answered correctly (What are the interactions?). The real answer is "it depends."

The metaphorical emphasis in this study addresses our use of representational language to portray reality. As Meyer (2005) points out, distance education and blended learning are metaphors themselves that in many respects constrain our thinking and creativity. These two labels are good examples of how language creates a context in which we operate. Meyer raises an interesting question: What if asynchronous learning networks or online learning and blended learning simply became *learning?* This creates a whole new theory suggesting that education transpires by multiple means, modalities, and approaches that incorporate the sociology, psychology, and metaphorical language of education.

The Interactions

The interplay of generational cohorts, Long types, and ambivalence creates the measurement model for the study. Each of these categories involves a prototype. For example, our characterization of Millennial students defines what Lakoff (1990) terms a stylized best example. Not every student in the Millennial age group acts like the Millennial students we have characterized as valuing personal technologies and a digital lifestyle. What, then, are the mediating variables that create these variations in students? The answer lies in the Long reactive behaviors and the ambivalence levels of students in blended learning courses. Passive Dependent, phobic students, for example, do not follow typical Millennial characteristics in their behavior because they show more uncertainty towards blended learning than their more aggressive peers. When we created student satisfaction categories for blended learning, we suggested that ambivalence was the prevailing posture. By "trichotomizing" student evaluations, we arbitrarily created a device that portrays the complexity of satisfaction with blended learning.

Expertise

To blend well takes time and experience for students, instructors, and the institution. Berliner (1998) argues that there is taxonomy of expertise in teaching and learning that begins with the novice, in which case the elements and tasks must be defined so that the instructor can operate in a set of context-free rules. Frequently, instructors who are experts in their discipline areas are novices with technology. Initially, they focus on the materials to present online rather than what to present face-to-face. Invariably, the novice instructors define their courses as part face-to-face and part Web-based. When more experienced, however, they begin to develop a more strategic approach to their teaching and focus more on the course as a whole, rather than two distinct segments: online vs. face-to-face. According to Berliner (1998), they develop a sense for the situation and begin to recognize general patterns. Intuitively, they describe a dynamic environment, guided by student participation and reflection with a self-sustaining energy.

After more than a decade, many instructors no longer think in terms of blended learning courses. They have become experts, operating in a fluid teaching and learning space. They have made the transition from literacy to fluency, managing difficulty extremely well. These instructors do not consciously choose how to integrate technology into their teaching, but operate in an effortless flow that is only interrupted when an anomaly occurs, at which time they evoke analytic skills derived from their years of experience. Like fluency, expertise takes time.

The Instructor Role in Student Satisfaction

It may seem odd to conclude a paper on student satisfaction by discussing faculty progression toward expertise, but we have argued (Hartman, Dziuban, & Moskal, 2000) that student satisfaction depends on faculty satisfaction and vice versa. Adams (1997), however, finds little evidence to relate student satisfaction to learning outcomes or persistence, and Kolitch and Dean (1999) contend that most approaches to student evaluation of instruction particularize items that correspond to the transmission of information models for teaching and learning. This defines an effective course in an excessively narrow context.

We believe, however, that student expression of satisfaction with their blended learning courses is an accurate and reliable measure of quality, valid against many external indicators such as course quality, and impervious to potentially biasing factors, such as class size, level, discipline, and required vs. elective. Many instructors, working in the online learning environment, use Garrison's (2005) work in cognitive, social, and teaching presence as the benchmark for quality and satisfaction. Decades earlier and prior to the advent of Web-based teaching and learning, researchers such as Feldman (1976) suggested presentation, facilitation, and regulation as

198

components to measure student satisfaction. These components have a distinctive correspondence to cognitive, social, and teaching presence, although developed in a different context. March and Roche (1997) designed a much more complex model of assessment and satisfaction that includes learning value, instructor engagement, organization, interaction, rapport, breadth, learning assessment, class assignments, and workload. Dziuban, Wang and Cook (2004) provide the methods for this paper and advance that the predictors of student satisfaction in any modality include the instructor's ability to facilitate learning, communicate ideas and concepts effectively, show interest in student learning, show respect for students, organize his or her course, and assess student progress. The work of all these authors, whether in blended learning or not, corresponds closely to the components of the National Study of Student Engagement (Kuh, 2001). That study identifies quality and satisfaction in terms of interaction, collaborative learning, active learning, supportive environments, and academic challenge. All of these, in turn, correspond to the Chickering and Ehrmann's (1996) work on the seven principles of effective instruction in undergraduate online learning. Our modification notes interaction, cooperative involvement, learning by doing, iterative feedback, recognizing multiple thinking patterns, engagement, and high expectations. The confluence of all these models forms a workable theoretical base for the pedagogy of blended learning.

The Millennial Generation—Learning Styles and Metaphors

Tailoring instruction to Reactive Behavior is not realistic in the present day dynamics of higher education. We believe that it is important to understand that different energy levels and need for approval dictate how students prefer to interact with instructors. Independent students want little more than information. Dependent students need the approval of their peers and instructors. High energy students will be engaged online and in the classroom. Lower energy students will not make nearly as strong a connection. Long's model provides instructors with more appropriate communication approaches so that students can accommodate their learning preference. As Stenberg and Grigorenko (1997) report, a learning style is a natural transition between cognition and personality. This is particularly true in blended learning.

By attending and accommodating the reactive behavior of the Millennial generation students and their representational language for blended learning, the academy will undergo several positive side effects. Blended learning is a major contributor to the transformation from the university as a bastion for learning to the university as an institution that accommodates the lifestyles of its students. Blended learning encompasses the best of the classroom and the best of online learning.

Already, this phenomenon is becoming a reality with multimedia classrooms, students' personal technologies, online library resources, and technology visible in classrooms, student unions, and dining halls. Students are connected and blended learning helps them connect. This wide world of technology is experiencing a creeping normalcy where more and more of its presence is hardly noticed. We have difficulty remembering when the campus was not technology-rich. Our forgetfulness is evidence of what Diamond (2005) calls landscape amnesia.

Our data suggest that many students enter these new learning environments with conflicting feelings. A healthy sense of skepticism, especially about new technologies, facilitates critical thinking skills and problem solving. Effective problem solving includes resolving conflicts when complete information might not be readily available. The blended learning classroom is the perfect environment for students to constructively engage in cooperative assessment of their work with their instructors and peers. Concrete information must be transformed into abstract constructs that are, in turn, manipulated to create new constructs that form the basis of a workable solution. The solution may not necessarily be the best, but can be tested and defended in the classroom and workplace.

Blended learning creates a whole set of new metaphors for higher education: a language less constraining and more facilitative toward the emerging dynamics of university campuses. Howe and Strauss (2000) suggests that this new representational language will characterize institutions that acknowledge students, who believe they will have a special place in history, have unlimited potential, learn collaboratively, cope with previously inexperienced pressure to achieve, and contribute to the common good. Blended learning will help these students mature. The wisdom of the traditional academy and technology will accelerate their learning and sophistication at "warp speed." Because of blended learning, things are "looking up." We are "right on target."

References

AASCU, Microsoft & EDUCAUSE Key to Competitiveness Conference. (2004, June). University of Central Florida, Orlando, June 9–11, 2004.

Adams, J. V. (1997). Student evaluations: The ratings game. *Inquiry, 1*(2), 10–16.

Berliner, D.C. (1998). *The development of expertise in pedagogy*. American Association of Colleges for Teacher Education, Washington, DC. (ED298122).

Bonk, C. J. & Graham, C. R. (2006). *The handbook of blended learning: Global perspectives, local designs*. San Francisco: Pfeiffer.

Breiman, L., Friedman, J. H., Olshen, R. A., & Stone, C. J. (1984). *Classification and regression trees*. New York: Chapman & Hall.

Chickering, A. & Ehrmann, S. C. (1996, October). Implementing the seven principles: Technology as lever. *AAHE Bulletin*, 3–6.

Chopin, K. (1899). *The awakening*. Chicago: Herbert S. Stone & Co.

Coupland, D. (1991). *Generation X: Tales for an accelerated culture*. New York: St. Martin's Griffin.

Diamond, J. (1999). *Guns, germs, and steel: The fates of human societies*. New York: W.W. Norton & Company.

Diamond, J. (2005). *Collapse: How societies choose to fail or succeed*. New York: Viking.

Dziuban, C. D., Hartman, J., Juge, F., & Moskal, P., Sorg, S. (2006). Blended learning enters the mainstream. In C. J. Bonk & C. R. Graham (Eds.), *The handbook of blended learning: Global perspectives, local design* (pp. 195–208). San Francisco, CA: Pfeiffer.

Dziuban, C. D., Hartman, J., Moskal, P. (March 30, 2004). Blended learning. *ECAR Research Bulletin*. Available online at http://www.educause.edu /ecar/.

Dziuban, C. D., Moskal, P. D., & Dziuban, E. K. (2000). Reactive behavior goes online. *Journal of Staff, Program, & Organization Development, 17*(3), 171–182.

Dziuban, C. D., Moskal, P. D. & Hartman, J. (2005). Higher education, blended learning, and the generations: Knowledge is power: No more. In J. Bourne & J. C. Moore (Eds.), *Elements of Quality Online Education: Engaging Communities*. Needham, MA: Sloan Consortium.

Dziuban, C. D., Wang, M. C., & Cook, I. J. (2004). *Dr. Fox rocks: Student perceptions of excellent and poor college teaching*. Unpublished manuscript, University of Central Florida.

Feldman, K. A. (1976). The superior college teacher from the students' view. *Research in Higher Education, 5*, 243–288.

Garrison, D. R. (2005). Facilitating cognitive presence in online learning: Interaction is not enough. *American Journal of Distance Education, 19*(3), 133–148.

Hartman, J. & Dziuban, C., Moskal, P. (2000). Faculty satisfaction in ALNs: A dependent or independent variable? *The Journal of Asynchronous Learning Networks, 4*(3).

Hendrickson, A. E. & White, P. O. (1964). Promax: A quick method for rotation to oblique simple structure. *British Journal of Statistical Psychology, 17*, 65–70.

Hotelling, H. (1933). Analysis of a complex of statistical variables into principal components. *Journal of Educational Psychology, 24*, 417–441 & 498–520.

Howe, N. & Strauss, W. (2000). *Millennials rising: The next great generation*. New York: Vintage Books.

Joyce, J. (1916). *A portrait of the artist as a young man*. New York: Viking Penguin, Inc.

Kolitch, E. & Dean, A. V. (1999). Student ratings of instruction in the USA: Hidden assumptions and missing conceptions about 'good' teaching. *Studies in Higher Education, 24*(1), 27–43.

Kuh, G. D. (2001). Assessing what really matters to student learning: Inside the national survey of student engagement. *Change, 33*(3), 10–19.

Lakoff, G. (1990). *Women, fire, and dangerous things.* Chicago: University of Chicago Press.

Lakoff, G. & Johnson, M. (2003). *Metaphors we live by.* Chicago: University of Chicago Press.

Likert, R. (1932). A technique for the measurement of attitudes. *Archives of Psychology, 140,* 55.

Long, W. A., Jr. (1975). Adolescent maturation: A clinical overview. *Postgraduate Medicine, 57*(3), 54–60.

Long, W. A., Jr. (1985). The practitioner and adolescent medicine. *Seminars in Adolescent Medicine, 1,* 85–90.

Long, W. A., Jr. (1989). Personality and Learning: 1988 John Wilson Memorial Address. *Focus on Learning Problems in Mathematics, 11*(4), 1–16.

Marsh, H.W. & Roche, L.A. (1997). Making students' evaluations of teaching effectiveness effective: The critical issues of validity, bias, and utility. *American Psychologist, 52*(11), 1187–1197.

McHugh, J. (2005). Synching up with the iKid: Educators must work to understand and motivate a new kind of digital learner. *Edutopia, 1*(7), 33–35.

Meyer, K. A. (2005). Common metaphors and their impact on distance education: What they tell us and what they hide. *Teachers College Record, 107*(8), 1601–1625.

Morrison, T. (1973). *Sula.* New York: Alfred A. Knopf, Inc.

Oblinger, D. (2003, July/August). Boomers, gen-exers, & millennials: Understanding the new students. *EDUCAUSE Review,* 37–45.

Oblinger, D. G. & Oblinger, J. L. (Eds.) (2005). *Educating the net generation.* EDUCAUSE.

Prensky, M. (2001, October). Digital natives, digital immigrants. *On the Horizon, 9*(5), np.

Senge, P. M. (1990). *The fifth discipline: The art and practice of the learning organization.* New York: DoubleDay Currency.

Shakespeare, W. (1603, 1992). *Hamlet.* New York: Washington Square Press.

Sternberg, R. J. & Grigorenko, E. L. (1997). Are cognitive styles still in style? *American Psychologist, 52*(7), 700–712.

Thurstone, L. L. (1935). *The vectors of mind: Multiple-factor analysis for the isolation of primary traits.* Chicago: University of Chicago Press.

Vail, K. (2005). The world of e-learning: How the National Education Technology Plan can help you teach today's 'technology natives.' *American School Board Journal, 192*(9), 30–31.

Wendover, R.W. (2002). From Ricky & Lucy to Beavis & Butthead: Managing the new workforce. *Center for Generational Studies.*

Student Perceptions of Blended Learning in a Traditional Undergraduate Environment

Robert Woods, Ph.D.
Spring Arbor University
Diane M. Badzinski, Ph.D.
Colorado Christian University
Jason D. Baker, Ph.D
Regent University

Abstract

This study explores students' patterns of use, perceptions of usefulness, and outcomes related to instructor use of a web-based course management program to supplement face-to-face instruction. Students' suggestions for improving the quality of online instruction were also solicited. The findings revealed that group discussion boards and announcements were the most popular features and perceived to be most important for learning. Students also perceived web-based instruction as enhancing the quality and quantity of class discussion, promoting a sense of connectedness among classmates and instructor, and contributing to their enjoyment and the effectiveness of the course. In terms of predicting course performance, the actual number of posts emerged as most salient predictor of course grade, indicating that the greater frequency of posts predicts success in course. Study results are discussed in terms of on-campus students' willingness to embrace blended instruction and the resulting instructional implications.

Introduction

The use of web-based technologies to enhance teaching and learning has not been limited to distance education; rather, the rapid acceptance of learning management systems (LMSs) such as Blackboard, eCollege and WebCT in undergraduate institutions has affected the face-to-face learning experience. Numerous faculty are incorporating online technologies into their campus courses to produce web-enhanced or blended learning experiences (Osguthorpe & Graham, 2003; Dziuban, et al., 2005). In such approaches, teaching and learning occur both in traditional and online environments, such that "the online component becomes a natural extension of traditional classroom learning" (Rovai & Jordan, 2004, p. 3).

Within the spectrum of technology-rich education, there are a number of models currently in use. *Web-enhanced* courses use the Web in an incidental manner to provide students with a repository for course materials and resource links or for threaded discussions, conferencing, and email. *Blended* or *mixed-mode* courses make more significant use of the web as an integral element of course delivery than web-enhanced courses. More significantly, blended courses typically incorporate a reduced amount of face-to-face contact (i.e., reduced seat time) in exchange for suitable online learning activities (Dziuban, et al., 2004).

The convergence of two teaching and learning media—face-to-face and online—has been seen by many as an attempt to address some of the limitations inherent in a any single medium of delivery (Bunker & Vardi, 2001). The convergence enables instructors to combine the advantages of online class learning with the benefits of face-to-face interaction with relatively limited technological sophistication (Edling, 2000; Strambi & Bouvet, 2003). Furthermore, the reduced seat time of blended learning is attractive as a cost savings approach for institutions coping with shrinking budgets and reduced classroom space (Brown, 2001).

Such approaches are likely to increase in popularity in the coming years. Brown (2001) posits that universities will eventually design courses using a "90–10 Rule" with neither face-to-face nor online instruction being exclusive but rather some combination between 90% face-to-face and 10% online to 10% face-to-face and 90% online (p. 22). Similarly, Young (2002) reports that 80–90% of traditional undergraduate courses are expected to become web-enhanced or blended within the next five years (Young, 2002). Clearly institutions are moving in this direction as 81% of all institutions of higher education, and 97% of all public institutions, currently offer at least one blended course (Allen & Seaman, 2003).

Preliminary reports indicate that this educational approach holds significant benefits for students and instructors regardless of their level of technological expertise (Black, 2001; Brakels et al., 2002) and regardless of whether the classroom is hard-wired for live Internet access (Bento & Bento, 2000). Web-enhancement of traditional classes may benefit faculty by improving efficiency of classroom management, especially for large classes (Papo, 2001), increasing the degree of student-led learning (Saunders & Klemming, 2003), enhancing information skills acquisition and student achievement (Kendall, 2001; Novitzki, 2000), influencing the quality and quantity of in-class discussions (Kendall, 2001; Rutter & Matthews, 2002; Saunders & Klemming, 2003), and reducing student withdrawals and absenteeism (Sorg, Juge, & Bledsoe, 1998; Riffell & Sibley, 2003; Dziuban et al., 2004).

Similarly, students in such courses have demonstrated improved morale and overall satisfaction with the learning experience (Byers, 2001; Twigg, 2003), increased motivation to learn (Cameron, 2003), greater levels of peer collaboration across different learning modalities (Story & DiElsi, 2003), and the development of a sense of classroom community (Rovai & Jordan, 2004). Students appear to enjoy the blended experience in part because it allows them to compare their thoughts and conclusions both in and after classes for additional discussion and debate. Some report finding the blended experience helpful in collecting valuable websites and resources that bring to life the material and connect it to every day life (Chuang, 2002).

Black (2001) reported that blending web-based instruction into the face-to-face setting was actually preferred by some students over face-to-face instruction, particularly as students' computer expertise increased. The incorporation of discussion boards and daily journals fosters students' critical reflection and increases instructors' ability to quickly assess students' knowledge and understanding of course material (Chuang, 2002). "Just-in-Time" teaching lets instructors post questions related to course content in discussion (bulletin) boards, review students' interaction and understanding related to those questions "just" prior to a particular face-to-face session, and then adapt classroom teaching accordingly (Wheeler, 2002).

Literature Review

The literature reviewed suggested that the use of web-based courseware to supplement traditional instruction would not only increase students' perception that learning was occurring in the course, but would also enhance their camaraderie with others in the class and bolster their overall satisfaction with the course. Over the past three years, the researchers received several positive comments from students in course evaluations for the ways they used Blackboard to supplement their teaching. Students said that the instructors' use of Blackboard helped to create a friendly and relaxed classroom environment and allowed them to interact more about course content and in ways they didn't expect. Furthermore, students who used Blackboard more often and in a greater variety of ways reported learning more and perceiving the course as more effective than those who used Blackboard less often and with less variety. Most students, however, regardless of their classroom performance, had an expectation that Blackboard would be used in some way to support the traditional classroom activities.

Faculty can use web-based courseware to augment traditional instruction in at least four main ways: presentation of course content, assessment of student learning, increased interaction among students, and development of a learning community. In a blended environment, faculty can use the online environment to make information available to students and more effectively administer classroom procedures (Bento & Bento, 2000, Bunker & Vardi, 2001). Course outlines, Power Point Presentations, and streaming video clips are typically posted. Links to course-related websites, professional and academic journals, and other news items and current events are also made available. Next, faculty can use the online environment to improve assessment of student learning. Rather than waiting until students arrive to class to take a quiz or begin discussion, instructors can mandate online activities and then review the results prior to the face-to-face class and make "just in time" instructional changes (Wheeler, 2002). Furthermore, faculty can develop online quizzes and tests which benefit both themselves and their students. Faculty benefit because such exams are typically graded by the computer, thus sparing the instructors this tedium. Students benefit because they can receive immediate results and detailed feedback on incorrect answers rather than waiting until the next scheduled class when the material may not be as fresh (McGroarty et al., 2004).

Next, online activities may also be incorporated into traditional classes in order to promote increased interaction among the students. Online discussions that extend classroom conversations throughout the week or address topics omitted in the limited face-to-face class meeting time increase the opportunity for student interaction. The online learning literature is rife with the pedagogical value of learner-learner interaction (e.g., Moore & Kearsley, 2005; Kearsley, 2000; Palloff & Pratt, 1999, 2001). Furthermore, several instructors have reported that the use of online discussion to enhance traditional classes may actually improve the quality and quantity of the face-to-face discussions (King, 2001; Rutter & Matthews, 2002; Saunders & Klemming, 2003). Second, the faculty regularly use Blackboard for class and small group discussion. It is well supported that effective learning in web-based environs requires interaction and collaboration among learners (Kearsley, 2000, Palloff & Pratt, 2001). Most instructors in the blended model make use of asynchronous discussion (bulletin) boards and live chatrooms for such interactions (Chuang, 2002). Many faculty, following the model used by most online instructors, randomly assign students into discussion groups (about 5–7 students) and create individual group pages where members of a particular group can go to discuss and reflect on assigned course material or work on group projects. Several researchers and practitioners have reported that the combination of face-to-face instruction with online discussion and reflection in various formats may actually influence the quality of interaction in the face-to-face settings (Joia, 2001; Rutter & Matthews, 2002;).

Finally, faculty incorporate personal, non-subject-matter-specific folders in an attempt to foster additional social interaction and foster a sense of classroom community. One of the challenges in the blended approach relates to the loss of some face-to-face student contact, which means that instructors must pay careful attention to personalizing the online exchange (Sorg, et al., 2000). The decision to use personal discussion folders in this study as online gathering places was also based on previous research demonstrating the effectiveness of such tools in building a sense of "togetherness" among learners in the online setting (Woods & Ebersole, 2003). Such folders allow for more opportunities for social interaction. Social information processing theory posits that increased opportunities for social interaction may result in increased opportunities for content related exchanges as relationships among learners develops (Walther, 1992).

Research Questions

While such blended approaches are growing in popularity, few delivery systems reflect a mixed approach that combines live instruction with web-based systems, and few studies to date have quantitatively described specific student perceptions or preferences of online-user education or have sought to identify patterns of use or outcomes associated with the use of such web-based integrated courseware (Parker, 2000). Toward this end, this study attempts to describe student use, perceptions and the effects of blending online Blackboard usage into a traditional undergraduate classroom environment. The following questions were proposed in an attempt to identify students' patterns of use, perceptions of usefulness and outcomes related to the instructors' use of a web-based course management platform to supplement face-to-face instruction:

RQ1: *What are students' primary Blackboard use patterns based on accesses or "hits" in the various course areas made available by the instructor?* Which course areas and features do students use most frequently? Such patterns of use may suggest pedagogical priorities for instructors, including principles of design.

RQ2: *What are students' perceptions of how certain Blackboard features enhance their learning experiences and overall effectiveness of the course?* Do students perceive certain course areas and features as helping or hindering them in the learning process? Do such features enhance the quality of classroom discussion or contribute to their enjoyment of the course?

RQ3: *What are students' perceptions of how the use of Blackboard affects their relationships with other students and the instructor?* Online facilitators often incorporate special course areas or features designed to build connectedness or foster a positive social dynamic among learners (Woods & Ebersole, 2003; Palloff & Pratt, 2001). Immediacy-inducing or prosocial communication behavior has also been studied in traditional course settings (Richmond, McCroskey, Kearney, & Plax, 1987) and has been adapted by online instructors in many instances (Woods & Baker, 2004; Woods & Ebersole, 2003). How a learning management system such as Blackboard can be used to foster prosocial behaviors in the blended model, and the effect of such immediacy on students' perceptions of the blended experience, has yet to be explored.

RQ4: *Will students who participate in Blackboard with greater frequency perform better in the course, as measured by final course grade and Richmond, et al's (1987) cognitive learning scale?* Researchers in both traditional (Richmond, Gorham, & McCroskey, 1987) and online (LaRose & Whitten, 2000) classroom settings have found that learning outcomes are directly and positively related to frequent student participation and engagement in the learning enterprise.

Research Participants

The study under consideration used an undergraduate level media literacy course at Spring Arbor University, Spring Arbor, Michigan. On-campus courses at Spring Arbor are offered on a regular semester calendar over 14–15 weeks except in January (J-term) and May (May Term), where a traditional semester is compressed into an intensive three week schedule. Courses during J-term and May Term meet every day (Monday – Friday) for 3 hours. During J-term, students are allowed to take only one course at a time. In order to enhance the J-term course offering, a blended learning model was selected.

Spring Arbor University is a private liberal arts undergraduate institution affiliated with the Free Methodist Church of America. There are approximately 1300 full and part-time students enrolled at Spring Arbor University's campus and another 1200 students enrolled in courses and programs at one of its various satellite campuses throughout the state of Michigan and in some parts of Ohio. Spring Arbor has been developing and delivering online courses and programs since 1996. The institution uses E-college to deliver most of its external online programs and uses Blackboard to deliver internal online courses and to supplement instruction in on-campus courses. Of the nearly 70 full-time faculty at Spring Arbor, nearly half are actively engaged in using Blackboard to supplement traditional courses in some way.

The blended model of this J-term undergraduate media literacy course included a combination of lecture, class and group discussion, guest speakers, video demonstrations accompanied by online discussion groups, and web scavenger searches. To reduce in-class seat time, course lectures, Powerpoint slides, and a number of additional resources were made available to students in Blackboard. Three personal, non-subject matter discussion folders were created along with one general information discussion folder on the main discussion board list. Face-to-face sessions were typically accompanied by discussion questions and other online activities (carried out in randomly assigned groups) designed to serve one of two purposes: 1) to follow-up on or extend discussion and debate on issues raised during the face-to-face session, or 2) to prepare students for the assigned readings and lecture for the following day. Online group discussion was graded on the basis of frequency, quality and timeliness of posting. Group discussion (online and face-to-face) constituted nearly 20% of the overall course grade, while performance on written (essay) papers, daily media logs, website reviews, and group projects determined the rest of the evaluation of student work

The population for this study consisted of all full and part-time Spring Arbor University students enrolled in the J-term course. The researchers employed a convenience sample of 151 students in RHE 102, a media literacy course taught by one of the researchers during this term. Students who completed the survey ranged in age from 17 to 23, mean age = 18.56; 73 were male and 78 were female. Nearly all of the students (91%) were freshmen, and while the students were familiar with the Blackboard LMS, none had previously taken a formal blended learning course at Spring Arbor.

A survey (see Appendix) was administered to students in a traditional undergraduate media literacy course to answer the research questions related to student perceptions of, and outcomes associated with, web-based augmentation (via Blackboard). Also, content analysis was performed on available Blackboard course areas to determine frequency and patterns of use. The authors were interested in developing practical guidelines and principles for using web-based courseware to supplement traditional instruction.

Instructional Design and Research Procedures

The instructor reviewed the syllabus on the first day of class and explained that classroom instruction would be a combination of face-to-face and web-based strategies. Students were instructed to log in and check Blackboard daily. They were also informed that they had been randomly assigned to one of seven discussion groups (6–7 students each) (described in greater detail below, see no. 4, Group Communication Area). The instructor further described the following course areas and features that were planned or otherwise made available for student use:

1. **Main Content Area** — All students had access to the following sections in the main content area:

   a) Announcements;

   b) Syllabus: the syllabus handed out in class was posted here for review and update;

   c) Staff Information: this section included a photograph of the instructor along with his personal background information and professional experience;

   d) Course Information: in this section the instructor gave students access to course lectures, Powerpoint slides, grading rubrics, sample assignments, online quizzes, and other information related to course assignments and procedures.

2. **Main Communication Area** — In addition to the main content area, all students, regardless of the discussion group to which they were assigned, had access to the following sections and features in the main communication area: a) main class discussion board with 4 discussion folders, b) virtual classroom (for live chat), c) email, and d) class roster.

As just noted, there were 4 discussion folders created for students that were posted on the main class discussion board. Three of these folders were personal, non-subject-matter specific folders designed to foster a sense of classroom community. Students were not "required" to make any posts in or access any discussion folder created on the main class discussion board. The instructor created these non-subject-matter specific folders because they are proven ways in the online setting to help students feel connected to others in the class (see discussion, *supra*, p. 2). A brief description of the discussion folders and the order in which they appeared on the main discussion board list follows:

(a) *Prayer Requests/Praise Reports*: a gathering place where students shared personal struggles, concerns or problems and could ask for their colleagues' thoughts and prayers. Students could also report good news of a personal nature in this folder occurring at any time throughout the semester. Note that this folder was labeled as such given Spring Arbor University's religious affiliation. However, although Spring Arbor is religiously affiliated with the Free Methodist Church, students are not required to be religiously affiliated in any way to attend. Students in this course represented a variety of Christian and non-Christian traditions.

(b) *Autobiographies*: in this folder students were given an opportunity to introduce themselves to one another in a safe environment by sharing basic background information along with 2–3 things about themselves that others might not know. Such a space lets students construct their "electronic personality" (Pratt, 1999, p. 22) form impressions of others (Hancock & Dunham., 2001) and meet-and-greet their fellow classmates in a safe environment.

(c) *SAU Cafe*: this discussion folder was a virtual café where students commented on or discussed anything that was of personal relevance or interest to anyone in the class that did not otherwise fit into Autobiographies or one of the other folders. The café folder functioned as a gathering place much in the same way that student unions or college coffee houses function as social venues on face-to-face campuses. Online instructors regularly construct virtual cafés (Harasim, Hiltz, Teles, & Turoff, 1995, p. 137) for students to meet apart from formal, required discussion formats.

(d) *General Class Information*: The description of the folder invited students to ask any questions they might have related to course procedures or requirements; answers to these questions might be helpful to their colleagues.

3. **Student Course Management Area** — Again, as with the first two areas listed above, all students had access to the check grade function and several other tools to assist them in the management of course requirements: digital drop box, create and edit personal home page, calendar function, and personal profile and contact information.

4. **Group Communication Area** — This course area included the group pages that functioned as the home page for each group. Each assigned discussion group's page contained several communication and file exchange features available only to that group. Other groups did not have access to any other group's page. Group features accessible via this area included the following: group discussion (bulletin) board area (where assigned groups could discuss questions posted by the instructor), group virtual classroom area, file exchange between members of the same discussion group, and email to members in a student's individual group.

Students were required (as clearly stated in the syllabus) to reply to any discussion questions posted in their individual discussion group area at the close of a particular class session. Each group received the same questions for discussion. Students in one group could not observe the discussion being carried out in another group, although students were encouraged to discuss their group deliberations with other groups outside of class time and to share them as part of regularly scheduled face-to-face session. The facilitator reviewed discussion posts and made comments where he deemed appropriate. Minimum posting and time requirements were established for group discussion questions. Students were told that they could continue with posting and replying as often as they wanted in response to a particular set of discussion questions (even after the forum had been closed).

The instructor's communication in each of the discussion folders on the main discussion board list constituted less than 10% of the total posts and replies in any given folder. His communication was less than 5% of the total in each discussion group bulletin board area.

Upon completion of the course, data for analysis was collected using the following procedures:

1. *Content Analysis*: The physical units counted were the total number of accesses that each course area and feature received throughout the semester. This analysis let researchers determine Blackboard use patterns: course areas and features used most often by students. At the end of the semester the statistical tracking function available in the Blackboard control panel was used to calculate frequencies and percentages of accesses in each of the four course areas described above. Course areas were then ranked according to frequency of accesses to identify use patterns.

2. *Survey*: At the conclusion of the course, a survey measuring perceptions of Blackboard's usefulness was sent to all 151 students who had successfully completed syllabus requirements. Prior to administration, the survey received human subjects' approval and was submitted to a panel of faculty currently using Blackboard. Changes were made to the wording and order of several questions based on feedback provided. The main survey questions were pre-tested on 32 students in another class.

The survey included questions related to students' use and perceived helpfulness of various Blackboard course areas and features that were set up by the instructor prior to the first day of class. Responses were measured using Likert-style rankings. Students were asked to report whether available Blackboard features employed by the instructor either helped or hindered the effectiveness of their learning and performance in the class (1 = Significant Hindrance and 5 = Significant Help). Additional questions asked on a Likert Scale were related to the effect of Blackboard on both quantity and quality of group discussion, the effect of Blackboard on the overall effectiveness and enjoyment of the course, and the way Blackboard affected students' relationships with other students in the class and with the instructor.

Finally, to help determine the relationship to course performance outcomes, relationships were considered between Blackboard usage and self-reported perceived learning and final grades. Originally, the cognitive learning scale developed by Richmond, Gorham and McCroskey (1987) was used. Due to concerns with the use of gain scores, only one item from the scale was used as a self-report measure of assessment: "On a scale of 0–9, how much have you learned in the class you are in now, with 0 meaning you have learned nothing and 9 meaning you have learned more than any other class you ever had." The final course grade was computed (as described in the syllabus) from a combination of quiz scores, daily media logs, participation, attendance and a final group oral presentation. Three open ended questions were added at the end of the survey: 1) What was the highlight of this course? 2) What features/functions would you like to see added to the Blackboard system to enhance the learning experience? 3) How do you imagine that this course will look different in five years?

Correlations were computed to determine the significant relationships, if any, between frequency of Blackboard use and performance. Multiple regression analysis was performed to determine the relationship between frequency of use, area of use, perceived effectiveness of learning, and course performance. Content analysis was performed on the open-ended data to identify common themes or categories of responses. SPSSX was used for statistical analysis.

Results and Discussion
Research Question 1: Students' Primary Blackboard Use Patterns

The first research question considered students' primary Blackboard use patterns based on accesses or "hits" in the various course areas made available by the instructor. In other words, which course areas and features do students use most frequently? As shown in Table 1, the group communication area had a far greater number of hits (26,100) than did the other three areas: main course (8,566), main content (7,836) and student course management (1,215).

Within the group communication area, the most popular feature was the group discussion board. Seventy-nine percent of all accesses occurred in this area, with less than 1% of the accesses to group virtual classroom, send e-mail, or file exchange. Within the main communication area, students visited the discussion board more than any other area. Over 90% of accesses were to the discussion board, with less than 2% of the accesses to roster, send e-mail, virtual classroom, or enter virtual classroom. Within the main content area, announcements was the most popular area with about 80% of the total accesses. Course information also appears to be an important area, with about 14% of the total accesses. There were relatively few hits to staff information and syllabus, although this isn't too surprising since there are certain areas within Blackboard that don't require multiple visits; once the students read about all the accomplishments of their instructor, for example, there's little need to re-read them. Finally, within the student course management area, about one third of the accesses were to check grades, with the remaining accesses to various other tools.

Table 1: Frequency and Percentage of "Hits" in Course Areas

	Hits	Percentages
Group Communication Area		
Group Discussion Board	20688	79%
Group Pages	3099	12%
Group (Main Course Page)	2203	9%
Group Virtual Chat	64	>1%
Send E-mail	62	>1%
File Exchange	44	>1%
Total	26160	
Main Communication Area		
Discussion Board	7881	92%
Communication	390	5%
Roster	131	2%
Send E-mail	108	1%
Virtual Classroom	37	>1%
Enter Virtual Classroom	19	>1%
Total	8566	
Main Content Area		
Announcements	6262	80%
Course Information	1100	14%
Staff Information	254	3%
Syllabus	220	3%
Total	7835	
Student Course Management Area		
Tools	782	64%
Check Grade	433	36%
Total	1215	

Research Question 2: Students' Perceptions of Blackboard Features Enhancing Learning

The second question considered students' perceptions of how Blackboard features enhance learning experiences and overall effectiveness of the course. In other words, do students perceive certain course areas and features as helping or hindering them in the learning process? Do such features enhance the quality of classroom discussion or contribute to their enjoyment of the course? Of the twelve Blackboard services, students indicated that the group discussion boards and daily announcements were most important for enhancing learning, with 95% of the students indicating that group discussion boards added or significantly added to their learning experiences, and 89% of the students thought daily announcements added or significantly added to their learning. The majority of students also felt that the online syllabus (84%), online gradebook (82%), general course information forum (77%), course information (77%), and external links (54%) contributed to learning.

In contrast, the majority of students felt that the prayer/praise forum (78%), SAU café forum (75%), virtual classroom (72%) autobiographies forum (65.5%), and faculty information (58.3%) had no effect on student learning. With only one exception, no student felt that these Blackboard services subtracted from learning. The exception was that one student thought that the prayer/praise forum, café, and virtual classroom subtracted from one's learning experiences.

In terms of students' perceptions of how Blackboard affects the quantity and quality of class discussion, the majority of the students indicated that Blackboard was helpful in terms of affecting the quantity (86%) and quality (87%) of classroom discussion, with nearly half of the students indicating that Blackboard was of significant help in terms of quantity (44%) and quality (45%) of class discussions. A very small percentage of the students thought that Blackboard hindered the quantity (3%) and quality (3%) of discussion.

A vast majority of students indicated that Blackboard helped in their overall enjoyment of the class (79%) and in the effectiveness of the class (85%), with nearly half of the students (45%) indicating that Blackboard was of significant help in the overall effectiveness of the course. Only a few students felt that Blackboard negatively impacted the enjoyment (8%) and effectiveness of the course (1%).

Research Question .3: Students' Perceptions of Blackboard Features Affecting Relationships

The third question considered students' perceptions of how Blackboard features affect their relationships with other students and instructors. In other words, do students think Blackboard helps build a sense of connectedness among class members? How does Blackboard foster the development of online relationships? The students' responses clearly indicated that Blackboard fosters connectedness among learners. A vast majority of students thought that Blackboard was of help in developing a relationship with instructor (60%) and classmates (87%). Nearly half of the students indicated that Blackboard was of significant help in developing relationships with classmates (43%). In comparison, 15% of the students thought Blackboard was of significant help in developing relationships with instructor. Only a few students indicated that Blackboard hindered their relationship with instructor (3%) and classmates (2%).

Research Question 4: Blackboard Participation and Course Performance

The fourth question considered whether students who participate in Blackboard with greater frequency perform better in the course, as measured by final course grade and self-report assessment on amount of learning.

215

Several observations can be made by examining the zero-order correlation matrix (see Table 2). The actual number of posts and quality of posts correlated positively with course grade, indicating that the greater number and quality of posts are associated with higher grades. In contrast, no relationship exists between self-report frequency of logging onto Blackboard or self-report frequency of posts and course grade. The only other variable that related to course grade was student perceptions of Blackboard affecting their relationships with classmates. The negative correlation (-.27) indicates that more favorable ratings of how Blackboard impacts relationships with classmates are associated with poorer course performance. Course participation was not associated with self-perception of learning. In addition, student perceptions of learning and course grade were not correlated.

Table 2. **Partial View of the Zero-Order Correlation Matrix**

	X_4	X_{17}	X_{18}	X_{19}	X_{20}	X_{21}	X_{22}	X_{23}	Y_1	Y_2
Activity										
Actual # of Postings (X_4)	-	.05	.05	.17*	.11	.16*	.11	.03	.08	.40*
Perceptions										
Quantity of Posts (X_{17})		-	.69**	.09	.07	.09	.02	.09	.13	.20*
Quality of Posts (X_{18})			-	.03	.09	.03	.02	.08	.10	.09
Relationship with Instructor (X_{19})				-	.86**	.99**	.86**	.57**	.77**	.01
Relationship with Classmates (X_{20})					-	.86**	.74**	.48**	.65*	-.27**
Enjoyment of Class (X_{21})						-	.86**	.57**	.77**	.01
Effectiveness of Class (X_{22})							-	.48**	.66**	.01
Computer Efficacy (X_{23})								-	.43**	.01
Performance										
Self-Assessment of Learning (Y_1)									-	.00
Course Grade (Y_2)										-

Note: ** $p \leq .01$,   * $p \leq .05$.

In terms of self-perception of learning and student ratings, findings showed that self-perception of learning was positively correlated with student liking of computer technology (r = .43), perceptions of Blackboard affecting relationships with both instructor (r = .77) and classmates (r = .65), and perceptions of Blackboard impacting the overall enjoyment (r = .77) and effectiveness of the course (r =.66). Moreover, self-perception of learning was associated with student perception of the usefulness of two of Blackboard services: group discussion (r = .16) and announcements (r = .19). Interestingly, students who held more favorable attitudes towards computer technology assigned more favorable ratings to several Blackboard services including group discussion (r = .21), announcements (r = . 25), online syllabus (r = .19) and online gradebook (r = .17).

The findings also revealed that students' relationships with instructor correlated positively with course enjoyment (r = .99) and effectiveness (r = .86). Students' relationships with classmates also correlated positively with course enjoyment (r = .86) and effectiveness (r = .77). Student self-ratings of how much they like computer technology also related positively with actual number of posts (r = .40), usefulness of Blackboard for developing relationships with instructor (r = .57) and classmates (r = .48), as well as overall ratings of course enjoyment (r = .57) and effectiveness (r = .48).

Predictors of Course Performance

To further identify factors affecting course outcomes, ordinary least squared regression analysis (OLS) was run on each of the two outcome measures: course grade and self-perception of learning. This technique is appropriate because both grade and perception of learning were measured at interval/ratio scales that allow us to model linear associations between sets of predictors and each dependent variable. The overall regression analysis for course grade was significant (F [23,127] = 5.66, p <. 001), accounting for 42% of the variance (r squared adjusted = .42). The only significant predictors were the actual number of posts (B = .41, t = 5.46, p < .001) and student perceptions of how blackboard affected their relationships with classmates (B = -1.09, t = -8.06, p < .001). Thus, greater frequency of posts predicts success in course. The negative beta weight reveals that student perception that Blackboard hinders connection with classmates predicts success in the course.

The overall regression analysis for self-perception of learning was also significant (F [23,127] = 13.45, p < .001), accounting for 66% of the variance (r squared adjusted = .66). Only one significant predictor emerged: student belief that the course information function of Blackboard assists in learning predicts student perception of how much they have learned in the course (B = .30, t = 5.84, p < .001).

Content Analysis of Open-end Questions

Student responses to the three open-ended questions were examined to identify common themes. The student responses to the three questions were unitized into idea units. One of the researchers and a trained coder divided the students' responses to the question into idea units, or "the smallest unit of meaning that has informational or affective value" (Stafford, Burggraf, & Sharkey, 1987, p. 214). The coders either agreed or disagreed on the units. The two coders agreed on 96% of the idea units. Through discussion the two coders resolved the disagreements. Next, the two coders identified common themes in student responses and classified the units in terms of the themes/categories. A reliability coefficient using Cohen Kappa was assessed for each main category for each of the questions separately, with the results ranging from $k = .74$ to $k = .94$; all of the kappas indicated an acceptable level of reliability (Landis & Koch, 1977). The results of the reliabilities suggest that the data were adequate for analysis. All disagreements were resolved through discussion between the coders.

In response to the first question, "What was the highlight of the course?" the student remarks were classified into one of the following five categories:

- *Instructor qualities* (e.g., "Having an instructor as passionate as Dr. _____.")
- *Course content* (e.g., "I really enjoyed having different speakers in class.")
- *Web-based instruction* (e.g., "The autobiography section of Blackboard.")
- *Classroom climate* (e.g., "The community of other students.")
- *Blank/irrelevant*

As shown in Table 3, the highlight of the course was its content (71%), with less than 10% of the responses indicating that the instructor, web-based instruction or classroom climate as its highlight.

Given the overwhelming number of responses relating to course content, further classification was done to identify what about course content was appealing. Thus, remarks related to course content were further classified into:

- *Lectures* (e.g., "Dr. _____ lectures.")
- *Media* (e.g., "All the video clips dealing with Reality TV shows.")
- *Class discussion* (e.g., "I just like sitting in class having discussions.")
- *Guest speakers* (e.g., "I really enjoyed having the different speakers in class.")

- *Assignments* (e.g., "Surprisingly I enjoyed presenting our speeches.")

Results indicated that students liked the assignments (33%), with media presentations (21%), class lectures (17%) guest speakers (15%), and class discussion (12%) also mentioned as course highlights. It should be noted that the course assignment that students most often mentioned (96%) dealt with class speeches/presentations, and the discussions that followed.

Table 3. **Frequency and Percentage of Responses to Open-ended Questions**

	Frequency	Percentage
Course Highlights		
Instructional Qualities	13	8%
Course Content	112	71%
Lectures	19	17%
Media	23	21%
Guest Speakers	17	15%
Class Discussions	13	12%
Assignments	37	33%
Other	3	1%
Web-based Instruction	8	5%
Classroom Climate	8	5%
Blank/Irrelevant	16	10%
n = 157		
Suggestions for Improvement		
Communication	9	6%
System Features	12	8%
Instructional	16	11%
Quality of Online Instruction	9	6%
No Change/Good "As Is"	34	22%
Blank/Irrelevant	71	47%
n = 151		
Imagine Course Differently in 5 Years		
Quality of Online Instruction	3	2%
Quantity of Online Instruction	30	20%
Advanced Technology	43	28%
Course Content	34	22%
Stay About the Same	7	5%
Blank/Irrelevant	34	23%
n = 151		

In response to the second question, "What features/functions would you like to see added to the Blackboard system to enhance the learning experience?" the student remarks were classified into one of the following five categories:

- *Communication* (e.g., "Maybe a type of instant messaging between people.")
- *System features* (e.g., "I'd improve the interface.")
- *Instructional* (e.g., "Need syllabus online with a calendar.")
- *Quantity of online instruction* (e.g., "More use of virtual classroom integrated to class work.")
- *No change/good "as is"* (e.g., "I think Blackboard is fine as it is.")
- *Blank/irrelevant*

The respondents clearly had difficulty offering suggestions for improving Blackboard. About half of the students (47%) had no comment and another 22% of the students offered no suggestions but indicated that the system is good as is. The suggestions that were offered dealt with improving communication (6%) suggesting changes such as instant messaging and a place to post questions just to professors, improving the system (8%) suggesting changes such as "I think colored font would make it more fun to look at" and "pictures of students as well as instructor, and enhancing instructional practices (11%) such as "more examples to help us understand what to write more clearly" and "grades posted in a more timely manner." Further, a small number of responses (6%) pertained to requiring more online interaction, with remarks such as "more use of virtual classroom" and "more virtual participation with class."

In response to the final question, "How do you imagine that this course will look differently in five years?" student remarks were classified into one of the following categories:

- *Quality of online instruction* (e.g., "Better in-depth Blackboard participation.")
- *Quantity of online instruction* (e.g., "We need more online discussion.")
- *Advanced technology* (e.g., "More advanced technology will be incorporated into the class.")
- *Course content* (e.g., "It will include new media.")
- *Stay about the same* (e.g., "Seems very modern now, I can't imagine it changing.")
- *Blank/irrelevant*

Results indicated that the students felt that a future course would incorporate more advanced technologies (28%) and that the quantity of online instruction would increase (20%). Students remarked that "web conferencing will probably be part of this course" and "the class will be more technologically advanced." Typical comments predicting greater online use include "I think that it will be possible to do it all online," and "There will probably be more online assignments and information." In addition, 22% of the responses pertained to changes in course content, often the result of changing technology. Students expressed, for example, "the course will discuss current issues as history in light of new developments that will be made," and "It will change to include any new media due to new technology."

Implications and Conclusion

The primary goals of the present study were to identify patterns of use, perceptions of usefulness and outcomes related to the instructors' use of a web-based management system to supplement face-to-face instruction. In addition, students' suggestions for improving blended courses were solicited. Based on student feedback, faculty should focus primary attention on group discussion boards and announcements. In terms of patterns of use, findings revealed that the group discussion boards and announcements were the most popular web-based services. Further, students perceived these two functions as most important for enhancing learning.

The workload associated with designing and implementing blended courses may seem overwhelming, especially for less-experienced online instructors. Our results show that pedagogical priority should be in constructing and facilitating group discussion questions as well as keeping students informed by regularly posting course announcements. Secondary priority should be given to posting an online syllabus and making grades available online. As the course develops, attention can be devoted to other course areas and features.

In promoting student participation in web-based courses, faculty should stress the benefits of such instruction. One benefit is that web-based instruction enhances classroom discussion. Our results show that students think web-based courseware enhances both the quality and quantity of classroom discussion. It is reasonable to suggest that students' grappling with course material prior to class promotes both greater and richer class discussions. Faculty struggling with student participation in class discussion, and struggling with generating responses from particular groups of students, should use web-based courseware to present questions requiring students to answer prior to class meeting.

Faculty attitudes toward technology can shape student attitudes about the benefits of technology in the classroom. The success of any new instructional technology effort depends strongly upon the support and attitudes of teachers involved (Woodrow, 1991). If faculty see the value of online education, such endorsement will likely carry over to student's perceptions of such instruction. Research that focuses on faculty perceptions of online education and ways to foster faculty willingness to embrace this type of instruction is therefore needed. The idea that attitudes toward technology affect implementation success not only makes sense intuitively but appears repeatedly in the literature (Choo & Cheung 1990–91; National Center for Education Statistics, 1999, 2003).

Another finding is that web-based instruction promotes a sense of connectedness among class members and instructor. Results showed that students perceive web-based instruction as helpful in developing relationships with their classmates and instructor. This sense of connectedness may help account for the finding that students enjoy such instruction. Our results revealed a third benefit of web-based instruction: such instruction adds to student enjoyment of the course. Nearly 80% of students indicated that Blackboard helped in their overall enjoyment of the course.

In addition to the attitudinal findings, it is valuable to realize that participation in web-based activities is associated with course performance. One important finding from this study is that greater numbers and higher quality of posts are associated with higher grades. Faculty should stress the link between active participation in online class activities and course grade. Regression analysis revealed that the actual number of posts is the strongest predictor of course grade. It should be kept in mind, however, that some students may be reluctant to fully participate. We found that students' self-ratings of how much they like computer technology correlate with the actual number of posts, student perceptions of the usefulness of Blackboard for the development relationships with instructor and classmates, and their ratings of how Blackboard affects their enjoyment and the effectiveness of the course. These findings suggest that perhaps faculty should assess student liking of computer technology for the purpose of identifying students that may need extra assistance and encouragement to participate fully in web-based activities.

Even students in the millennial generation or the "digital natives" (Prensky, 2001) have a sizable history with traditional classroom-based education. Accordingly, one would expect that their idea of learning in new environments would be influenced. While some students would likely relish a move toward increasingly blended learning, perhaps as a step toward fully on-demand education, others might be more comfortable with traditional models. These students need to be convinced of the educational benefits of web-based instruction. By stressing the positive outcomes of such instruction, faculty can increase the likelihood of students having positive attitudes toward blended learning, promoting the overall enjoyment and effectiveness of such instruction.

According to our research, students believe that the classroom of the future will include more online and blended activity. What we don't know, however, is whether they expect that such models will be enhanced versions of their current classrooms (as is typically the case with today's blended courses) or something entirely different that looks more like searching Google on a Blackberry. Perhaps the next generation looks toward blended and online learning activities with a less traditional view of the classroom and a different set of expectations. Accordingly, it's not only important to labor now to make blended courses learner-friendly but to conduct additional research to reveal biases inherent in current blended design strategies that include and exclude students based on educational expectations, technological literacy, learning style, cognitive style, motivation, subject, gender, or other factors. Since students and instructors lack a common history with blended learning, we must continue research into practice to develop ever better education.

References

Allen, I. E., & Seaman, J. (2003). *Sizing the opportunity: The quality and extent of online education in the United States, 2002–2003.* Wellesley, MA: The Sloan Consortium. Available from http://www.sloan-c.org/resources/sizing _opportunity.pdf

Bento, R. F., & Bento, A. M. (2000). Using the web to extend and support classroom learning. *College Student Journal, 34*(4), 603–609.

Black, G. (2001). A comparison of traditional, online and hybrids methods of course delivery. Paper presented at the Teaching Online in Higher Education Online Conference, November, 2001. Available at http://www.ipfw.edu /as/2001tohe/master.htm.

Brakels, J, van Daalen, E., Dik, W., Dopper, S., Lohman, F., van Peppen, A., Peerdeman, P., Peet, D. J., Sjoer, E., van Valkenburg, W., & van de Ven, M. (2002). Implementing ICT in education faculty-wide. *European Journal of Engineering Education, 27*(1), 63–76.

Brown, D. J. (2001). Hybrid courses are best. *Syllabus,* (1), 22.

Bunker, A., & Vardi, I. (2001). Why use the online environment with face-to-face students? Insights from early adopters. ERIC Document no. 467926.

Byers, C. (2001). Interactive assessment: An approach to enhance teaching and learning. *Journal of Interactive Learning Research, 12*(4), 359–374.

Cameron, B. (2003). The effectiveness of simulation in a hybrid and online networking course. *TechTrends, 47*(5), 18–21.

Choo, M. L., & Cheung, K. C. (1990–1991). On meaningful measurement: Junior College pupils' anxiety towards computer programming. *Journal of Educational Technology Systems, 19*(4), 327–343

Chuang, W. (2002). An innovative teacher training approach: Combine live instruction with a web-based reflection system. *British Journal of Educational Technology, 39*(2), 229–232.

Dziuban, C. D., Hartman, J., Juge, F., Moskal, P. D., & Sorg, S. (2005). Blended learning enters the mainstream. In C. J. Bonk & C. R. Graham (Eds.), *The Handbook of Blended Learning: Global Perspectives, Local Designs* (pp. 195–208). San Francisco: Pfeiffer.

Dziuban, C., Hartman, J., Moskal, P., Sorg, S., & Truman, B. (2004). Three ALN modalities: An institutional perspective. In J. Bourne & J. C. Moore (Eds.), *Elements of Quality Online Education: Into the Mainstream* (pp. 127–148). Needham, MA: The Sloan Consortium.

Edling, R. J. (2000). Information technology in the classroom: Experiences and recommendations. *Campus Wide Information Systems, 17*(1), 10.

Hancock, J., & Dunham, P. (2001). Impression formation in computer-mediated communication revisited: An analysis of the breadth and intensity of impression. *Communication Research, 28*, 325–32.

Harasim, L., Hiltz, S. R., Teles, L., & Turoff, M. (1995). *Learning networks: A field guide to teaching and learning online.* Cambridge, MA: MIT Press.

Joia, L. A. (2001). Evaluation of a hybrid socio-constructivist model for teacher training. *Journal of Teacher Training and Technology, 9*(4), 519–549.

Kearsley, G. (2000). *Online education: Learning and teaching in cyberspace.* Belmont, CA: Wadsworth/Thomson Learning.

Kendall, M. (2001). Teaching online to campus-based students. *Education for Information, 19*(4), 325–346.

Landis, J. R., & Koch, G. G. (1977). The measurement of observer agreement for categorical data. *Biometrics, 33*, 159–174

LaRose, R., & Whitten, P. (2000). Re-thinking instructional immediacy for web courses: A social cognitive exploration. *Communication Education, 49*, 320–338.

McGroarty, E., Parker, J., Heidemann, M., Lim, H., Olson, M., Long, T., Merrill, J., Riffell, S., Smith, J., Batzli, J., & Kirschtel, D. (2004). Supplementing introductory biology with on-line curriculum. *Biochemistry and Molecular Biology Education, 32*(1), 20–28.

Moore, M.G., & Kearsley, G. (2005). *Distance education: A systems view* (2nd ed.). Belmont, CA: Wadsworth.

National Center for Education Statistics. (1999). *Distance education at postsecondary education institutions: 1997–98,* NCES 2000-013. Retrieved from http://nces.ed.gov/surveys/peqis/publications/2000013/.

National Center for Education Statistics. (2003). *Distance education at degree-granting postsecondary institutions: 2000–2001,* NCES 2003-017. Retrieved from http://nces.ed.gov/surveys/peqis/publications/2003017/.

Novitzki, J. E. (2000). Asynchronous learning tools in the traditional classroom—A preliminary study on their effect. Paper presented at the International Academy for Information Management, Annual Conference, Brisbane, Australia.

Osguthorpe, R. T., & Graham, C. R. (2003). Blended learning environments: Definitions and directions. *Quarterly Review of Distance Education, 4*(3), 227–233.

Palloff, R. M., & Pratt, K. (2001). *Lessons from the cyberspace classroom: The realities of online teaching.* San Francisco: Jossey-Bass.

Palloff, R. M., & Pratt, K. (1999). *Building learning communities in cyberspace: Effective strategies for the online classroom.* San Francisco: Jossey-Bass.

Papo, W. (2001). Integration of educational media in higher education large classes. *Educational Media International, 38*(2–3), 95–99.

Parker, M. J. (2000). Web-based extended learning through discussion forums. Paper presented at the National Education Computing Conference, Atlanta, Georgia.

Prensky, M. (2001, September/October). Digital natives, digital immigrants. *On the Horizon, 9*(5), 1–6.

Richmond, V. P., Gorham, J. S., & McCroskey, J. C. (1987). The relationship between selected immediacy behaviors and cognitive learning. In M. L. McLaughlin (Ed.), *Communication Yearbook 10* (pp. 574–590). Newbury Park, CA: Sage.

Richmond, V. P., McCroskey, J. C., Kearney, P., & Plax, T. G. (1987). Power in the classroom VII: Linking behavior alteration techniques to cognitive learning. *Communication Education, 36*, 1–12.

Riffell, S. K., & Sibley, D. F. (2003). Student perceptions of a hybrid learning format: Can online exercises replace traditional lectures? *Journal of College Science Teaching, 32*, 394–399.

Rovai, A. P., & Jordan, H. M. (2004). Blended learning and sense of community: A comparative analysis with traditional and fully online graduate courses. *International Review of Research in Open and Distance Learning, 5*(2). Retrieved from http://www.irrodl.org/content/v5.2/rovai-jordan.html.

Rutter, L., & Matthews, M. (2002). InfoSkills: A holistic approach to on-line user education. *The Electronic Library, 20*(1), 29–34.

Saunders, G., & Klemming, F. (2003). Integrating technology into a traditional learning environment: Reasons for and risks of success. *Active Learning in Higher Education, 1*, 74–86.

Sorg, S., Juge, F., & Bledsoe, R. (2000). Institutional change through a web-enhanced course model. Paper presented at the Florida Educational Technology Conference, Orlando, Florida, March, 2000. Retrieved from http://distrib.ucf.edu/present/FETCpresentation030100/index.htm.

Stafford, L., Burggraf, C.S., & Sharkey, W.F. (1987). Conversational memory: The effects of time, recall mode, and memory expectancies on remembrances of natural conversations. *Human Communication Research, 14*, 203–229.

Strambi, A. & Bouvet, E. (2003). Flexibility and interaction at a distance: A mixed-mode environment for language learning. *Language Learning & Technology, 7*(3). Retrieved from http://llt.msu.edu/vol7num3/strambi/default.html.

Story, A. E. & DiElsi, J. (2003). Community building easier in blended format? *Distance Education Report, 7*(11), 2–7.

Twigg, C. A. (2003). Improving learning and reducing costs: New models for online learning. *Educause Review, 38*(5). Retrieved from http://www.educause.edu/ir/library/pdf/erm0352.pdf.

Walther, J.B. (1992). Interpersonal effects in computer-mediated interaction: A relational perspective. *Communication Research, 19*, 52–90.

Wheeler, S. (2002). Around the Globe. *Quarterly Review of Distance Education*, *3*(2), 227–30.

Woodrow, J. (1991). A Comparison of four computer attitude scales. *Journal of Educational Computing Research, 7*, 165–187.

Woods, R. H., & Baker, J. D. (2004). Interaction and immediacy in online learning. *International Review of Research in Open and Distance Learning*, *5*(2), Retrieved from http://www.irrodl.org/content/v5.2/woods-baker.html.

Woods, R. H., & Ebersole, S. (2003). Using non-subject matter specific discussion boards to build connectedness in online learning. *American Journal of Distance Education, 17*(2), 99–118.

Young, J. R. (2002, March 22). "Hybrid" teaching seeks to end the divide between traditional and online instruction. *Chronicle of Higher Education*, p. A33.

Appendix

Survey Instrument

1. Age: _____
2. **Gender: ( ) Male   ( ) Female**
3. Year in School: (   )Freshman   (   )Sophomore   (   )Junior   (   )Senior

BLACKBOARD SURVEY

Please answer the following questions, based on your experiences using the Blackboard Web site in the Freshman Rhetoric (RHE102) course, by placing an X in the box below the statement that reflects your response.

	Never	Once	Once per Week	2–3 Days per Week	4–6 Days per Week	Daily
4. How frequently did you log into the Blackboard site?						
5. How frequently did you post a message on the Blackboard site?						

How did the following Blackboard services affect your learning experience in this course?

	Added Significantly to Learning	Added to Learning	No Effect on Learning	Subtracted from Learning	Subtracted Significantly from Learning
6. Prayer/Praise Forum					
7. SAU Café Forum					
8. Autobiographies Forum					
9. General Course Information Forum					
10. Group Discussion Boards					
11. Daily Announcements					
12. Online Syllabus					
13. Faculty Information					
14. Course Information					
15. Online Gradebook					
16. Virtual Classroom (Chat)					
17. External Links					

18. How did the use of Blackboard affect the *quantity* of class discussion?

Significant Hindrance	Minor Hindrance	No Impact	Minor Help	Significant Help

19. How did the use of Blackboard affect the quality of class discussion?

Significant Hindrance	Minor Hindrance	No Impact	Minor Help	Significant Help

20. How did the use of Blackboard affect your relationship with the instructor?

Significant Hindrance	Minor Hindrance	No Impact	Minor Help	Significant Help

21. How did the use of Blackboard affect your relationships with your classmates?

Significant Hindrance	Minor Hindrance	No Impact	Minor Help	Significant Help

22. How did the use of Blackboard affect your overall enjoyment of this course?

Significant Hindrance	Minor Hindrance	No Impact	Minor Help	Significant Help

23. How did the use of Blackboard affect the overall effectiveness of this course?

Significant Hindrance	Minor Hindrance	No Impact	Minor Help	Significant Help

24. Where would you place yourself on this continuum?

Technophobic/ I Hate Technology	------------------ ------------------	------------------ ------------------	------------------ ------------------	Technophiliac/ I Love Technology

25. On a scale of 0–9, how much have you learned in the class you are in now, with 0 meaning you learned nothing and 9 meaning you learned more than any other class you ever had?

0	1	2	3	4	5	6	7	8	9

26. How much do you think you could have learned in this class had you had the ideal instructor, with 0 meaning you could have learned nothing and 9 meaning you could have learned more than in any other class you ever had?

0	1	2	3	4	5	6	7	8	9

27. What was the highlight of this course?

28. What features/functions would you like to see added to the Blackboard system to enhance the learning experience?

29. How do you imagine that this course will look different in five years?

Educational Equivalency

Renee Welch

> With the introduction and proliferation of instructional technologies, equivalency based on time in the classroom is of minimal relevance to learners and instructors who supplement educational opportunities through technology. (Watkins & Schlosser, 2000a, p.1)

The question of educational equivalency has become a growing topic of concern as institutions integrate traditional classroom instruction with technology enhanced instruction. While various components between the traditional classroom and online classroom have been examined, many continue to question the notion of educational equivalency between the two delivery formats. For nearly a century, the standard for determining the equivalency of academic courses and degrees has relied on time in the classroom, also known as the Carnegie Unit, as the primary indicator. Though widely accepted and convenient, time as the standard offers little value for today's institutions of higher education as the use of learning technologies become prevalent.

Currently, the credit hour is a measure of performance and a vehicle for translating complex activities into quantifiable units (Wellman and Ehrlich, 2003) such as: faculty workload, student learning, enrollment, graduation rate, time to degree, and the cost per student. Although the Carnegie Unit alleges to measure faculty effort and student accomplishment, it does not measure learning based on course goals or student results.

Currently, the standard formula for determining the number of credit hours to be awarded to various types of education for a lecture/discussion is that one 50-minute period per week for 15 weeks is equal to 1 semester credit hour. Or put another way, when connected to course work, credit earned is usually defined by seat time in the classroom, which means 1-hour each week for 15 weeks equals 1 academic credit hour.

In the design and execution of a conventional curriculum, time has been a powerful element in determining content (Wellman and Ehrlich, 2003). For instance, contact hour seat time is measured as the actual time students are expected to sit in a traditional classroom. The semester hour is determined by the amount of time spent in the classroom during each week. However, neither seat time or semester hour in the classroom can easily be measured when a class is conducted on the Internet.

Recent findings from Wellman and Ehrlich (2003) indicate that colleges are trying to modify the credit hour to measure learning goals and not time-on-task. However, this has proven difficult and most institutions continue to enforce standards based on centuries-old, time-linked measures.

Wellman and Ehrlich (2003) argue that using time to measure 21st century learning is ineffective. Furthermore, they posit that competency-based education models using course goals and objectives, offer a better solution for online courses.

The purpose of this study was to explore a basic model for the transformation of academic equivalency in online education, shifting from a unit of measurement that relies on time in the classroom to one that focuses on learner achievement. Looking for a way to make assigning appropriate academic credit consistent across courses, this study examined a large enrollment course using the Capabilities Based Educational Equivalency (CBEE) Unit framework in providing a sample application to highlight this research. An intended outcome of this research was to offer higher education administrators and faculty insight into some of the issues that surface when transforming a traditional course (taught in a face-to-face environment) into a blended or online course. As the instructional designer for the course described, my responsibilities included providing instructional support to the faculty member in developing and redesigning his traditionally taught course into a blended offering. My role as instructional designer was my entry point to this study.

Conceptual Framework

Equivalency Theory

Equivalency theory advocates designing a collection of equivalent learning experiences for distant and local learners, even though experiences will be different for each student. "The more equivalent the learning experiences of online learners are to those of local learners, the more equivalent the outcomes of the educational experiences for all learners" (Simonson, 1995, p. 12). In elaborating on this theory, Simonson (1995) states that it should not be necessary for any group of learners to compensate for different, possibly lesser, instructional learning experiences. Learners should have learning experiences that are tailored to the environment and situation in which they find themselves. Thus, developing virtual learning environments should strive for equivalency in the learning experiences of all learners, regardless of how they are linked to the resources or the instruction they require. Key elements to equivalency theory include the concepts of equivalency, learning experiences, appropriate application, learners, and outcomes.

Capabilities-Based Educational Equivalency (CBEE) Unit

Currently the Carnegie unit is a time based measurement used to show the equivalency of traditional courses. Researchers Watkins and Schlosser (2000c) found this unit of measure to be inappropriate for distance courses. They propose a CBEE "unit" to replace the hour as the measure of a task's efficient completion. The CBEE Units approach suggests a standardized formula for relating instructional objectives to academic credit. The research of Watkins and Schlosser (2000a,c) indicates that CBEE is a more practical instrument and can be used for both traditional, blended, and online courses relying on academic achievement rather than time to measure the class equivalency.

The CBEE Units model offers an "alternative approach that is not time-dependent but is responsive to emerging technologies, supportive of systematic instructional design, and focused on the achievement of learners" (Watkins & Schlosser, 2000c). This model puts forward a framework of academic equivalency that is founded on valid and useful instructional design objectives and permits the comparison of student achievement in classroom and online learning formats, as well as between programs delivering instruction using a wide variety of media. By making "quantitative approximations (units) for the qualitative description of what learners will achieve (objectives) the CBEE Units approach offers educators a 'ballpark' standard for how many instructional objectives should be attained in a course that is worth a given number of academic credit hours" (Watkins & Schlosser, 2000a).

This model offers a viable alternative to institutions that supplement educational opportunities through technology and focuses on the determination of equivalency on capability-based objectives rather than seat time (Gagne, Briggs, & Wager, 1992). As illustrated in the table below (Watkins & Schlosser, 2000 a,b,c), this model distinguishes instructional objectives as academic credit hours, and instead allocates a unit value to the demonstration of human capabilities as specified in Gagne's (1977) taxonomy:

Table 1. **Human Capabilities and the Proposed CBEE Units**

Human Capabilities (Gagné, 1977)	Objective Verb (Gagné, 1977)	CBEE Units
Intellectual Skills		
Discrimination	Discriminates	1 unit
Concrete Concepts	Identifies	2 units
Defined Concept	Classifies	3 units
Rule	Demonstrates	4 units
Problem Solving	Generates	5 units
Cognitive Strategy	Originates	6 units
Information	States	1 unit
Motor Skill	Executes	4 units
Attitude	Chooses	4 units

With a proposed standard of 30 CBEE Units per academic credit hour, a determination of educational equivalency can be based on the attained knowledge and skills of learners (as specified by the instructional objectives of courses and degrees) rather than time in the classroom. By relating the number and scope of objectives to the credit hour value of a course, instructors (and instructional designers) are provided with an approximate benchmark when determining the scope and sequence of a course regardless of the instructional delivery system chosen (Watkins & Schlosser, 2000a, p.3).

They suggest that the number of attained capabilities per credit hour would differ among academic disciplines and recommend that within an academic discipline a standard ratio should be set for equivalency. In an initial application, the 30 CBEE Units per credit hour ratio appeared to be appropriate for graduate level courses in education.

Bloom's Taxonomy

Bloom's Taxonomy, among the most widely accepted hierarchical arrangement of this sort in education, can be viewed as a continuum of thinking skills starting with knowledge-level thinking and moving eventually to evaluation-level thinking. The taxonomy is neither a developmental model nor a rubric for assessing online activities, but a classification of educational objectives used in the creation of lesson plans and educational goals and assessments. This framework was chosen because of its familiarity and because of its extensive research and theoretical base that can be helpful in grounding results. The cognitive levels of Bloom's Taxonomy are knowledge, comprehension, application, analysis, synthesis, and evaluation. The projected relationship between Bloom's Taxonomy and CBEE Units (Watkins & Schlosser, 2003) follows:

Table 2. **Adapted from Bloom's Taxonomy of Educational Objectives and the Proposed CBEE Units**

Bloom's Objectives	Action Verbs	CBEE Units
Knowledge	list, define, tell, describe, identify, show, label, collect, examine, tabulate, quote, name, who, when, where, etc.	1 unit
Comprehension	summarize, describe, interpret, contrast, predict, associate, distinguish, estimate, differentiate, discuss, extend	2 units
Application	apply, demonstrate, calculate, complete, illustrate, show, solve, examine, modify, relate, change, classify, experiment, discover	3 units

Analysis	analyze, separate, order, explain, connect, classify, arrange, divide, compare, select, explain, infer	4 units
Synthesis	combine, integrate, modify, rearrange, substitute, plan, create, design, invent, what if?, compose, formulate, prepare, generalize, rewrite	5 units
Evaluation	assess, decide, rank, grade, test, measure, recommend, convince, select, judge, explain, discriminate, support, conclude, compare, summarize	6 units

While debate exists as to the comparability of learning in traditional classrooms versus online courses, a basic assumption in this study is that the level of cognition is equal in both instructional formats. Discussions as such also support the need for further research in this area to investigate what implications the course content and technology used has on the requirements for activities and the delivery of a course.

Methodology

A case study methodology was followed using the redesign of a single course in criminal justice at the University of Illinois-Chicago. The author of this study functioned as the instructional designer working with the instructor of record for the course.

The Course: Criminal Justice 121

Criminal Justice 121: Violence in America, a course in the College of Liberal Arts and Sciences/Department of Criminal Justice, explores the history and varieties of violence. An historical and multi-disciplinary overview of violence is combined with an examination of how the varieties of violence are exemplified in the history of Chicago. In the traditional format, students attend two lectures and one discussion session per week for 3 credit hours. The instructor of record delivers the (2) one-hour lectures to classes of approximately 100 students while a teaching assistant facilitates the discussion sections of about 30 students each. The teaching assistant also holds office hours and grades exams.

This traditional course configuration faced several academic problems including decreasing class attendance (attendance at the large lecture sections averages approximately 70%) and uneven student participation and engagement with the material. In the lecture format, while some students engaged in lively dialogue, most did not, and some were clearly intimidated from discussing a topic like gangs in front of so many other students. Some of these students participated more fully in the discussion section, but there were many students who were not engaged in either of the lectures or discussion sessions. Although students could meet individually and in small groups with the teaching assistant or with the instructor during office hours, only a small number of students availed themselves of these. Most students attended lectures, took notes, studied the text, turned in their homework, and took the quizzes and exam. According to the faculty member, and part of his rationale for wanting to redesign this course offering, the traditional large-lecture format does not always provide the means for students needing to interact in a smaller, less intimidating manner.

This course was re-designed from a two lecture, one discussion format to a blended course based on the instructor's extensive use of web resources and the Blackboard course management system (CMS). To best take advantage of multiple approaches and allow students space to anonymously and individually react to images of violence, this would be the first offering of this course in a technology-enhanced format. The major assumption was that having an online component would allow for different learning styles and improve completion of course requirements.

The instructor decided to incorporate three online sessions as a pilot during the initial semester in order to gather data on both the blended course design and its suitability to teaching about sensitive subjects. The primary goal of the redesign was to restructure the large-lecture sections to increase active learning and interactivity in a large lecture format through the use of technological enhancements that stressed peer interaction and asynchronous learning.

He began the process by creating an interactive syllabus in an effort to map out instructional strategies in relation to the course objectives, assignments and assessments. Each weekly module consisted of an introductory Monday lecture, required readings, group work, and assigned activities. The modules integrated classroom activities and online activities. The Monday lecture included information on how to proceed through the week's activities and reviewed and incorporated reactions from the online discussions and assignments. The online resources were presented, discussed, and reviewed during the face-to-face lectures and discussion sections of the course using Blackboard as the course's management tool. Students underwent an orientation prior to their online experience.

The discussion forum was designed to foster conversation and assignments integrated with articles and web sites linking supplementary resources and enrichment materials. By sequencing assignments that moved students from the lecture to discussing and responding online, from written reflections about their responses and readings to group projects that were developed in the discussion forum, students were engaged in learning. Each discussion board question was made available on Monday and remained open for the remainder of the course so students could always retrieve information and discussions. The teaching assistant facilitated the online discussions and the Friday face to face discussion sessions throughout the semester, as well as monitored the group discussion in preparation for group presentation. The discussion sections provided opportunities for students to discuss and deepen their understanding of the lectures, prepare their presentations, and receive feedback.

Two online quizzes, two papers, a group project, and short essay final exam were incorporated as a means for assessing learning. Students were expected to use online texts and other documents during the course, as well as identify written resources related to their specific area of professional interest. Significant learning activities were web-based and discussion was required of students.

In summary, the redesigned course implemented the following changes:

- Change in three lecture sessions to online meetings
- Offer interactive, online materials and computerized testing
- Offer collaborative and hands-on learning opportunities for students
- Eliminate some of the time that TAs spend grading exams
- Expand the instructor role from mainly instruction to learning facilitation.

Findings

Date Collection and Analysis

As a new offering, this course would have to meet the approval of the College of Liberal Arts and Sciences Educational Policy Committee. In an early meeting the Committee shared concerns about face-to-face time being reduced in a course that handled such controversial content. The majority of the committee felt that first-year students would need more face-to-face time in handling such content and not less. Another concern was the number of hours that were associated with online work. Some thought that the students might be working more than a typical 3 credit-hour class, while some thought there would be less work. To triangulate findings and answer their concerns, data collection methods included an end-of the course survey, peer assessment techniques, and analysis of Blackboard course statistics and web-based student responses and activities.

Aside from student evaluations (and) the final exam, a debriefing session was held to discuss content and the effectiveness of this offering from an instructional perspective. In a debriefing session with the faculty member after the course, his thoughts could be summarized as follows:

Large enrollment courses have problems, such as students with widely varying skills and knowledge, and the lack of interaction within these courses. Lost in a sea of faces, they sit with other strangers whom they understandably perceive as competitors for the all-important grade. Anonymity breeds apathy: without supportive, encouraging, motivating relationships among learners and instructors, students often do not prepare for, or even come to lecture. Even when they have access to small discussion groups, led by junior instructors, these 'sections' usually are haphazardly taught and not well integrated into the curriculum, sometimes students don't even attend. Students simply do not like this type of course and overwhelmingly give large lecture courses low evaluation ratings... What I learned was that the 3 hybrid sessions significantly enhanced learning and made the course more effective pedagogically. While a model of 3 or 4 online sessions does not create more classroom space, it does seem to produce better education. What I would like to do for the next time the course is offered is to formally pilot it as a blended course, add a chat session, video, and up to four additional online sessions and present the course as one model for teaching large lecture classes in the social sciences. (Debriefing Session of John Hagedorn).

"Large lecture course have a reputation as being poor learning settings, especially among educators who advocate a predominately student-centered approach to learning" (Harley, Maher, Henke, Lawrence, 2003, p. 32). Their study provides data on the costs and utility of current technology enhancements in a large lecture course at a major public research university. One of their most important findings about "student behavior and technology was the degree to which students embraced the multiple opportunities technology provided for curricular resource access and scheduling flexibility" (Harley et al., 2003, p. 32).

The redesigned format allowed students to participate in traditional ways in lecture or discussion groups and gave them the additional choice of participating online and observing the discussion by fellow students with no pressure to participate in ways that were uncomfortable. For example, the online discussion component, particularly on sensitive topics, allowed students to go over the material at their own pace, and react online rather in a difficult face to face manner. It also allowed for "lurking" or learning by reading others' responses and only participating when the student felt safe. The time spent on these online activities surpassed the 50 minute lecture that was being replaced.

There were 95 students enrolled in this course, with 88 students finishing. In the end of the course survey, 64 students participated, and the responses indicate that students liked the online discussion because it was easier for them to speak their minds. The online forums became very popular and they had 15,942 hits, a hit being any time a student posted a response or read another student's response. This is an average of 178 hits per student. There were 766 postings, or an average of almost 9 per student. In the most participatory face-to-face lectures, typically fewer than 25% of the class will ask questions or comment. The survey and responses are summarized in the appendix.

According to the students, the online discussion component allowed for opportunity to go over the material at their own pace, and gave time to interact online more so than in a face to face manner. It also allowed them to learn by reading others' responses. Eighty-one percent of the students responded it was a good way to deal with sensitive topics.

The Friday discussion section was seen as important. The students recommended replacing between 3 and 8 lectures with online discussions, and indicated that they did not want them eliminated. Overall they liked the course and its hybrid nature — 95% would recommend the course to others and 86% would recommend continuing to offer it as a blended course.

Various learning activities were used to reach the course's goals and objectives. Web based reading assignments and supplemental resources and videos provided a foundation of information about the content of the course. Online discussions were used to ensure an understanding of ideas and concepts. Most important, student activities focused on allowing each student to concentrate on course content that was most applicable and useful to them. Student questions and responses were shared and integrated into lecture sessions.

In an effort to provide an explanation for the amount of work students would do online, I used the CBEE Units model as the framework, applying Bloom's taxonomy, and the proposed 30 CBEE Units per academic credit hour. Relating the number and scope of objectives to the credit hour value of a course provided an approximate benchmark for determining the scope and sequence of a course regardless of the instructional delivery format (Watkins & Schlosser, 2000 a, c). Watkins and Schlosser's initial application highlighted a graduate level course, had not been applied to an undergraduate course, and did not incorporate Bloom's taxonomy and instructional strategies, as shown in Table 3.

Table 3. **Aligning Course Objectives in Relation to Bloom's Taxonomy and CBEE Units**

Objective	Instructional Strategies	Activity Assessment	Bloom/ CBEE
The student will learn: different types of violence and the centrality of race and the dehumanization of the "other" in violence	The thesis of Exterminate the Brutes was that the holocaust was not a unique event. Using examples from the lectures, readings, and discussions, critique this viewpoint. This is a controversial assertion, so feel free to agree or disagree, but use materials from the class to support your views.	Final exam	Evaluation 6 units
	The projects are intended as a means for students to investigate and report on an aspect of violence that interests you. Presentations should be multi-media and educational. Projects are graded both on their educational content as well as the effectiveness of their presentation. *Possible topics include…*	Group project weeks 13–15	Synthesis 5 units
	Online discussion of slavery and the annihilation of the native peoples of North America. Online discussion about genocide. *Jefferson Davis in his speech defined slaves as property, or as non-human. American Indians. According to your reading, were they victims of white settler genocide? Are these attitudes basically horrors of the past that have*	DQ	Application 3 units

239

	"faded away" with the advance of civilization? How might they manifest themselves today?		
The student will learn: How these different types of violence are exemplified by events in Chicago	Phillipe Bourgois classified violence into several types. Classify the violence portrayed in the media and the sweatshops group presentations, and from one other group's topic of your choosing. Explain how the classification fits in two paragraphs or so for each topic.	Final exam	Analysis 4 units
	CVL History. History Channel movie *Is this story believable? Explain, how can gang transform into a community organization?* Music videos—review and critique assignment	Movie and online discussion. Friday discussion Chapters Five and Six of People & Folks	Analysis 4 units
The student will gain: An understanding of the central role violence plays in modern life.	This class has argued a controversial thesis that the advance of Western civilization has meant an increase of violence against the other. The most current example would be the war on terror and war against Iraq. Using materials from the class, give your opinion on this thesis and support it. Grading will not be based on your point of view, but solely on how well you can incorporate the materials and discussion in class to support your argument.	Final exam	Evaluation 6 units
	Gentrification, housing and violence in Chicago. Variations in urban homicide http://www.chicagohomeless.org/factsfigures/facts.htm	In class Friday Discussion/ Reviews. Online quiz on Violence in Chicago	Compre-hension 2 units

Although the information from this table does not report time spent on task, it does highlight the instructional strategies, in relation to assignments and assessments for the face-to-face and online components of this offering. When this course is offered again, a question will be added to the student survey to gauge the time students spent on class assignments.

Conclusion

Education at a distance should be built on the concept of equivalency of learning experiences. With the onset of technologies in the classroom, time is no longer a fixed constant equivalency for coursework. Furthermore, definitions of coursework centered on classroom seat time is of minimal relevance to learners and instructors who supplement educational opportunities through technology (Watkins & Schlosser, 2000a,c). Although the Carnegie Unit has been a convenient standard of equivalency since 1902 and purports to gauge faculty effort and student accomplishment, it does not measure learning based on goals or results. The growing requirement due to technology-delivered instruction, blended and online learning necessitates a re-examination of this time-based standard.

Universities should begin to explore a basic model for the transformation of academic credit in blended and online education, shifting from the Carnegie Unit as a unit of measurement that relies on time in the classroom to one that focuses on learner achievement.

Rob Reynolds (2004) in *How to Measure Time for Online Activities and Courses*, observes that traditional classroom environments are "instructor-mediated." The instructor serves as timekeeper (constantly available to adjust time) and mediator for student progress on activities and projects. The online learning environment offers much less instructor mediation and when it does occur, it is typically asynchronous. Without the ever-present instructor as an experienced interpreter of the learning context for an activity, the student is dependent on the system itself to measure how long he/she should spend on a given section of the course. The absence of a teacher as timekeeper and mediator, as well as the general variation between course delivery structures makes it difficult to determine accurately how long digital assignments will take learners to complete.

The effectiveness of teaching in a blended or online learning environment is dependent on planning and organization. There should be a focus on the equivalency of learning experiences rather than on which format is better—the traditional classroom versus the virtual environment. Faculty and administrators should focus on learning experiences versus the vehicle used to deliver instruction and keep in mind that in online delivery time is on the side of the learner (Ross, 2001, p. 44). Therefore, faculty and instructional designers should tailor learning experiences based on the environment of the learner by incorporating objectives, activities, and assessments that make the sum of experiences for all learners equivalent.

The purpose of this study was to explore a model for the transformation of academic equivalency in online education, shifting from a unit of measurement that relies on time in the classroom (the Carnegie unit) to one that focuses on learner achievement. An intended outcome of this study was to offer insight into some of the questions faced by institutions when attempting to transform a traditional course to an online or blended format. Such information could be useful in determining strategies, procedures, and processes necessary for delivery of instruction in an online or blended course environment at Brigham Young University, as well as provide new knowledge accessible to other institutions engaged in similar efforts. As institutions consider and adopt blended and online education models, the topic of educational equivalency calls for further research and dialogue.

References

Black, E. J. (1992). Faculty support for university distance education. *CADE: Journal of Distance Education, 7*(2), np.

Bloom, Ben. S. (1984) *Taxonomy of educational objectives*. Boston, MA: Allyn and Bacon Pearson Education.

Driscoll, M. (1991) *Psychology of learning for instruction*. Boston, MA: Allyn and Bacon.

Gagné, R. (1977). *The conditions of learning* (3rd ed.). New York, NY: Holt, Rinehart and Winston, Inc.

Gagné, R. (1972). Domains of learning. *Interchange, 3*(1), 1–8.

Gagne, R., Briggs, L. & Wager, W. (1992). *Principles of instructional design* (4th ed.). Fort Worth, TX: HBJ College Publishers.

Harley, D. (2003). An analysis of technology enhancements in a large lecture course. In M. Maher, J. Henke, and S. Lawrence (Eds.), *EDUCAUSE Quarterly 26*(3). Retrieved from http://www.educause.edu/ir/library/pdf/eqm0335.pdf.

Hagedorn, J. (2005). Faculty interview/debriefing. Equivalency theory and distance education: A new discussion Michael Simonson, Charles Schlosser, and Dan Hanson *The American Journal of Distance Education, 13*(1), np. Retrieved from http://www.uni-oldenburg.de/zef/cde/found/simons99.htmTheory.

Ross, V. (2001). Offline to online curriculum: A case-study of one music course. *Online Journal of Distance Learning Administration, 4*(4). State University of West Georgia, Distance Education Center. Retrieved from http://www.westga.edu/~distance/ojdla/winter44/ross44.html.

Reynolds, Robert. (2004). How to measure time for online activities and courses. Retrieved from http://www.xplanazine.com/archives/2004/06/this_brief_stud.php.

Simonson, M. (2000). Equivalency theory and distance education. *TechTrends Journal, 43*(5), 5–8.

Simonson, M. (1995). Does anyone really want to learn at a distance? *TechTrends Journal, 40*(5), 12.

Watkins, R., & Schlosser, C. (2003). It's not about time: A fresh approach to educational equivalency. *TechTrends Journal, 47*(3), 35–39.

Watkins, R. & Schlosser, C. (2000a). Moving past time as the criteria: The application of capabilities-based educational equivalency units in education *Online Journal of Distance Learning Administration, 5*(3). State University of West Georgia, Distance Education Center. Retrieved from: http://www.westga.edu/~distance/ojdla/fall53/watkins53.html.

Watkins, R. & Schlosser, C. (2000b). The impact of technology on educational equivalency: Capabilities based educational equivalency units. *Educational Technology, 40*(6), 49–54.

Watkins, R., & Schlosser, C. (2000c). Capabilities based educational equivalency units: Beginning a professional dialogue on useful models for educational equivalency. *American Journal of Distance Education, 14*(3), 34–47.

Wellman and Ehrlich. (2003). How the student credit hour shapes higher education. San Francisco: Jossey-Bass Publishers.

Appendix

Student Survey and Responses (N=64)

Question 1 Multiple Choice

The use of the discussion board in weeks 3, 5, and 10 was

Answers	Percent Answered
Very useful	34.375%
Useful	51.562%
Didn't make a difference	9.375%
Not useful	4.688%
Unanswered	0%

Question 2 Multiple Choice

The best feature of the discussion board was

Answers	Percent Answered
You could express your opinion	76.562%
You didn't have to attend class	12.5%
You could interact with other students	10.938%
Other	0%
Unanswered	0%

Question 3 Multiple Choice

The main problem with the discussion board is

Answers	Percent Answered
There are too many threads to read	39.062%
Some of the responses weren't focused on the assignment	15.625%
Not enough feedback from the instructor	12.5%
The lectures presented more information	12.5%
Other	20.312%
Unanswered	0%

Question 4 Multiple Choice

If you were designing this course for next year, how often would you replace a face to face lecture with Blackboard (Bb) activities:

Answers	Percent Answered
Weekly — keep a face to face lecture and discussion, and replace one lecture with online activities each week	10.938%
Every other week or so — have 5-6 sessions online throughout the semester	40.625%
Only a few — Keep it like it was done this semester (3 sessions)	42.188%
None — have two lectures each week.	6.25%
Unanswered	0%

Question 5 Multiple Choice

Would you recommend this course to other students?

Answers	Percent Answered
Yes — Highly	75%
Yes	20.312%
Maybe	4.688%
No	0%
Unanswered	0%

Question 6 Multiple Choice

Would you recommend a "blended" course like this for other students?

Answers	Percent Answered
Yes — Highly	51.562%
Yes	34.375%
Maybe	12.5%
No	1.562%
Unanswered	0%

Question 7 Multiple Choice

Does the discussion board promote more participation in discussions about sensitive topics like genocide and rape than in a class with two lectures and a discussion group?

Answers	Percent Answered
Promotes more participation on sensitive topics	81.25%
Promotes about the same amount of participation	15.625%
Promotes less participation	3.125%
Not sure	0%
Unanswered	0%

Question 8 Essay

Please write any other comments you have on the course and the on line discussion board component. Explain your "other" answers if you like here.

Thank you for your participation this semester.

Blended Learning – Complexity in Corporate and Higher Education

Robert Albrecht and Judy Pirani
Educause Center for Applied Research (ECAR)

Blended learning is taking place in education from segment to segment, small to large, research to specialized, and K–12 to post-graduate. While not yet as pervasive as online learning—as far as we know!—anecdotal evidence suggests rapid growth. Since many institutions do not identify or track blended learning offerings, data is typically missing or unreliable. However, some programs are data driven, seeking and collecting information that supports the development of blended learning. Among these are corporate training companies and universities that recognize the need for data based decisions. The case studies of two such entities illuminate the advantages of embracing blended learning, managing it and incorporating it into the strategic goals of a company or a higher education institution.

A university with ambitious growth plans looks for opportunities to expand enrollments at acceptable cost while maintaining its base of offerings. A very large corporation necessarily manages its assets to maximize revenues. Both need to track enrollments, student/customer satisfaction, revenues, return on investment (ROI) and learning effectiveness. One has established a flourishing blended learning structure; the other is embracing an opportunity to meet student expectations and to achieve new strategic goals. Both are committed to seeking financially viable and pedagogically effective programs that can be offered through a mix of delivery modes appropriate to both audience and content.

In higher education the labels blended (and hybrid) learning have a relatively short history. The common definition in higher education—substituting face-to-face class sessions with web-based activity—is somewhat restrictive. Other patterns can be found, just as broader definitions reveal examples from some years ago. Corporate training programs are using a mixture of delivery systems to present effective learning.

The case studies illuminate some of the differing practices between higher education and corporate training. While academics may look askance at the corporate training segment, case studies can suggest useful comparisons and the potential benefits of becoming more familiar with the "other" side.

The examples chosen for this comparison are IBM and the School of Extended Studies at Arizona State University (ASU). These very large organizations present significant contrasts. However, they offer examples of how large scale offerings of blended learning can succeed. Convenience is such a major feature of blended learning in both that it can't be over-stated. The lessons learned at the end of this chapter summarize those features particularly applicable to higher education.

While IBM is both a vendor and a provider of corporate training, its use of blended learning internally reveals a strong commitment to delivery patterns that bring together face-to-face delivery with various technology delivery systems—Internet, e- mail, chat rooms, and so forth. In fact, blended learning has become so popular, and its results so significant, that programs throughout the company (and its large variety of customer companies) employ it. The example presented in this chapter is one of the basic IBM programs, Basic Blue for Managers. For IBM, cost savings make a difference, and training costs are closely monitored. Beyond dollar costs is the return-on-investment (ROI) which includes increased learning effectiveness that translates to higher skills in employees. Evidence from IBM sources indicates that blended learning has advanced the effectiveness of training, increased ROI and significantly improved the satisfaction of the students (employees).

The ASU case study presents a university that, like IBM, is an entity of great size and complexity with issues of cost, effectiveness, and student satisfaction. While IBM may seem more centralized, ASU is organized in order to permit functions to be delivered globally—beyond its four campuses. The attraction of blended learning courses has driven very significant growth among on campus students and certainly among the off campus students served by the School of Extended Education in University College. Students at ASU, and elsewhere as suggested by evidence from the Educause Center for Applied Research (ECAR) survey (Kvavik, 2005), want the convenience of accessing content and other material outside the classroom when that is appropriate. Like IBM employees (and its customers), they would prefer to receive certain kinds of information at the desktop at home or at work at their convenience rather than travel to a classroom to hear that same information in a lecture. The challenge for IBM as much as for ASU is how to package,how to choose and to structure elements of course work,for appropriate delivery. "Appropriate" must be defined as educationally effective, leading to better learning. Faculty support at ASU, like that at IBM, is available in both a central and a distributed fashion; that is, it supports the faculty who are involved in constructing and teaching the blended learning courses. The strategic task for ASU, and particularly for University College, is to serve members of the diverse communities in Phoenix, in Arizona and beyond. To do that, ASU must listen to students and to potential students.

Methodology

The methodology for the case studies began with extensive personal contacts and searching of print and online sources for appropriate organizations. This work led to the key contacts at IBM and Arizona State University. The sources were interviewed by telephone, and precise transcripts of those conversations were preserved. Relevant web sites and publications of both organizations were searched for other material. Follow-up telephone conversations confirmed the accuracy of the data in interviews, and interviewees reviewed the draft manuscript.

Arizona State University Organization and Distributed Learning

Arizona State University (ASU) a public metropolitan research university and the 4th largest university in the United States, with over 60,000 students is structured with four campuses (Tempe, Polytechnic, West and Downtown Phoenix). The Downtown Phoenix Campus, the newest of the four, includes University College, although various University College programs are housed on all four of the campuses. The School of Extended Education, which includes 300 community outreach programs at 480 locations, is a center for blended learning (hybrid learning in the ASU lexicon) and is organizationally housed with the ASU University College. Blended learning courses offered at ASU come from departments and programs throughout the University.

The website, ASUonline (http://asuonline.asu.edu/FacultySupport /Hybrid.cfm), in the "Overview of Hybrid Courses," defines blended learning offerings: "A hybrid course combines face-to-face instruction and web- or computer-based learning in an educational environment that is non-specific as to time and place. . . . In a hybrid course, a significant part of the course interaction takes place online and students can expect to spend at least as much time as they would in an on-campus section of the course."

The School of Extended Education (formerly the College of Extended Education) includes a distributed learning area with academic technology headed by Samuel DiGangi, Associate Vice President for Academic Technology and Executive Director of ASU's Applied Learning Technologies Institute. Following ASU's mantra, "one university, geographically distributed," distributed learning is centralized through a partnership between the School of Extended Education and ASU's University Technology Office (formerly Information Technology).

The School of Extended Education now has strategic enrollment goals, according to DiGangi (S. DiGangi, personal communication, March 6, 2006). "When we looked at our extended campus or official educational offerings, we found that a large number of the students who were enrolled in our '100% online courses' under the College of Extended Education, were already matriculated," explains DiGangi. "They were in essence ASU students who were taking courses online. We were not hitting a truly extended campus, rather we were servicing the residence halls." The challenge given to DiGangi was to create a global campus of students beyond the campuses. The reorganization includes a new business plan and a new entrepreneurial spirit.

ASU Blended Learning—History, Patterns, Policies and Plans

Blended learning has been part of the University offering for some years. "In the early days of networking ASU's College of Education was using online discussion groups to supplement traditional instruction," says DiGangi (S. DiGangi, personal communication, March 6, 2006). With BitNet e-mail and computer-based bulletin-boards, blended learning courses were introduced. But it was with the Web that blended learning as it is commonly practiced today came to ASU. By 1996 or 1997, the University was hosting multiple course management systems. Blended learning courses are presently hosted in Blackboard, although a Sakai implementation has begun.

While online offerings tend to cluster in specific areas or programs, blended courses are spread across the campuses with no single college dominating the offerings. DiGangi estimates the current offerings of distributed learning at 4000 courses, with approximately 40,000 students (S. DiGangi, personal communication, March 6, 2006). ASU defines an active hybrid student as a student who accesses the course at least once a week. The use of Blackboard permits the School to track the offerings since they are hosted centrally. "All student and faculty access as well as the faculty course creation takes place in the ASU portal environment," states DiGangi. ASU runs a "U Portal" point of entry and employs a single sign-on to Blackboard, as well as other ASU services and resources (see http://my.asu.edu) that allows them to track both the type of course as well as collecting data at that U Portal point of entry.

Currently, the number of blended courses is rapidly growing, while the number of wholly online courses seems to have leveled out. Since blended courses are not transcribed separately, precise numbers have not been available. However, the new business model has led to the need for more precise data collection for analysis.

If the online enrollments have leveled out, what is driving the increase in blended learning enrollments, and how does that fit into the new plans for distributed learning at ASU? DiGangi believes the growth in blended learning comes from "a pull from the student side" (S. DiGangi, personal communication, March 6, 2006). ASU has surveyed 3000 new students who will be attending the downtown campus in Phoenix which opens in the summer of 2006. The students indicate a preference for blended courses and a desire for the faculty to be supported in offering such courses effectively. One area of particular of student interest is enhanced podcasting.

According to DiGangi, ASU has no formal policies requiring faculty to move to blended learning, but the student pull is manifest through the enrollments (S. DiGangi, personal communication, March 6, 2006). There is strong central support for course design. A "train-the-trainer" program is provided by the central IT organization—ASU's University Technology Office—to support course and program development. Support and training programs are provided for students through the colleges. Some colleges also have their own faculty support units. For those colleges, the University Technology Office provides "a central infrastructure, media server access, as well as training and materials on how to use resources and facilities for Blackboard, Sakai and other resources," DiGangi reports. For those faculty members in colleges without program- or college-based support resources, a central support lab is available, although that facility is now geared primarily to provide college, department or program based support.

Another change has been to move the University College effort towards support for developing programs rather than individual courses. DiGangi said, "This enables the college or a group of faculty to develop reusable modules, to tie their design together we so are not building a series of individual, freestanding courses. They are leveraging the group investment from within their college or department" (S. DiGangi, personal communication, March 6, 2006). Such planning helps bring faculty together in joint efforts. DiGangi also points out that this approach enables the "construction of courses that constitute programs" and allows better scaling of those programs. Given the ambitious enrollment goals for distributed learning, scalability is a key issue.

ASU Data Collection and Decision Making

Such innovation requires careful evaluation and assessment of student learning as well as of new structures and support systems. "There is an opportunity for all of us to make data-based decisions on how we combine and choose approaches and tools within this environment," explains DiGangi (S. DiGangi, personal communication, March 6, 2006). "There is great opportunity there and we have overlooked it over the years." Data collection and analysis at ASU is being used to support data-based decision making to an extent beyond typical practices in large public universities.

ASU has a central learning research group, the Applied Learning Technology Institute. Its purpose, DiGangi notes, is to look "at central/overall effectiveness indicators as well as a college's or a program's instructional design and delivery components (S. DiGangi, personal communication, March 6, 2006). The University recognizes the need to develop "refined web analytics, where students and faculty go in the overall environment, and how they behave in the course management systems."

The push for assessment comes from the recognition of "the need to look at measures at as granular level as possible." Student grades or enrollment retention are not sufficient. "We need to look at how specific tools are used and in what combinations, and in what specific programs. The degree to which an institution can collect that degree of data—as well as analyze it—is very important."

Given the entrepreneurial nature of the School of Extended Education, it is not surprising that cost as well as learning effectiveness drives the significant effort to gather necessary information. "We are looking at an open-ended side to potential enrollment growth and we don't really have any algorithms to calculate and to evaluate whether we are making effective decisions—in everything from staffing to equipment to licensing," DiGangi explains (S. DiGangi, personal communication, March 6, 2006). "We are focusing on a budgeting model and a costing and evaluation model. We are closest to having that information and figures on the University College's Distributed Education component because we are going through a [business plan development] process in response to our enrollment goals. We are breaking down central costs and attempting to attach them to programs, courses, and ultimately, to students." This analysis, he further explains, applies to blended learning offerings as well as fully online offerings. ASU is attempting to break or slice the components of the courses down into six categories that range from a standard text-based Blackboard offering up to a boutique category that would cover very esoteric course applications and investments.

This effort to understand the costs and learning effectiveness of blended learning as well as other delivery systems has led to an effort to create a "calculator model" to determine the cost of individual courses depending upon enrollment, for example. The program must maximize its return on investment (ROI) in order to achieve enrollment goals. In other words, only by knowing costs and revenues can it successfully financially support the expansion of enrollment.

While the colleges on the (now) four campuses operate somewhat independently, we asked DiGangi about faculty attitudes towards blended learning (S. DiGangi, personal communication, March 6, 2006). Some difficulties have occasionally developed over the adoption of course management systems, particularly when several were being used at the University. Some faculty members were concerned over the effect of the CMS on pedagogy. However, "with the increased use of ancillary and other types of products nesting within the portal, there is less reluctance to use the systems and less resistance to offering blended learning courses and programs," explains DiGangi. "Faculty members are no longer restricted to the look, feel, and delivery of a specific course management system. Initial resistance was more in line with the limitation perceptions derived from the design, delivery, and pedagogy imposed by using a specific system."

"While this seems to be a diverse collection of applications and resources, our approach to authentication and authorization enables users to easily and securely access services through one user id and one password," DiGangi asserts, "ensuring that ASU does not duplicate account creation and maintenance (S. DiGangi, personal communication, March 6, 2006). Through this approach, we strive to provide a learning environment that is nimble, able to incorporate new technologies and resources that can scale to meet current and emerging needs. Our goal is to ensure production-level quality, reliability, and security while anticipating and controlling resource costs."

As ASU continues to evolve its extended learning program, DiGangi offers the following success factors:

- There is the need to look at measures and evaluations at as granular a level as possible. "Don't accept overall indicators such as students' grade levels or enrollment retention as sufficient," he explains. "We need to look at a more specific level: how specific tools are used and in what combinations, and what in specific programs. The degree that an institution can collect that degree of data—as well as analyze, interpret and apply the findings—is very important."

- DiGangi also sees great potential in looking at course design— hybrid design, or 100% online—at the integrated program level, not at the individual course level. This facilitates a strategic viewpoint about blended learning in general and promotes faculty buy-in at the outset (S. DiGangi, personal communication, March 6, 2006).

A Corporate Perspective on Blended Learning

Corporate employee training programs continue to gain importance as companies strive to maintain a competitive workforce. As Michael King, Director, Market Development, IBM Education Industry and Learning Solutions notes, "Senior managers are escalating their focus on this issue. For example, an IBM survey revealed that 75% of CEOs said that organizational skill improvement is one of their top management issues" (M. King and C. Davia, personal communication, February 21, 2006). A further indicator of training's importance is the increasingly common role of the Chief Learning Officer (CLO) to manage company programs and to monitor their effectiveness. Corporate training activities differ from higher education in that many employees learn new job skills during their day-to-day work activities as well as during a formal course setting. Blended learning tools are ideally suited to bridge these diverse educational requirements.

The size and scope of IBM's education and training activity marks it as one of the nation's leading models of teaching and learning, albeit in a world seen as distinct from higher education. However, IBM's concern for learning effectiveness and quality, cost of education and the return on investment (ROI) in teaching and training are counterparts of the issues found at ASU and its peers. Further, the blending of delivery modes to increase learning effectiveness and student satisfaction are directed towards the same purposes as those at ASU.

The web site, www.ibm.com/learning, opens to a number of related sites that reveal the breadth of interest and activity for the company in this area. For example, white papers include such topics as "aligning strategy with organizational outcomes," and "blended learning for today's evolving workforce." The marketing rhetoric includes statements such as, "At IBM, learning is in our DNA." But the topics and slogans that are designed to sell the IBM products and services also put forward ideas that are recognizable to a higher education audience: "If you can measure it, you can manage it;" "there is no credible way to link what you put in with what comes out;" "why learning impact is so difficult to measure;" "at IBM we developed the Learning Effectiveness Measurement methodology to establish causal linkages between training initiatives and business results." Underneath the marketing rhetoric, as heard by an audience from higher education, are the themes and the issues with which higher education in an age of accountability must also wrestle. The measurement of learning, for example, leads to the issues of assessment which accrediting agencies are pressing. In other words, while IBM and ASU may face different problems, the underlying issues are remarkably similar. Blended learning happens to represent a common ground where the challenges facing each entity can be recognized and discussed.

"Measuring effectiveness is fairly straightforward in the education world, but not so with corporations," states King (M. King and C. Davia, personal communication, February 21, 2006). "In K–12, each state sets the skill level. In higher education, the faculty may set degree standards. But in the corporate area, most CEOs would agree that an employee's competitive skill set is a key organization success competency. It is quite difficult, however, to map a firm's investment in learning accordingly. It is not a matter of looking at the reduced costs, but it is much more about the resumes and the skills of the people who are driving your revenues. At IBM, we sell our skills on the open marketplace and if we are not world class, then we can't compete effectively. As Christopher Davia, Senior Architect, further explains, "It is not only a matter of leveraging technology, but how you leverage technology to most effectively improve learning outcomes, to find greater efficiencies, and to lower costs of learning delivery."

IBM's Perspective

IBM is particularly qualified to offer perspectives about corporate training and blended learning as IBM's educational services extend from the thousands of IBM employees to many more thousands who are served through IBM's vendor business.

Ted Hoff, CLO, manages IBM's internal learning program. "IBM currently invests more than $700 million annually to develop the knowledge and expertise of its workforce. Employees spend an estimated 16 million hours each year (about 50 hours per employee) in formal training—either through online learning activities or in a traditional classroom." In 2005, the IBM earned the top spot in *Training* magazine's 2005 'Training Top 100'.

Each IBM employee takes ownership of the supervision of his or her skill set, working with his or her manager to create a skill enhancement plan as part of his or her annual review and assessment cycle. All managers are responsible for reviewing and signing off on their subordinates' plans as well as keeping them up-to-date. "It is our mission and mandate to identify the key skill sets that we need in the marketplace, to provide an outlook to each employee as to where he or she can their enhance skills, and to make the supporting educational opportunities available to them," explains King. Employees' skill enhancement can cover diverse areas, delivery requirements, and time expectations—e.g. one-on-one or group mentoring, formal classroom sessions, or just in time information delivery—all of which can benefit from blended learning delivery systems.

IBM's 4-Tier Learning Model

To match educational requirements with appropriate tools, IBM uses its 4-Tier Learning Model™ to design its learning solutions. The model "provides a blueprint for training and support planning, development, and implementation. With the 4-Tier Learning Model framework, IBM can help an organization establish the way in which training content is designed and delivered" (IBM's 4-tier, 2006).

An example of IBM's use of blended learning in the 4-Tier Learning Model is its own "Basic Blue for Managers," a program for new managers. The program rests on a model of leadership development "that incorporates four distinct instructional approaches (tiers) to provide an array of technology-enhanced learning to support the standard classroom intervention" (Lewis). In the 4-Tier Learning Model:

- Tier 1 supplies "awareness and information" online to managers at their desktops. The tier offers both information and just-in-time support.
- Tier 2 promotes "understanding" through simulations and scenario based problem solving.
- Tier 3 moves to "group learning" based on online collaboration.
- Tier 4 focuses on "higher order skills" and develops people skills, relying on face-to-face interaction.

In general, the progression through the tiers moves managers from desk top, to online sources, to interactive online work through to face-to-face interaction. The blended model mixes online resources and interaction with classroom learning. "Basic Blue for Managers" rests on IBM's "4-Tier Learning Model." (Lewis, 2006) The program has three phases:

- Phase I: 26 weeks of self-paced, online learning within a cohort of 24 new managers. The Phase includes simulations, tutors and digital interaction with others.

- Phase II: A 5-day "learning lab" at an IBM learning center. The learning exercises include experiential learning founded on the Phase I work. Simulation and teaming work allows students to learn from one another.

- Phase III: A combination of Phases I and Phase II work in requiring demonstration of competency within the workplace. It rests on the blended learning—the online and face-to-face components—of Phases I and II. An elaborate Kirkpatrick model of evaluation permeates all three Phases.

The blended 4-tier learning approach has achieved such success at IBM that all the company's business units are using the approach. The careful and precise evaluation of the learning has convinced the internal users of the efficacy of the approach. The lessons learned are instructive for both corporate and higher education adopters and apply significantly to blended learning and not to e learning alone (Lewis, 2006):

- Learning preferences are poor predictors of e-learning acceptance. IBM found that its employees were not able to accurately (and successfully) predict their preference for e learning, suggesting that students are simply not aware of the potential match for their preference and its learning effectiveness.

- The relative advantage of e learning must be salient and promoted. Students must be persuaded of the advantages of an innovation.

- The compatibility of e-learning with already existing tools, navigation, and usability is important to students. If innovations are compatible with familiar interfaces, learners are immediately comfortable: e.g., if an innovation resembles email, students are quite comfortable.

- The simplicity of an e-learning application, as perceived by its potential adapters, will speed its rate of adoption. The 'perceived complexity' of an innovation can significantly slow adoption.

- Trialability is also important. The degree to which e-learning can be experimented with on a limited basis helps to dispel uncertainty and to drive its adoption. New e-learning features such as simulations can best be introduced with 'no risk trials' before students are required to use them.

- Observability is also key. The degree to which the innovation's results are visible to others speeds the innovations' adoption. Building accessible and useable content into a program early gives the student confidence in the whole program.

A critical aspect of the success of the 4-tier programs has been student acceptance, as important at IBM as in any educational situation.

Typical responses included praise for the blended model: "The key thing was the 'hybrid' model . . . they decided to take a 'best of both worlds' approach, and it really worked" (Lewis, 2006). Students praised the model for allowing them to work through some kinds of material at home or at the desk while learning others through face to face interaction."

IBM's Formal, Enabled and Embedded Learning Methods

When using its 4-Tier model design, IBM considers whether formal, enabled, or embedded learning are required to accommodate employees' various training needs. For example, one important aspect of corporate learning is its 'just-in-time' nature. Davia referred to studies where only 10% of employees' training occurs in a formal, classroom setting. Instead, employees, tend to require training during the course of their normal work day (M. King and C. Davia, personal communication, February 21, 2006). The three learning method characteristics include:

- *Formal learning* is the traditional learning that is most familiar. It occurs mostly outside of the work context, and usually involves instructor-led activities, whether in physical classrooms, in seminars or online, as in virtual classrooms. It also refers to self-study, which occurs increasingly online. Formal learning requires a break from work. It's learning in preparation for a need that may arise later. It plays an important role for deep learning needs, because it allows for reflection and idea generation. It facilitates basic knowledge and skill acquisition.

- By contrast, *enabled learning* happens in the context of work. This is what most of us do most of the time . . . . Unlike formal learning, work-enabled learning is done in the office and on the job. This approach leverages the work environment to combine knowledge and skill acquisition with work. It facilitates the contextual acquisition of knowledge and skills from collaborative experiences in the workplace.

- *Embedded learning* also happens in the context of work, but it occurs as an integral part of a specific business task or set of tasks. It is embedded in that, at each step of a business process, modular learning is available to help users execute specific tasks. For example, when a user is unsure about how to execute the next step in an online process, the system offers a short learning module to guide the user through successful completion.

Blended learning activities—such as simulation or collaboration—can be infused throughout the methods as necessary.

"It is a spectrum," explains King (M. King and C. Davia, personal communication, February 21, 2006). "Blending learning activities could be part of formal learning, an enabled learning, or an embedded learning process. An employee, for example, can use Instant Messaging to access an expert or mentor—even during an embedded learning activity." IBM also incorporates learning objects and metadata programmable learning content to make the content searchable and reusable in different kind of models.

King sees an opportunity, too, for a similar blend of formal, enabled and embedded learning in higher education (M. King and C. Davia, personal communication, February 21, 2006). "You can think about the student's skill development as a continuum. Technology is used to acquire new skills and certifications as needed," King explains. "Obviously the faculty will drive the formal learning process, but wouldn't it be great if the students participated in a broader learning experience, remediating themselves when necessary and accessing core content or knowledge that is delivered in a more enabled or more embedded model."

Interestingly, both King and Davia point to non-technical successful factors that promote successful learning method implementations (M. King and C. Davia, personal communication (February 21, 2006):

- Senior management support and engagement is important. "In terms of technology-enablement, culture is a big – if not the biggest – impediment or facilitator to success," states King. "It involves changing the process and getting people's buy-in. When you get senior sponsorship and support, it makes a big difference."

- Implementation should encompass the human as well as the technical elements. "I am a technologist/architect," explains Davia. "The technology is really exciting and you can have the best technology in the world, but the enablement of the technology is probably more important than the technology itself. Effort must be spent in the learning the best practices for using the system, the most effective way to use the system, and training individuals to use the system."

- A long term viewpoint is also essential in planning. "You have to view this as a long term journey," states King. "You find quick successes, but the real value here is the things that will emerge from investments made over the long term, as for example, building a standards-based and flexible learning infrastructure to repurpose formal course content in an enabled way."

The Next Generation: Mix and Matching Pedagogy and Environments through Blended Learning

King has gained a unique vantage point about blended learning from his experiences working with corporate, higher education, and K–12 clients. He has observed that each market tends to operate in its own sphere, emphasizing blended learning in a different fashion. For example, the 'just-in-time' delivery found in the corporate sector differs from many higher education institutions and K–12 applications.

However, standards and open source options provide an opportunity for technology convergence across all three markets, creating a new generation learning solution that promotes a further mixing of technology and pedagogy, which in turn supports opportunities for blended learning applications. "Each segment—corporate, higher education, and K–12—all have elements that each could borrow from the other," he believes (M. King and C. Davia, personal communication, February 21, 2006). "But I am starting to see a lot of bleed through the segments already." For example, community colleges borrow corporate training techniques for their self-paced corporate training contracts or distance learning education programs.

The maturation of broad-based, middle-level capabilities and functions around some core standards for learning content design, content packaging, learning object definition, and interoperable tools could create a common technology platform with plug and play tools that can be tailored accordingly. "We approached this initially from a pedagogical frame of mind on how things worked by segment," explains King (M. King and C. Davia, personal communication, February 21, 2006). "As we move into a model of formal, embedded, and enabled learning, we are finding that you can use the technology in different ways: to collaborate with others, deliver information, do self-paced training or simulations, access to experts, or coaching. It gets back to emphasizing the flexibility of blended learning. You build a set of resources wrapped around a technology infrastructure, environment, and process which facilitates strategic pedagogical decisions at the top all the way down to fulfilling individual needs." In higher education, blended learning applications could then evolve from course-related activities to a configurable tool set to facilitate broader institutional, collegian, or departmental objectives.

Technology enhances individual corporate, higher education, and K–12 learning applications. In addition, it is propagating tomorrow's vision of tailoring plug and play blended learning elements according to specific learning and pedagogical requirements. The result will be greater individualization to address an employee's or student's unique educational needs.

The size and scope of IBM's educational and training operations marks it as one of the nation's leading examples of teaching and learning, albeit in a world seen as distinct from higher education. IBM's concern for learning effectiveness and quality, for the cost and the return on investment in teaching and training are counterparts of the issues found at ASU and its peers. Further, the blending of delivery modes to increase learning effectiveness and student satisfaction apply to both sectors.

Lessons Learned

The two case studies illustrate some of the advantages to be gained through blended learning courses and programs. The lessons learned also suggest issues that any offering of blended courses or programs must take into account. Beyond the brief descriptions here, each of these topics holds a wealth of detail that requires careful consideration in order to meet the requirements of over-all institutional strategy and structure.

Convenience

Convenience, as demonstrated by the major ECAR study on students and technology, is a primary factor for the student pull, as Sam DiGangi calls it, for blended learning (S. DiGangi, personal communication, March 6, 2006). But the word "convenience" hides the multiplicity of advantages to students, faculty and institution. The convenience to students of being able to access information from home or desk top obviously appeals to them. The convenience to faculty may be less obvious—less time spent traveling to provide lecture information, more flexibility in schedule as they control the course pattern, less time spent providing information in formats that are not interactive and often not well attended. The convenience to institutions in scheduling courses, using classroom facilities and reaching off-campus audiences can be managed to considerable advantage. The corporate management of the convenience factor may be even greater: employees need information and skills at differing times and locations. Often no single location can provide the training opportunities of just-in-time, human interaction, job skill building, background information, and training for future positions.

Cost

In their separate worlds, IBM and the School of Extended Education at ASU are necessarily cost conscious organizations. Without clear advantage, neither would embrace blended learning. IBM saves millions of dollars of employee travel through blended learning. Identifying what skills and information can be delivered through blended learning and other modes of e learning has lead to significant cost savings. Both have further examined costs and benefits to show that learning effectiveness for managers has substantially increased the ROI. Colleges and universities cannot easily determine such benefits but the IBM model may suggest further avenues to explore.

ASU, in its efforts to increase its off-campus populations, is pressed to determine costs with increasing precision. The efforts to determine costs for accurate budgeting for expansion have lead ASU to examine various models, including the categories of delivery from text-based to fully mediated.

Learning Effectiveness

Learning effectiveness remains an issue for both IBM and ASU. While some colleges and universities have made significant progress to determine learning effectiveness across student populations and among multiple delivery systems (e.g., face-to-face classroom, blended, and online), few institutions have sufficient assessment tools and structures to measure student learning within or across programs. IBM regards the metrics to gauge learning success among its leading topics; aligning training skills with ROI is a challenge that can serve the company as well as its innumerable customers. ASU has assessment and learning research groups at central, campus and college levels, recognizing the importance of measuring learning effectiveness.

Marketing

Both IBM and ASU face the inevitable issues of marketing courses and services to a large public. The School of Extended Studies at ASU has been given a specific goal, some part of which can be reached with blended learning courses. Over the next few years, the goal of 100,000 enrollments must be met by reaching potential students who are not enrolled at any of the four campuses. With blended learning offerings, students can choose courses and programs that mix face-to-face sessions with e learning opportunities. The faculty members who teach these classes have college and university support resources to help them design curricula to maximize the effectiveness of the blending.

IBM, as both provider and vendor, must offer education and training that appeal to its own employees and to thousands of potential customers whose own employees must be served. As an award winning leader in the industry, IBM must offer the full range of services that its customers may want. Furthermore—to a large extent unlike higher education—IBM must provide data on the assessment and effectiveness of the program it delivers or designs for its customers. Blended learning provides alternative delivery modes to increase convenience, lower cost and maximize learning effectiveness in training and education.

These lessons learned suggest the parallels between two very different organizations. Each offers examples applicable to many other organizations—attending to the convenience factor; measuring costs, satisfaction, and learning effectiveness; and marketing to those for whom blended learning has great appeal. The initiatives at both IBM and ASU suggest that successful efforts will be highly managed with extensive assessment and evaluation, strong attention to learners, analysis of cost and ROI, and well-supported instructional design.

References

IBM earns #1 ranking in training magazine's 'Training Top 100' award. Retrieved March 3, 2006, from http://www-03.ibm.com/press/us/en/pressrelease/6773.wss.

IBM's 4-Tier learning model. Retrieved March 3, 2006, from http://www-304.ibm.com/jct03001c/services/learning/ites.wss/zz/en?pageType=page&contentID=a0003032.

Kvavik, R., & Caruso, J. (2005). ECAR study of students and information technology. *Chapter 4 Information Technology in the Classroom.*

Learning infrastructure: Architecting a formal and informal learning environment. *IBM Learning Solutions Executive Brief.* Retrieved January 2006, from http://www-304.ibm.com/jct03001c/services/learning/solutions/pdfs/learning_infrastructure.pdf.

Lewis, Nancy, and Peter Z. (2006). Orton Blended Learning for Business Impact—IBM's case for learning success. In Curtis J. Bonk, Charles R. Graham, Jay Cross, Michael G. Moore (Eds.), *Handbook of Blended Learning Global Perspectives, Local Designs.* San Francisco: Wiley.

Concluding Comments

Everything I Need to Know about Blended Learning I Learned from Books [2]

Charles Dziuban
Director, Research Initiative for Teaching Effectiveness
Joel Hartman
Vice Provost, Information Technologies and Resources
Patsy Moskal
Associate Director, Research Initiative for Teaching Effectiveness
University of Central Florida

Online learning has become ubiquitous among U.S. institutions of higher education, with nearly 90% of them offering online courses (Allen & Seaman, 2005). Institutions that initially offered only fully online courses are increasingly being drawn to develop blended learning formats. The phenomenon is becoming an area of intense investigation by many institutions, as evidenced by the number of recent publications on the subject, as well as attendance at events such as the Sloan-C Invitational Workshops on Blended Learning held in 2003, 2004, and 2005 (http://www.sloan-c .org/publications/view/v3n5/blended.htm).

It appears, however, that many institutions are finding their attempts to initiate programs challenging, because unlike fully online courses, blended learning has the potential over time to impact nearly all students and faculty, as well as campus support services. While face-to-face and fully online instruction involve only one instructional format, blended learning combines the two, raising a host of new questions. How should blended learning be positioned by the institution as an instructional strategy? Is it necessary to displace classroom time with online activities? If so, what is the appropriate division between face-to-face and online? What are effective methods for preparing faculty to develop and teach blended learning courses? How will we know if our blended learning program is succeeding?

There are no simple answers to these questions; moreover, approaches that work well in one institutional setting may be unsuccessful in another. How, then, can those responsible for planning and implementing blended learning programs approach this challenge with confidence? The answers—or at least useful insights—can be found in books.

---

[2] Authors in alphabetical order

"Once I Figure Out What Blended Learning is All About, How Can I Get Others to Understand?"

In *The Fifth Discipline,* Peter Senge (1990) labels organizations capable of transformational change as "learning organizations." Such organizations are characterized by mastery of five "disciplines": personal mastery (continuous personal learning and clarifying personal vision), mental models (representations of reality that help explain how something works in the real world), shared vision (diffusion of mental models and creating common understanding and purpose), team learning (sharing and mutual development of mental models), and systems thinking (the fifth discipline) (Bonous-Hammarth & Smith, 2001, p. 58). According to Senge (1990) learning organizations are "organizations where people continually expand their capacity to create the results they truly desire, where new and expansive patterns of thinking are nurtured, where collective aspiration is set free, and where people are continually learning to see the whole together" (p. 3). Learning organizations are thus capable of conceptualizing, growing, and transforming.

Personal mastery is continuous individual learning. It means approaching life with vision, purpose, and an intent to grow intellectually—to develop and refine new personal mental models that are based on "how things really work." Organizations can learn only when their leaders and employees learn.

Mental models have been closely linked with change theory. For organizational transformation to occur, old mental models must be revised or replaced with new models that are consistent with the direction the organization wishes to move. Senge (1990) states, "[Mental] models, if unexamined, limit an organization's range of actions to what is familiar and comfortable" (pp. 186–187). Mental models determine individuals' propensity to change: limited, tacit, negative or rigid models obstruct change, while robust, shared, positive and flexible models can help support it. Without conscious articulation, reflection, refinement, and enhancement of individuals' mental models they become incapable of changing their beliefs, attitudes, and behaviors; they become resistant to change and unable to share their personal visions with others, limiting the power of whatever personal vision they may possess (Senge, 1990, p. 175).

Mental models alone are insufficient to transform organizations. They must be accompanied by systems thinking (Senge, 1990, p. 203). Systems thinking focuses on relationships, interconnections, and interdependencies, and allows individuals to apply and adjust their mental models in the context of their own roles, those of their departmental units, and those of the organization as a whole (pp. 203–204). Systems thinking is necessary if individuals are to shift from a personal to an organizational worldview, and to refine and improve their personal mental models (p. 203). As Senge (1994, p. 48) states it, "...every organization is a product of how its members think and interact."

Organizations such as colleges and universities are arguably very complex systems. Senge observes that we often do not fully comprehend the level of complexity or the interrelationships between elements present in our organizational environments. Systems thinking is an attempt to perceive an organization as a whole and understand the relationships and interactions between its parts. We talk more about systems thinking later in this chapter.

Assessment (research) is a critical component of both systems thinking and mental models (Senge, 1990). Systems thinking focuses on interconnectedness and feedback loops. Assessment enhances the flow of information and helps leaders make decisions based on facts rather than wishful thinking. Likewise, mental models require assessment so that new information can be collected and employed to improve upon previously-held models.

As online learning practitioners within an institution prepare to launch a blended learning initiative, it will be useful to consider the attributes of learning organizations as described by Senge. Through gaining personal mastery, the initiative's leaders become better informed regarding the attributes of successful blended learning programs. They seek to create a vision for blended learning based on clear institutional objectives with well-defined outcome expectations, and they develop models of practice that describe the program's key elements. They conceptualize mental models for each of the service and support areas that will be required: program development, faculty development, course development, assessment, learner support, and infrastructure. These mental models are shared and refined, leading to team learning. The team then broadens model sharing to include faculty members and administrators. Over time, as implementation and assessment occur, new information is generated that helps refine the model, leading to organizational learning.

In discussions about blended learning questions often arise, such as "should we call it hybrid or blended?" or "At what percentage of online learning does a face-to-face course become blended?" In terms of project success, the answers to such questions are of minor significance; it is far more important to have a well-defined model that fits the institution's needs and can be understood, explained, and adopted than it is to choose the best label for the activity or to be overly concerned about minor implementation details. No mental model is perfect, and any initial flaws can be addressed as the initiative moves forward.

"Why Can't I Get _____ to Even Consider Blended Learning?"

Individuals within an organization differ in regard to their ability and propensity to accept or adopt an innovation such as blended learning. Some of these individuals may be administrators, and some may be faculty members. Some faculty members, for example, may be eager to modify their courses to encompass the tools and techniques associated with blended learning, while others may strongly resist the notion. In *Diffusion of Innovations,* E.M Rogers presents a model, depicted in Figure 1 below, suggesting that members of an organization (e.g., faculty members or administrators) are not homogeneous, but rather can be classified as sub-populations based on their personal characteristics and the relative order in which they are willing and able to adopt an innovation (Rogers, 1995). Rogers labels these sub-populations as innovators, early adopters, early majority, late majority, and laggards. Innovators are the few pioneers who are first to experiment with a new concept. They are generally bold and curious individuals who are willing to take risks. Often possessing advanced technical skills, innovators bring attention to the innovation within the organization, where it may subsequently be observed and then attempted by the early adopters. Early adopters are the first to begin moving an innovation into the mainstream, and the greater the visibility and credibility of this group, the more likely the innovation is to be adopted by the early majority. The early and late majority groups are progressively less likely to be convinced of the value of the innovation. However, by the time the innovation has passed through the early majority segment, it has likely achieved sufficient momentum that it will sweep through the rest of the organization. The final category, laggards, is labeled in recognition of its members' unwillingness to give up their traditional beliefs and practices.

Figure 1. **The Diffusion of Innovation, from Rogers, E. M. (1995),**
Diffusion of Innovations, 4th ed. p. 262.

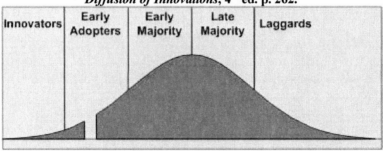

Applying the Rogers diffusion model to blended learning, several points become apparent. The motivations, incentives, and support required for each population of adopters differ. At each stage, the adopters become more pragmatic, less likely to adopt the innovation for its own sake, and more entrenched in their traditional beliefs and practices. It will therefore take higher levels of persuasion and resources to support an innovation such as blended learning as it moves through an institution. A second point is evident from Figure 1: the "tipping point" at which the rate of adoption of an innovation begins to grow rapidly occurs during the early majority phase. Once an innovation passes from the early adopters to the early and late majorities, the size of the population that must be supported increases dramatically. A third observation is that at the later stages of diffusion there are large populations at multiple stages of adoption, bringing on the new challenge of supporting large groups of people with widely differing needs.

The blended learning explorations of innovators are often solo ventures, and thus can be idiosyncratic, especially in the absence of institutional standards, guidelines, and support mechanisms (i.e., mental models). Some early adopters are motivated to continue to pursue their involvement because of the results, or the personal satisfaction it brings. Others become frustrated by a perceived lack of institutional support and recognition, eventually ceasing their involvement and moving on to other, more rewarding endeavors.

As blended learning advocates begin to interact with both faculty and administrators, Rogers reminds us that neither is a "one size fits all" group. The models that are developed, and the resources put in place to implement them, must be cognizant of the inherent differences that exist among individuals.

"We're Just Starting Out and Have Only a Few Support Staff. How Can We Prepare and Support All of these Faculty Members and Their Blended Courses?

Well qualified and trained faculty members are the key to the success of blended learning programs, and faculty development is therefore an essential part of any blended learning initiative. But as we have seen from the Rogers discussion, not all faculty members are alike.

In *Managing Technological Change,* Bates (2000) identifies a prominent characteristic of faculty innovators and early adopters: the tendency (or need) to "go it alone." He refers to them as "Lone Rangers." The Lone Ranger approach can lead to faculty understanding of the potential of blended learning; however, Bates cites several negative characteristics of many projects developed by Lone Ranger faculty: poor user interfaces and graphics, excessive technical time demands, failure to complete the project, and limited dissemination of results. Such initiatives generally do not scale well because they are heavily dependent on the ideas and energy of one or a few individuals. Self-direction can appear to work well for innovator and even many early adopter faculty members because they are enthusiastic and self-reliant. However, enthusiasm alone is not sufficient to scale these efforts institution-wide, as early and late adopter faculty become engaged.

The "Lone Ranger" model is one of three general approaches to engaging faculty in blended learning, as described by Bates (2000). The second is the boutique approach, in which one-on-one support is provided to faculty members as each comes forward seeking assistance. This can be satisfying to both faculty members and professional staff, but is not scaleable to large numbers of faculty.

As the number of individual faculty members embracing blended learning increases, the time requirements for both faculty and staff can become unsustainable. When development efforts shift from individual courses to full programs, faculty members at several stages of Rogers' diffusion curve may become involved as a team, further complicating the requirements for planning and support. Although boutique projects may themselves be scalable, the support structure is not, eventually leading to the "support crisis" present on many campuses.

In the third approach described by Bates (2000)—the systemic approach—campus support resources, including instructional designers, programmers, and digital media specialists, are brought together and supported by scalable systems and processes for dealing with increasingly demanding and complex support needs. A successful response may require the development of new organizational structures or working relationships involving the institution's information technology, instructional technology, library, and assessment units.

The three basic support approaches are not mutually exclusive, nor is the existence of Lone Rangers or boutique support approaches necessarily harmful. The question is one of how to achieve scalability while maintaining quality as the number of faculty requiring support increases. All campuses have their faculty innovators, or Lone Rangers, and from them come many excellent and creative ideas. To be made scalable, these ideas must be institutionalized and brought within a systemic support structure.

Boutique support is, in many ways, the optimum solution, and it might be preferred if not for its lack of scalability. But even in systemic support environments boutique elements are useful. For example, as a systemic support organization begins to serve new faculty members, a one-on-one approach is often used to assess faculty, determine project needs, and establish a trust relationship. Individual faculty members may also be identified as leaders and given special support to carry their innovative ideas forward to be developed and shared with others.

Ideally, expertise increases until a critical mass of adoption and dissemination exists, liberating the support staff to keep up with constantly changing technologies. Control over the instructional process is shared as synergy develops between faculty members and support staff. In the interest of institutionalization, faculty members should not be totally dependent on support staff, nor completely independent (Lone Rangers), but rather interdependent, doing what they do best and allowing staff to provide support and mentoring. Return on investment is improved by designing systems that scale for enterprise-wide delivery as opposed to developing what Chris Dede (1996) calls "Islands of innovation." Although individual "islands" may be successful, they may be difficult or impossible to disseminate throughout an institution. The learning organization strategies discussed by Senge may prove helpful in fostering and sustaining dissemination.

Faculty members who are experienced in blended or fully online learning have found that it cannot be accomplished effectively as an "add-on," but instead requires fundamental re-thinking of objectives and instructional strategies (Bates, 2000). Such changes require a shift in personal theories of teaching and in instructional behaviors (new mental models)—becoming a "coach" rather than a "teacher"—especially in environments that emphasize active student learning. Blended learning environments also change the "division of labor" required to develop and offer courses, and institutions need to respond by creating a new class of instructional technology personnel who support the online efforts of faculty.

Many faculty development programs employ workshops, software training classes, and guest speakers, in combination with walk-in consultation and support. These offerings are relevant and useful, but often do not lead to the cultural change required to achieve a transformative integration of technology into teaching and learning. Individual consultation is not scalable, as Bates (2000) points out in his discussion of the "boutique approach."

Interest, as Rogers and Bates suggest, derives naturally from individuals' discovery and application of an innovation. However, lacking an institutional context and resources, interest alone is not sufficient to drive an innovation such as blended learning throughout an institution. Direction gives form and scope to blended learning initiatives. From where does direction originate? It can come from institutional planning, faculty-led initiatives, in reaction to external competition, as a means to improve teaching and learning, and as a response to student expectations. It can also come from individuals with vision and authority. This is where leadership, personal mastery, mental models, and team learning converge.

Just as "interest" implies a bottom-up approach, "direction" implies top-down. A top-down approach can have advantages, such as a place on the institutional agenda and dedicated resources. However, lacking faculty interest and acceptance, administratively initiated efforts can be counterproductive, resulting in faculty avoidance or pushback. It is therefore desirable to have both faculty interest and administrative direction, with the two being in harmony. Yet, even a beneficial combination of faculty interest and administrative direction are insufficient to move an innovation through the institution. Facilitation is also required.

In describing facilitation, Bates (2000) lists components that are required to achieve quality in technology-assisted learning: content, media production, instructional design, faculty and student support, and assessment. Facilitation can come from internal resources, or from external partners under outsourcing arrangements. As an example, the majority of institutions see a need to assist faculty with developing, delivering, and updating their blended courses; however, the locus of this support may not be immediately apparent. The rapidity with which interest in blended teaching and learning is growing is finding many campus support units scrambling to understand and support the phenomenon. The information technology or computing organization may have extensive experience with Web-based resources and services, but may not be accustomed to working with faculty to develop and support courses, and may have no pedagogical perspective to tell them what approaches are sound.

A similar dilemma exists for media services units, teaching and learning centers, and instructional technology units. Very few possess the range of resources or skills necessary to fully support online teaching and learning. Consequently, many campuses are finding it necessary to reorganize or develop new, specialized support units as a means of bringing to bear the expanded range of expertise and resources necessary to grapple with the needs of blended teaching and learning. At a minimum, needs include instructional designers, HTML programmers, digital media designers and producers, trainers, systems support staff, and assessment experts.

An examination of the institutions that are regarded as leaders in the blended learning arena finds a new organizational model emerging: units bringing together the two "ITs"—Information Technology and Instructional Technology—to develop scalable, sustainable support strategies for blended teaching and learning. These units may stand alone, or be an extension of other entities. They are characterized by bringing under one roof the range of expertise needed to perform the diverse tasks required to support blended teaching and learning. A second characteristic of the leaders, and the new organizational models, is the prominent role of instructional designers. Often absent in traditional information technology organizations, teaching and learning centers, and media centers, instructional designers can play a dual role. They not only work with faculty to design and implement effective technology-assisted instruction, but also create professional development materials and training that support scalability and sustainability, reducing future support needs. The effectiveness of faculty development programs based on the central role of instructional designers often distinguishes systemic efforts from boutique.

The next required element is capacity. Capacity includes the human and technical infrastructure, systems, and processes needed to support an ever-increasing number of faculty members wishing to become involved in blended learning, and the associated course redesign projects. Technical capacity encompasses elements such as servers, course management software, network bandwidth (campus network and Internet access), multimedia-equipped classrooms, and administrative processes for maintaining performance and reliability. Course and faculty development capacity is a measure of the level of facilitation available.

As the number of blended learning courses grows from the tens to the hundreds to the thousands, how will the faculty be trained, the courses created and maintained, and the increasing pool of online students supported? As adoption of blended learning expands, these needs are typically met by an expansion of support staff, decentralization of support into academic units, or outsourcing. Processes that work well with the first few courses can begin to collapse under the weight of hundreds or thousands of courses. Therefore, one of the most important capacity issues is process scalability. Scalability requires both human and technological elements, as well as effective processes and approaches. Human resource issues include creating new and effective organizational models capable of accommodating the diverse range of expertise required to support faculty development, course redesign, production, student support, and assessment.

The final element is the involvement of one or more champions—leaders with vision. Champions bring energy and direction; they help develop and share the necessary mental models, they help keep blended learning on the institutional agenda, and they facilitate communication and team learning among the various entities involved. Innovations that have credible champions disseminate more rapidly through the organization than those that do not.

"Some Say that Traditional Institutions will be made Obsolete by the Upstart Online Institutions; Others Say that the Traditional Institution is Eternal. Who's Right?"

In *The Innovator's Dilemma*, Christensen (1997) describes how large, successful organizations that grow by responding to the continuing needs of their key customers are at risk from technologies that create

273

alternatives whose capabilities are initially more limited and whose costs are lower. Sustaining technologies, according to Christensen, offer current customers more of what they have historically wanted and valued. A sustaining example from education might be classroom multimedia, which provides faculty members with improved tools with which to present content in more clear and engaging ways to students.

Disruptive technologies, on the other hand, usually deliver worse performance, at least in the near term, according to the values of mainstream users. Disruptive technologies are generally cheaper, simpler, smaller, or more convenient. Such technologies are therefore usually employed by emerging or niche markets. Mainstream users generally do not want or cannot use a disruptive technology at first. The ultimate uses or applications for disruptive technologies are not knowable in advance, because their markets have not been identified. Disruptive technologies, therefore, are initially adopted by markets that are regarded as insignificant.

Mainstream users are often over served, and sustaining innovations exacerbate the problem by providing improvements or enhancements beyond a level that such customers can effectively use. Disruptive technologies also improve over time, and eventually become capable of serving new customers and new markets. The price or performance advantages of disruptive technologies continue to drive them upstream, until the established technologies can no longer afford to improve and are replaced.

Normally, as in the case of sustaining technologies, plans must be made before action is taken. In the case of disruptive technologies, action must be taken before plans can be made. Plans must be made for learning rather than implementation, suggesting a certain level of risk.

Christensen suggests several management strategies that are appropriate for dealing with disruptive technologies:

1. Set up a separate organization to manage the disruptive technology and focus the technology on markets with a different set of values from those of the parent organization.
2. Keep the separate organization small, so that even minor gains will be important.
3. Design the separate entity as a learning organization, and focus on learning opportunities. Revise mental models as more information becomes available. Anticipate early failures.
4. Explore new markets. The attributes that make disruptive technologies unattractive to mainstream markets are those upon which new markets will be built.
5. Customer expectations shift from functionality to reliability to convenience to price.

Are blended and online learning disruptive or sustaining technologies? It is the position of the authors that blended learning is clearly a sustaining technology, and fully online learning can be either sustaining or disruptive depending on certain conditions. Blended learning is an enhancement of face-to-face teaching and learning, and it relies at least in part on all of the elements that are common to classroom-based instruction. It is highly unlikely, therefore, that in the hands of a competitor blended learning poses a threat to colleges or universities because they could easily respond to external competition by offering blended courses or programs. Further, it is well established that students (current customers) value and seek blended learning opportunities.

Fully online learning initially had many of the attributes of a disruptive technology; however, it has been adopted by the vast majority of institutions and in many cases made a mainstream offering, thereby providing a defense against external competition. Online learning can be disruptive in cases where brick and mortar institutions do not provide online offerings, thereby making themselves subject to competition from those that do, including commercial providers. Notable successes in fully online learning that have followed Christensen's recommendation to place potentially disruptive technologies within separate organizational structures include the University of Maryland (UMUC), the Pennsylvania State University (Penn State World Campus), and the University of Massachusetts (UMass Online). A number of institutions have achieved success through offering fully online and blended courses as a standard course delivery option.

"Without Systems Thinking There is No System."

Effective blended learning involves the interaction of many elements: pedagogical transformation, new roles for both instructors and students, technology infrastructure, support mechanisms, and strategic planning to name just a few. In turn, each one of those elements requires the support of several components that interact with each other. Pedagogical transformation, for instance, demands faculty development, student and faculty support, reconfigured assessment models, and differing expectations for students and faculty members. Therefore, blended learning is a prototype for what Forrester (1995) referred to in *System Dynamics and the Lessons of 35 Years* as a complex system–the implications of which cannot necessarily be understood through a direct cause and effect relationship.

As we pointed out earlier in this chapter, educators think about blended learning in terms of mental models, a prime example of which might be the Sloan-C pillars: access, learning effectiveness, student satisfaction, faculty satisfaction, and cost effectiveness (Moore, 2002). Using these elements to develop a systemic model of blended learning requires recognition of their confluence featuring three predominant idiosyncrasies. First, it is virtually impossible to predict how an intervention such as blended learning will develop in complex systems represented by colleges or universities. Second, many outcomes will be counterintuitive, unexpected or overlooked in the planning process. Finally, there will be many unanticipated side effects, both positive and negative that will require systematic response and accommodation. Complex systems are dynamic. Higher education is a complex system; therefore, blended learning in higher education is a dynamic process.

What are the defining characteristics of a complex system (Forrester, 1991)? A useful distinction might come from comparing complexity to a simple system where direct cause and effect relationships are readily discerned. A classic example of simple systems thinking for a complex model can be found in the protocols of many educational accrediting agencies requiring colleges and universities to demonstrate that their instructional strategies result in improved student learning outcomes (problem + action + expected result = simple system). Certainly, student learning is much more complex than assuming that there is a direct cause and effect relationship between what transpires in class and what students learn. Such accreditation requirements ignore the complexity of present day learning dynamics in higher education such as co-curricular and social environments.

In a complex approach to blended learning the primary differentiator is the presence of systematic feedback loops that inform original assumptions, identify counterintuitive results, and respond to side effects. This is a structured approach that iterates in a responsive way to the original problem.

What is it then that makes blended learning a complex system? First of all the effects of blended courses and programs are not necessarily closely related in time and space. Blended learning, however, because of its learner-centered emphasis makes it possible to track tangential effects. Some examples might include the establishment of a scholarship of teaching and learning reward program, the impact blending has on the growth of branch campuses, or the evolution of blended learning into a strategic initiative for the university. While these are not direct objectives, they are side effects related to the blended learning initiative.

As a complex system, blended learning can result in actions that facilitate unanticipated long term planning. An example is discovering that blending responds to the needs of millennial generation students who naturally harbor some ambivalence toward technology-mediated learning (e.g., they enjoy the flexibility provided by the asynchronous environment but lament the lack of face-to-face contact with the instructor). Blending can help students use their personal, mobile, and virtual technologies in the learning space thereby enhancing student engagement and meeting their personal and educational needs.

Complex systems such as blending learning force instructors, students, and policymakers to optimize decisions. The often cited oversight that students make when they assume that there is somehow less required of them in blended courses is quickly overcome by a modified and more effective study protocol that migrates into other aspects of their academic lives. Interestingly and counterintuitive, when faculty members encounter redefined and expanded workloads, they experience a rededication to the teaching enterprise. Finally, when policymakers spend substantial resources attempting to develop a strict sense definition of blended learning, the process usually results in a flexible and effective mental model.

Students function more effectively when they receive regular, consistent, and incremental feedback about their performance in class (Pascarella & Terenzini, 2005). The traditional teach-then-test assessment models are not consistent with the feedback loops of blended learning. The interpretive nature of assessment in the blended environment allows students to know where they stand, what progress they are making, and to benchmark where they need to be at the end of the course or program. Blending facilitates this outcome where complete face-to-face or online environments may not be as effective at helping students understand the academic implications of their classroom activities. As a complex system, blending helps students balance their long- and short-term goals. For instance, they are able to better understand that the intermediate step of specific course objectives is really the facilitation of their becoming information fluent in the discipline. Fluency in these instances is a long term goal defined as the nexus of information literacy, technology literacy, and critical thinking mediated with effective communication skills.

Blended learning is a prototypical example of a complex system in which mental models become the operative constructs. Certainly all of us use models for our decision-making processes. Those decisions must be made based on our assumptions about the components of blending and the intuitive fit we make about its' instructional effectiveness. Blended learning helps us decide how things will change based on the decisions we make, as well assess the consequences for those decisions in an effectively functioning and dynamic system.

"Blended Learning is an Idealized Cognitive Model, or The Balinese Tell Time Differently."

In a recent white paper, Mayadas (2006) introduced the "localness" construct as an underpinning of blended learning. In its broadest interpretation, localness considers a student population on campus, near campus, and far from campus. Using some combination of face-to-face and asynchronous modalities in blended learning courses, universities are able to "localize" education for a much larger constituency of these populations, thereby increasing access. This notion draws some parallels to early pedagogical work with very large lecture sections of face-to-face courses where most strategies attempted to make large classes seem small to the students. Localness extends the campus metaphor to populations who may feel at the margins of higher education. Bourne (2006) extrapolated this notion to geo-localness where students at some physical distance to the university can experience a campus-like presence.

Blended learning and localness are examples of what Lakoff (1990) in *Women, Fire, and Dangerous Things* defines as idealized cognitive models (ICM). An ICM is a pattern of thought in which we try to define a complex situation in a rational, simplified way. Lakoff argues that idealized cognitive models (Senge's mental models) are the basis of human knowledge organization. At some level our search for a prototype definition of blended learning has to do with trying to idealize the definition. This comes from Fillmore's (1982) notion of a frame. Consider, for example, Monday as an idealized cognitive model that only exists within the concept of a week that doesn't exist objectively in nature. These models were arbitrarily created by human beings as an expediency for dealing with time. Obviously there can be many more ICMs dealing with the passage of time. For example, Lakoff demonstrates this by citing the Balinese culture that structures time through three individual week structures (one 5 day, one 6 day, and one 7 day—18 total days, each with a different name). These idealized models do not fit the world perfectly because they are oversimplified and based on over-restrictive background assumptions. There are some segments of society where the models fit very well and others where there is a considerable mismatch. Lakoff gives an example of this phenomenon. In most circumstances the ICM bachelor fits the category unmarried man, but it does not work well for the Pope or for celibate men from other religious sects.

Certainly higher education is abundant with idealized cognitive models. For example, critical thinking, creativity, motivation, satisfaction, learning style, cognitive presence, teaching presence, social presence, and of course, blended learning, comprise just a few obvious examples. They only exist through our efforts to define them. Actually, blended learning gives rise to an entire cluster of ICMs that fit the category to some degree but never actually converge to a singularity. We have blended activities, blended courses, blended programs, and blended institutions (Bonk & Graham, 2006), none of which have a strictly closed definition. Therefore, the term "blended learning" signifies an idealized cognitive mental model that facilitates our developing the notion of localness in an educational environment featuring rapid pedagogical and technological changes. Without the blended learning mental model we would have no way to conceptualize effective ways to interact with the student populations that are arriving from near and far away.

"We are Moving from Command and Control to Connect and Collaborate, Or Higher Education is Flattening."

In *The World is Flat: A Brief History of the Twenty-First Century*, Friedman (2005), asserts that the economic world is flattening, thereby causing the United States to lose its global economic advantage. He cites "In-Forming" as a major contributor to this phenomenon. By this, he means a democratization of content through digital resources so that information can be created by anyone and published virtually worldwide. Therefore, knowledge and information are no longer command-and-control functions where certain people who have information have the power to distribute or withhold it at their pleasure. Phenomena such as searches, wikis, blogs, and personal publishing capabilities allow the individual to compete with the large company on a more or less equal footing (Battelle, 2005). Consider this quote from Eric Schmidt (CEO of Google).

> *Search is so highly personal that searching is empowering for humans like nothing else. It is the antithesis of being told or taught, It is about self-empowerment; it is empowering individuals to do what they think best with the information they want. It is very different from anything else that preceded it. Radio was one-to-many. TV was one-to many. The telephone was one-to-one. Search is the ultimate expression of the power of the individual, using a computer, looking at the world, and finding exactly what they want-and everyone is different when it comes to that"* (Friedman, 2005, p. 157).

We have argued in other papers that this democratization of information renders the old adage "Knowledge is Power" moot (Dziuban, Moskal, & Hartman, 2005). Friedman (2005) speculates that the economic flattening of the world results from a convergence of three elements: a web-enabled playing field, horizontal collaboration, and new players from all over the world. Certainly, these factors are flattening higher education as well and blended learning is a large part of that process. The Web components of blended courses enable students to access information so that content acquisition is nearly instantaneous. Boolean algorithms replace the painful search through physically archived information. In blended learning, collaboration creates a collective cognition base where the teaming orientation of students increases the power of learning by an order of magnitude. The mobility of students' technologies creates a dynamic and responsive learning environment where they enjoy learning degrees of freedom that their technologies enable. Most certainly the metaphor for research has changed from "mining" to "surfing."

Blended learning is consistent with a horizontal democracy of learning where class, instructors, and students behave more like partners rather than masters and apprentices, programs become localized in the sense of worldwide access, and institutions of higher education are forced to collaborate rather than compete. Further, however, blended learning is consistent with the globalization of education where partnerships form horizontally across the world in higher education just as multinational corporations have become true global entities transcending national and regional boundaries. Blending can make students several thousand miles from campus local by creating a common Web course component and then outsourcing the face-to-face components to institutions in several areas around the world. In addition, blending is the natural transition to the new world of higher education maintaining some trappings of the original academy while embracing the technologies of the new flat world of learning. The primary question becomes, however, how will American higher education respond to the new democracy?

"We Read the Book—Now What?"

Blended Learning, Research Perspectives emerged from the inspiration of educators who discovered that precious little research was being conducted on blended learning in higher education. From this anthology, we hope the reader will agree on the need for sustaining such an inquiry base. With respect to a mental model, one possibility for conceptualizing blended learning is a coordinate position on a hypothetical continuum from the face-to-face classroom to fully online learning. However, blended learning, in its most effective form, involves courses with pedagogically transformed components.

A successful model for blending depends on an environment that is centered on the learner, knowledge, assessment, and community. Activities in this environment should focus on the goals, objectives, needs, and interest of the learner; use online and face-to-face resources in ways that support understanding and future transfer of knowledge; use assessment to help learners understand their thought process through feedback and revision; and promote a sense of connectedness and collaboration through integrated online and offline activities.

Individuals who were interested in online, but not necessarily blended learning, and those specifically interested in blended learning view blending as a means to offer the best of both online and face-to-face resources to their students. Equally important is enhancing the traditional classroom and meeting the students' need for more flexible learning experiences. Barriers that hinder the adoption of blended learning include the additional time requirements for developing and delivering a course, and the aversion that some faculty members have toward the opportunity costs associated with implementing new technologies.

Blended learning has the potential to transform instruction at private universities as well as public venues. Accordingly, we can apply lenses to the nature of the blending—*enabling* if the technology focuses on increased access and convenience for students; *enhancing* if the technology focus is on increasing instructor or student productivity; *transforming* if the technology focuses on facilitating an improvement in more active learning pedagogy, and *sustaining* if institutions employ blended learning to better meet the needs of their current students. We should, however, be wary of superficial blends that add nothing significant to instruction and use blended learning to focus on efficiency and productivity at the cost of pedagogy.

Rogers' innovation-diffusion process shows why faculty members choose to adopt and implement blended instruction; for instance, institutional initiatives provide information and design and implementation support. This generates awareness and understanding of blended courses as well as their potential benefits. Although in many cases instructors receive financial incentives to teach blended courses, they stress that teaching and learning benefits presented in faculty development workshops and discussions with experienced blended instructors are major factors in their decisions to go "blended." Instructors indicate that a comprehensive faculty development program is critical to their understanding of blended learning, providing them with necessary skills, a redesigned course, and the enthusiasm and motivation to forge ahead. In implementation phases, faculty members discover that trial and error, as well as the experience and wisdom of colleagues who have been through the process, is crucial. The experience of teaching blended courses allows faculty members to understand the change in student and faculty roles and the impact of technology on the teaching and learning process.

The impact of innovative teaching practices on both students and faculty members, shows that as students become more *experienced* learners, their perception of the efficacy of "school" assessments focusing on monotonic interaction between student and teacher such as multiple choice tests, term papers, and essays, diminishes. Less experienced learners prefer these objective assessment methods over "community" activities or tasks such as peer critiques. More experienced learners, however, see greater efficacy in collaborative, cooperative, and interpretative assessment. This foreshadows the growing necessity for authentic assessment in blended learning.

Blending offers immense potential for many special populations. Faculty members are able to focus on blended learning as a way to provide increased interaction among extremely diverse student constituents. Instructors further indicate that blended learning 1) offers multiple modes of communication, 2) provides more "even" participation from all students, 3) encourages peer-to-peer teaching and learning, and 4) allows faculty to become facilitators rather than dispensers of knowledge. Students in regular and special populations react positively to blended courses; those most satisfied are those who feel this environment levels the course playing field for them. However, student satisfaction appears to be an interactive combination of demographics, social and political influences on students, and preference for knowledge acquisition.

Students perceive class discussion groups and announcements as the most important features for blended learning. They believe that blended instruction enhances the quality and quantity of class discussion, promotes a sense of connectedness among students and instructor, and makes the class more enjoyable. Students' frequency of posts emerges as the best predictor of their performance in the courses. We have a sense that blended learning is effective in liberal education environments where the residential experience is so highly valued.

This book examines the Carnegie Unit as an indicator of instructional time in the online or blended modality. Seat time and semester hours can no longer be easily measured in a Web-based or blended class and a better index might be a learner achievement model. New models focus on learner accomplishment tying Capabilities Based Educational Equivalency units to Bloom's taxonomy or other cognitive theories in developing a framework for course equivalence.

Shifting gears a bit, comparing a major research university and a global corporation yields interesting similarities and differences. Many universities find that students in fully online courses are attending face-to-face sections as well, providing the impetus for blending. As universities' blended programs evolve, their advice includes examining not just overall indicators of success, but also how specific tools are used effectively. In addition, they also focus on examining course design at the program level. From the corporate perspective, employees learn job skills both at work and in formal courses; therefore blended learning is an ideal model. In both settings, convenience is the driving factor for students' desire for more blended courses. However, costs and learner satisfaction and effectiveness are primary goals that must be monitored constantly. Both organizations stress the importance of marketing to those who might find blended learning appealing.

"We Need More Research!"

The authors for Bonk and Graham (2006) examine blended learning from multiple perspectives: concept and construct formation, blended learning in the corporate cultures, the higher education perspective, for-profit blended learning, global perspectives, multinational models, and workplace blending. They make the point that because blended learning is the centerpiece of educational conversations in each of these venues it must be considered the next import agenda in learning theory and practice. The volume and quality of papers in *The Handbook of Blended Learning* (Bonk & Graham, 2006) attest to the importance of the blended mental model as a vehicle for response to Friedman's (2005) issues for America and its higher education system:

1. The declining number of American students pursuing mathematics and science careers compared to the rest to the emerging world;
2. A growing lack of ambition in America's young people; and
3. The exodus of higher level research positions from the United States.

With books like *Educating the Net Generation* (Oblinger & Oblinger, 2005) and *Millennials Rising* (Howe & Strauss, 2000) trying to facilitate our understanding and engagement of a new generation of American college students, we might well turn our attention to blended learning as a way of reengaging America's youth. Further, a growing body of research has shown women to be far outstripping men in ambition and success in higher education (Lewin, 2006). Bok (2005) warns us of an entire higher education system that is underachieving. Certainly, these and Friedman's (2005) concerns must be high on the agenda for blended learning research in the coming decades if we are to stem the worrisome decline in achievement.

Bonk, Kim, and Zeng (2006) predict future trends in blended learning around such issues as: mobility, visualization, individualization, connectedness, collaboration authenticity, employment-based learning, and blending specialization, among others. Certainly, many of these are underway with some of them emerging rapidly. Therefore, building on Friedman (2005) and Bonk, Kim and Zeng (2006), we end this book with a series of questions that may help define the blended learning research agenda for the years ahead. How will we move assessment models to adopt methods that are interpretive, contextual, and authentic? Through blended learning models will it be possible to move students' learning from knowledge acquisition and problem solving to information fluency in their disciplines? How will blended learning become a strategic initiative for American higher education? How can we make critical thinking an operational construct in higher education through blended models? In what ways can blended learning foster industry and university partnerships? What is the proper role for technology in the blended learning environment? What metaphors will develop for blended colleges and universities? Does blended learning have the potential to better serve under-represented populations in higher education? Is it possible that blended learning will help ameliorate the growing gender gap in higher education? How will faculty and student roles evolve in the blended environment? What is the impact of social networking on blended learning? What is the potential systemic impact of blended learning on higher education? Finally, what are the empowering constructs of blended learning?

This series of questions is not exhaustive but perhaps some of our readers will establish a blog, wiki, or some other communication mechanism so people around the United States and the world can build a much more comprehensive and functional agenda for blended learning research in the coming years. We will be the first to "sign on".

References

Allen, I. E. & Seaman, J. (2005). *Growing by degrees: Online education in the United States, 2005*. Needham, MA: Sloan Consortium.

Bates, A. W. (2000). *Managing technological change*. San Francisco, CA: Jossey-Bass, Inc.

Battelle, J. (2005) *The search: How Google and its rivals rewrote the rules of business and transformed our culture*. New York: Penguin Group.

Bok, D. (2005). *Our underachieving colleges: A candid look at how much students learn and why they should be learning more*. Princeton, NJ: Princeton University Press.

Bonk, C. J. & Graham, C. R. (2006). *The handbook of blended learning: Global perspectives, local designs*. San Francisco, CA: Pfeiffer.

Bonk, C. J., Kim, K., & Zeng, T. (2006). Future direction of blended learning in higher education and the workplace learning settings. In C. J. Bonk & C. R. Graham (Eds.), *The handbook of blended learning: Global perspectives, local designs* (pp. 550–567). San Francisco, CA: Pfeiffer.

Bonous-Hammarth, M. & Smith, M. J. (2001). Sustaining change efforts in higher education: A look at factors influencing organizational learning and renewal. In Alexander W. Astin and Helen S. Astin (Eds.), *Transforming institutions: Context and process* (Higher Education Research Institute). Los Angeles, CA.

Bourne, J. (2006). *The Babson strategy: Blended online education enables localness and geo-localness.* Sloan Consortium. Retrieved July 10, 2006, from http://www.sloan-c-wiki.org/wiki/index.php?title=Babson_College_Blended_and_Localness.

Christensen, C. M. (1997). *The innovator's dilemma: When new technologies cause great firms to fail.* Boston, MA: Harvard Business School Press.

Dede. C. (1996). Distance learning-distributed learning: Making the transformation. *Learning and Leading with Technology, 23*(7), 25–30.

Dziuban, C. D., Moskal, P. D., Hartman, J. (2005). Higher education, blended learning, and the generations: Knowledge is power—no more. In J. Bourne & J. C. Moore (Eds.), *Elements of Quality Education: Engaging Communities.* Needham, MA: Sloan Consortium.

Fillmore, C. (1982). Frame semantics. In Linguistic Society of Korea, (Ed.), *Linguistics in the Morning Calm* (pp. 111–138). Seoul: Hanshin.

Forrester, J. W. (1991). System dynamics and the lessons of 35 years. In K. B. De Greene (Ed.), *The systemic basis of policy making in the 1990s.* Cambridge, MA: MIT Press. Retrieved July 10, 2006, from http://sysdyn.clexchange.org/sdep/papers/D-4224-4.pdf.

Forrester, J.W. (1995) Counterintuitive behavior of social systems. Systems Dynamics in Education Project. Massachusetts Institute of Technology. Retrieved July 10, 2006, from http://web.mit.edu/sdg/www/D-4468-2.Counterintuitive.pdf.

Friedman, T. L. (2005). *The world is flat: A brief history of the twenty-first century.* New York: Farrar, Straus and Giroux.

Howe, N. & Strauss, W. (2000). *Millennials rising: The next great generation.* New York: Vintage Books.

Lakoff, G. (1990). Women, fire, and dangerous things. Chicago: University of Chicago Press.

Lewin, T. (2006, July 9). At colleges, women are leaving men in the dust. *The New York Times*, pp. 1, 18–19.

Mayadas, F. (2006) *Blending, localness, and Sloan programs.* Unpublished paper, Alfred P. Sloan Foundation. New York.

Moore, J. C. (2002). Elements of quality: The Sloan-C Framework. Needham, MA: Sloan Consortium.

Oblinger, D. G. & Oblinger, J. L. (Eds.). (2005). Educating the net generation. EDUCAUSE.

Pascarella, E. T. & Terenzini, P. T. (2005). *How college affects students: A third decade of research.* San Francisco: Jossey-Bass.

Rogers, E. M. (1995). *Diffusion of innovations* (4th ed.). New York: Free Press.

Senge, P. M. (1990). *The fifth discipline: The art & practice of the learning organization.* New York, NY: Doubleday.

Biographies of the Contributors

Robert Albrecht, Chancellor Emeritus of Western Governors University, is a Senior Research Fellow of the EDUCAUSE Center for Applied Research (ECAR). Prior to his retirement as Chancellor of Western Governors University, he held faculty and administrative positions at the University of Chicago, the University of Oregon, the University of Northern Colorado, the Montana University System and the University of Colorado. His early publications were in American literature. More recently he has published chapters and articles on distance learning, information technology, online learning and academic administration. His work as an ECAR Senior Research Fellow has included numerous case studies (as supplements to ECAR research projects) as well as articles on blended learning, accreditation, and learning objects.

I. Elaine Allen is Associate Professor of Statistics and Entrepreneurship at Babson College. She is also Director of Research for the Sloan Center for Online Education at Babson College and Franklin W. Olin College of Engineering, Faculty Director of the Center for Women's Leadership at Babson College, and Co-Director of the Babson Survey Research Group at the Blank Center for Entrepreneurship at Babson College. Dr. Allen received her Ph.D. in Statistics from Cornell University and has published extensively on meta-analysis, data-mining applications, survey research, and evidence-based medicine. She serves on the editorial boards of a number of medical, statistical and applied research journals and is a Fellow of the American Statistical Association. Prior to joining Babson she was Vice President of Scientific Affairs at MetaWorks, where she produced meta-analyses and systematic reviews for pharmaceutical and biotechnology clients and for government agencies. Prior to joining MetaWorks, she was Co-Founder and Vice President of Biomedical Operations for ARIAD Pharmaceuticals and Director of Biomedical Operations at Centocor, Inc.

Diane M. Badzinski is Coordinator of Special Academic Terms at Colorado Christian University, Lakewood, Colorado, and affiliate faculty in the online Masters of Communication program, Spring Arbor University. Prior to her current positions, she was an Associate Professor of Communication at Bethel College and the University of Nebraska-Lincoln. She holds a MA in communication from University of California- Santa Barbara, and a Ph.D. in communication from the University of Wisconsin-Madison. Her research program has centered on mapping behaviors/attributes to communication outcomes. For example, she has mapped judges' nonverbal behavior to jury decision-making, faculty gender to use and perception of online course management systems, as well as media consumption to citizens' comprehension and perceptions of Megan's Law. She has co-authored a textbook in statistics and has published in a variety of research journals, including *Journal of Applied Communication, Communication Research, Human Communication Research, Western Journal of Communication, and Journal of Advertising.*

Jason D. Baker is Associate Professor of Education at Regent University where he serves as the distance education advisor in Regent's online Doctor of Education program and consults with institutions and individuals on the effective use of educational technology and online learning. He earned a B.S. in electrical engineering from Bucknell University, a M.A. in education from The George Washington University, and a Ph.D. in communication from Regent University. Dr. Baker has been published in a variety of academic journals including the *International Review of Research in Open and Distance Learning, The Internet and Higher Education,* and the *Journal of Computing in Higher Education.* He has authored or edited five books including *Parents' Computer Companion, Baker's Guide to Christian Distance Education* and *The Student Guide to Successful Online Learning.*

Gary Brown has in interdisciplinary Ph.D in Education, Communication, and English. He directs the Center for Teaching, Learning, and Technology at Washington State University, a program that was inaugurated in 1997 to help faculty integrate technology, assessment, and outcomes driven course designs that are learning centered, collaborative, and generative. Gary was lead developer of the WSU Guide to Critical Thinking, a FIPSE funded project for assessing and promoting students' critical thinking. In collaboration with the National Learning Infrastructure Initiative, Coalition for Networked Institutions, and the Teaching, Learning, and Technology Group, he led the Transformative Assessment Practices (TAPS) project. Gary has also worked with a variety of professional associations on the assessment of outcomes and costs of educational practices and innovations, and, with WSU colleagues, he has received National University Telecommunications Network award for best research in 2002, 2003, and 2005. Gary directs the CTLT Silhouette Project, which serves Flashlight Online, an online survey instrument sponsored by the Teaching, Learning, & Technology Group, which has recently received a FIPSE for developing the Better Education through Assessment (BETA) project. He was a National Learning Communities fellow and is the assessment section editor for *Innovate.* He was the leader on the EDUCAUSE New Academy project. He served on the Washington State Governor's Task Force presaging the establishment of a statewide Digital Learning Commons, and he is currently serving as Vice President of the Learning Curves Education Network. Gary has published over 50 articles on teaching, learning, and assessment.

Charles Dziuban is Director of the Research Initiative for Teaching Effectiveness at the University of Central Florida (UCF) where has been a faculty member since 1970 teaching research design and statistics. He received his Ph.D. from the University of Wisconsin. Since 1996, he has directed the impact evaluation of UCF's distributed learning initiative examining student and faculty outcomes as well as gauging the impact of online courses on the university. Chuck has published in numerous journals including: *Multivariate Behavioral Research, The Psychological Bulletin, Educational and Psychological Measurement, The American Education Research Journal*, the *Phi Delta Kappan*, the *Internet in Higher Education*, the *Journal of Asynchronous Learning Networks*, and the *Sloan-C View*. His methods for determining psychometric adequacy have been featured in both the SPSS and the SAS packages. He has received funding from several government and industrial agencies including the Ford Foundation, Centers for Disease Control, and the National Science Foundation. In 2000, Chuck was named UCF's first ever *Pegasus Professor* for extraordinary research, teaching, and service and in 2005 received the honor of *Professor Emeritus*. Currently, he is editing a book on blended learning research for the Sloan foundation, has a forthcoming chapter in the *Handbook of Blended Learning Environments* as well as in the Educause E-book *Educating the Net Generation*. In 2005 Chuck received the Sloan Consortium award for *Most Outstanding Achievement in Online Learning by an Individual*.

Linda Futch is the Lead Instructional Designer at the University of Central Florida. A In this position, her team is responsible for facilitating faculty and course transformation to the online environment. Futch has taught at the community college, high school, and business levels. She has presented at industry conferences. Futch has a bachelor's degree in secondary education and a master's degree in instructional technology-instructional systems. She received her doctorate degree from the University of Central Florida. Her dissertation was titled "A Study of Blended Learning at a Metropolitan Research University."

Charles R. Graham is an Assistant Professor of Instructional Psychology and Technology at Brigham Young University with a focus on technology-mediated teaching and learning. He has an MS in electrical and computer engineering from the University of Illinois, where he helped to develop an asynchronous learning environment used in undergraduate engineering courses. He earned his doctorate in Instructional Systems Technology at Indiana University, where he worked for the Center for Research on

Learning and Technology and helped to develop an online professional development environment for K–12 teachers. His research interests include the study of online collaborative learning environments and the use of technology to enhance teaching and learning. He has authored articles and book chapters in many venues including: *Quarterly Review of Distance Education*, *Small Group Research*, *Educational Technology*, *TechTrends*, *Educational Technology Research & Development*, *Computers in the Schools*, *Online Collaborative Learning: Theory and Practice*, and *The Encyclopedia of Distance Learning*. He recently co-edited the *Handbook of Blended Learning: Global Perspectives, Local Designs* (2005, Pfeiffer) which contains 39 chapters on blended learning in higher education, corporate, and military contexts from around the world.

Joel L. Hartman is Vice Provost for Information Technologies and Resources at the University of Central Florida in Orlando. As the university's CIO, he has overall responsibility for library, computing, networking, telecommunications, media services, and distributed learning activities. He was employed by Bradley University from 1967 to 1995, holding several information technology management positions, including CIO. He has been an active author and presenter at industry conferences. He previously served as treasurer and 2003 Chair of the EDUCAUSE Board of Directors, and currently serves as chair of the EDUCAUSE Learning Initiative (ELI) Advisory Committee. He also serves on the Florida Digital Divide Council, the Microsoft Higher Education Advisory Group, is secretary of the Seminars on Academic Computing Coordinating Board, and Vice Chair of the Board of Directors of Florida LambdaRail. Dr. Hartman graduated from the University of Illinois, Urbana-Champaign, with bachelor's and master's degrees in Journalism and Communications, and received his doctorate from the University of Central Florida.

Tom Henderson is the Director of Testing and Assessment at Central Washington University. His research interests include the efficiency and effectiveness of postsecondary educational processes, online survey design and analysis, learning outcomes assessment, and formative assessment techniques. Henderson consults with the WCET on Technology Costing Methodology projects and he is a Senior Associate of the Flashlight Program of the TLTGroup. His work at WSU designing and administering the Goals, Activities, and Processes formative assessment process was recognized in 2002 by the National Learning Infrastructure Initiative as an exemplar of transformative assessment. Two articles that he co-authored received the National University Telecommunications Network award as best research papers in 2002 and 2005. Henderson received his Ph.D. from the Washington State University Individual Interdisciplinary Degree Program in 1999, an

MBA in Finance from the University of Washington in 1981, and a B.S. in Accounting from the University of Idaho in 1975.

Joeann Humbert is Director of Online Learning at the Rochester Institute of Technology. In that capacity, she is responsible for all facets of online learning at RIT—from faculty and course development to online student support. Joeann also oversees the department's Teaching, Learning and Technology Lab; faculty training in and support of the campus-wide courseware system; development of online survey and course evaluation tools; blended learning; and a number of recent pilot projects that support the integration of technology in campus classrooms. Joeann has written and presented on educational technology for a wide variety of local, national, and international audiences. She is a member of the New Media Consortium and currently serves on its Horizon Project Advisory Board. Her higher education experience includes teaching positions, manager of distance learning student services and coordinator of the First Year student experience. Joeann has worked as a consultant in the areas of teamwork, communication, and career development, and was a small business entrepreneur.

Tanya Joosten is an Instructional Design Consultant in the Learning Technology Center at the University of Wisconsin-Milwaukee (UWM). She works with faculty on the pedagogical considerations in using instructional technology and has assisted in the development and coordination of various faculty development programs at UWM. Tanya teaches in the Department of Communication and has several years of experience designing and teaching technology-enhanced, blended, and fully online communication courses, covering such areas as communication technology and organizational communication. She has an interdisciplinary doctorate in Communication, Management, and Public Administration from Arizona State University. Her research interests include communication technology, virtual teams, organizational communication and technology, student response systems, gaming, and podcasting.

Robert Kaleta is director of the University of Wisconsin-Milwaukee's Learning Technology Center (LTC), the campus faculty development center for instructional technology. The Center focuses on assisting mainstream faculty with their efforts to effectively integrate technology into their courses and make the transition to blended and online teaching. Bob received his Ph.D. from the University of Texas at Austin. An instructor in the Department of Psychology at UWM, he has extensive personal experience using technology for teaching. Bob has presented papers and conducted a number of workshops on preparing faculty for blended teaching at national conferences, and his writings have focused on faculty development and faculty experiences in blended learning. Other areas of interest include the integration of student response systems for engaging students in large lecture courses and the use of portable rich media, such as MP3 and MP4, for teaching and learning. He is currently involved in research to evaluate student and faculty reactions to these technologies and assess their impact on learning.

Patsy Moskal is the Associate Director for the Research Initiative for Teaching Effectiveness at the University of Central Florida (UCF), where she has been a faculty member since 1989. She received an Ed.D. from UCF specializing in Instructional Technology and Research Methods and holds BS and MS degrees in computer science. Since 1996, she has served as the liaison for faculty research of distributed learning and teaching effectiveness at UCF. Patsy specializes in statistics, graphics, program evaluation, and applied data analysis. She has extensive experience in research methods including survey development, interviewing, and conducting focus groups and frequently serves as an evaluation consultant to school districts, and industry and government organizations. She has co-authored a number of book chapters and journal articles on research in online and blended courses.

Anthony G. Picciano is a professor in the graduate program in Education Leadership at Hunter College. He is also a member of the faculty for the Ph.D. program in Urban Education and the program in Interactive Pedagogy and Technology at the City University of New York Graduate Center. He has thirty-five years of experience in education administration and teaching and has been involved in a number of major grants from the U.S. Department of Education, the National Science Foundation, IBM, and the Alfred P. Sloan Foundation. In 1998, Dr. Picciano co-founded CUNY Online, a multi-million dollar initiative funded by the Alfred P. Sloan Foundation that provides support services to faculty using the Internet for course development. Currently he serves on the Board of Directors of the Sloan Consortium. His major research interests are school leadership, Internet-based teaching and learning, and multimedia instructional models. Dr. Picciano has authored numerous articles and seven books including *Data-Driven Decision Making for Effective School Leadership* (2006, Pearson), *Educational Leadership and Planning for Technology*, 4th Edition (2005, Pearson), *Distance Learning: Making Connections across Virtual Space and Time* (2001, Pearson), and *Educational Research Primer* (2004, Continuum).

Judith A. Pirani is a research fellow at the EDUCAUSE Center for Applied Research (ECAR) and president of Sheep Pond Associates. Her expertise focuses on educational technology issues, providing market research and best practices case studies. Sample research includes the use of e-learning to improve employee efficiencies and sales demand, the marketability of course management systems for corporate training applications, and Web site development strategies in higher education and government institutions. At ECAR she has authored several studies, including *Information Technology Networking in Higher Education: Campus Commodity and Competitive Differentiator*, *Supporting E-Learning in Higher* Education, and *Wireless Networking in Higher Education*, as well as conducting qualitative research and authoring numerous case studies in support of other studies. Ms. Pirani also developed ECAR's Roadmaps, which synthesize the research studies' issues and recommendations in a concise four-page format. Ms. Pirani has over 20 years of consulting experience. Previously she was Vice President at Lyra Research and Giga Information Group, where she managed worldwide research practices in digital imaging technologies.

Reid A. Robison is an instructor in the Organizational Behavior program at Brigham Young University. He is also Director of Alumni Activities for the BYU Alumni Association. He has taught courses at BYU for the past 6 years and personally directs the University's Alumni Tour Program, which provides educational travel experiences to more people than any other university within the United States. Dr. Robison earned his Ph.D in Educational Leadership from the University of Nebraska-Lincoln and his MBA from the Kellogg School of Management at Northwestern University. For 18 years he led the Canadian Operation for O. C. Tanner Company, the leading provider of corporate service awards in North America. His major research interests include distance education and educational travel. Dr. Robison has published articles in the *Quarterly Review of Distance Education* and in *Currents* magazine (Council for Advancement and Support of Education).

Jeff Seaman is the Chief Information Officer and Survey Director for The Sloan Consortium and Co-Director of the Babson Survey Research Group. He holds degrees in Demography/Statistics, Sociology, Electrical Engineering, and Housing, all from Cornell University. He created and ran the Computing Resource Center and served as Associate Vice Provost for Computing for the University of Pennsylvania and as Chief Information Officer for Lesley University. His industry experience includes serving as Chief Technology Officer at HighWired.com where he led the development of an online learning system and as the Vice President of Engineering for Vista Associates building course management systems. Dr. Seaman has been conducting research in the impact of technology on higher education and K–12 for over a decade, beginning with comprehensive national studies of technology use in U.S. Higher Education in 1991. His most recent work has included the annual Sloan Consortium surveys on the state of online learning;

Growing by Degrees: Online Education in the United States, 2005, Entering the Mainstream: The Quality and Extent of Online Education in the U. S. 2004 and 2004, and *Sizing the Opportunity: The Quality and Extent of Online Education in the United States, 2002 and 2003*.

Peter Shea is a member of the faculty of the Department of Educational Theory and Practice and the College of Computing and Information at the University at Albany, State University of New York (SUNY). Previously he served as the Director of the SUNY Learning Network, the online educational program for the 64 colleges of SUNY, and as the manager of the university system's Teaching, Learning, and Technology Program. He is currently co-principal investigator for two Sloan Foundation grants, investigating faculty and student motivations to teach and learn in asynchronous learning networks. He is co-author of *The Successful Distance Learner* and his research has appeared in *The Journal of Asynchronous Learning Networks, The Journal of Educational Computing Research, The International Review of Research in Open and Distance Learning,* and *The Internet and Higher Education* as well as the books *Learning Together Online,* and *Learner Centered Theory and Practice in Distance Education* published by Lawrence Erlbaum Associates. He is an associate editor for *JALN* and an effective practices editor for the Sloan Consortium for Online Learning.

Karen A. Skibba, a former corporate communication manager, is now a doctoral candidate in Adult and Continuing Education at the University of Wisconsin-Milwaukee (UWM), where her work focuses on instructional design and distance education. She also has experience teaching communication courses and has coordinated preparing future faculty programs for graduate students. Karen received her Masters Degree in Communication Studies from Marquette University. Her research interests include adult learning, hybrid/blended learning, distance education, instructional design, faculty development, learner-centered teaching, and the impact of technology on teaching and learning. Karen has conducted workshops and presented at international and national conferences, including: Distance Learning Conference; Professional and Organizational Development Conference, Lilly South Conference on College and University Teaching, Adult Education Research Conference, and Midwest Research to Practice Conference.

Tamara Smith is an Assistant Professor of Biology at University of Nebraska at Kearney. Her research interests include herpetology, animal behavior, and functional morphology. Dr. Smith also has a strong background in curriculum design and assessment and a current research focus in assessment of distance and blended education and service learning. She teaches several courses in the online Master's degree program at UNK, including Research in Biology, Current Issues in Biology, Behavioral Ecology, and Functional Morphology. Dr. Smith received her B.S. from University of California, Davis in Environmental Biology and Management and her M.S. and Ph.D. in Zoology from Washington State University. She conducted three years of postdoctoral work at the Center for Teaching, Learning, and Technology at Washington State University.

Michael Starenko is an Instructional Designer in the Online Learning Department at the Rochester Institute of Technology. He coordinated the department's Blended Learning Pilot Project and coordinates its ongoing Blended Learning Program. Prior to joining the department, he was Director of Curriculum Development for Synergistics, a Rochester-based higher education consulting company. His academic field is media studies, in which he has authored more than 100 articles and served as editor-in-chief of *Afterimage: The Journal of Media Arts*. Michael has extensive teaching experience, having taught online courses at Charter Oak State College and on-campus courses at the University of Rochester, RIT, Syracuse University, Columbia College, and the Rhode Island School of Design. He has a BA from Kalamazoo College and an MA in Humanities from the University of Chicago.

Karen Vignare currently serves as the Director of MSU Global Ventures at Michigan State University. In that role, Karen is responsible for creating online entrepreneurial approaches for extending both non-credit and credit programs at MSU. Before that, she was the Sr. Research Analyst for the Online Learning Department at the Rochester Institute of Technology. Before coming to RIT, Karen was a full-time faculty member at SUNY-Alfred State in the marketing, retail, and computer technology fields. She also served as a vice president and political economist for a Wall Street financial firm. She publishes regularly on various topics in online learning. She has an MBA from the University of Rochester's William Simon School of Business and a BS from Frostburg State University in political science and economics. She is currently attending doctoral classes at Nova Southeastern University.

Renee Welch is an Instructional Designer for External Education at the University of Illinois at Chicago. She is responsible for faculty support and course design, development, and delivery of blended and online university courses as well as professional education programs. Renee Welch joined UIC as a project researcher in 1996, providing project management and leadership in the coordination of research based projects focused on School

295

Improvement and Education. As a Research Associate Professor for the Institute for Mathematics & Science Education, she was responsible for creating online professional education courses for Chicago Public School teachers. As an Adjunct Instructor, she is constantly working to continue to develop best practices in the virtual classroom and has research interests in pedagogical and instructional aspects of asynchronous learning environments. Dr. Welch earned her Ph.D. on Educational Policy Analysis from the University of Illinois at Urbana-Champaign and is a certified Master Online Instructor.

Robert H. Woods, Jr. is Associate Professor of Communication at Spring Arbor University, Spring Arbor, Michigan, where he teaches media ethics and research at the undergraduate and graduate levels. He has a B.A. in communication from the University of New Mexico and an M.A. in communication and Ph.D. in communication from Regent University, Virginia. He also holds a J.D. (Juris Doctor) from Regent University and is licensed to practice law in the Commonwealth of Virginia. He has published journal articles and book chapters on distance education, computer-mediated communication, and the pedagogy of online learning.

Index

Print this Receipt

Transaction number: 105782
Order date: 03/28/08
CustOrderId: 1 copy Blended Learning Book

SCOLE
Olin Way Suite 262
Needham, MA 02492-1200
7812922523
info@sloan-c.org

MID: 5429298000895039
TID: LK310668

Bill to:

LESLIE SULLIVAN
792 Commercial Street
Braintree, MA 02184
United States
617-605-2036
leslie.sullivan@umb.edu

Ship to:

Quantity	Order Description	Unit Price	Total Price
n/a		n/a	$65.00
		Merchandise Subtotal	$0.00
		Shipping	$0.00
		Tax	$0.00
		Grand Total	$65.00

Invoice Number:: 1   Complete   Shipped :

Quantity	Order Description	Unit Price	Total Price
n/a		n/a	$65.00
		Merchandise Subtotal	$0.00

Card Type	MC
Ending digits of card number	X3231
Card Expiration Date	
Fraud Score	N/A